Michal Vít

THE EU'S IMPACT ON IDENTITY FORMATION IN EAST-CENTRAL EUROPE BETWEEN 2004 AND 2013

Perceptions of the Nation and Europe in Political Parties of the Czech Republic, Poland, and Slovakia

With a foreword by Andrea Pető

Bibliografische Information der Deutschen Nationalbibliothek
Die Deutsche Nationalbibliothek verzeichnet diese Publikation in der Deutschen Nationalbibliografie; detaillierte bibliografische Daten sind im Internet über http://dnb.d-nb.de abrufbar.

Bibliographic information published by the Deutsche Nationalbibliothek
Die Deutsche Nationalbibliothek lists this publication in the Deutsche Nationalbibliografie; detailed bibliographic data are available in the Internet at http://dnb.d-nb.de.

ISBN-13: 978-3-8382-1275-3
© *ibidem*-Verlag, Stuttgart 2020
Alle Rechte vorbehalten

Das Werk einschließlich aller seiner Teile ist urheberrechtlich geschützt. Jede Verwertung außerhalb der engen Grenzen des Urheberrechtsgesetzes ist ohne Zustimmung des Verlages unzulässig und strafbar. Dies gilt insbesondere für Vervielfältigungen, Übersetzungen, Mikroverfilmungen und elektronische Speicherformen sowie die Einspeicherung und Verarbeitung in elektronischen Systemen.

All rights reserved. No part of this publication may be reproduced, stored in or introduced into a retrieval system, or transmitted, in any form, or by any means (electronical, mechanical, photocopying, recording or otherwise) without the prior written permission of the publisher. Any person who does any unauthorized act in relation to this publication may be liable to criminal prosecution and civil claims for damages.

Printed in the EU

Soviet and Post-Soviet Politics and Society (SPPS) Vol. 206
ISSN 1614-3515

General Editor: Andreas Umland,
Institute for Euro-Atlantic Cooperation, Kyiv, umland@stanfordalumni.org

Commissioning Editor: Max Jakob Horstmann,
London, mjh@ibidem.eu

EDITORIAL COMMITTEE*

DOMESTIC & COMPARATIVE POLITICS
Prof. **Ellen Bos**, *Andrássy University of Budapest*
Dr. **Gergana Dimova**, *University of Winchester*
Dr. **Andrey Kazantsev**, *MGIMO (U) MID RF, Moscow*
Prof. **Heiko Pleines**, *University of Bremen*
Prof. **Richard Sakwa**, *University of Kent at Canterbury*
Dr. **Sarah Whitmore**, *Oxford Brookes University*
Dr. **Harald Wydra**, *University of Cambridge*

SOCIETY, CLASS & ETHNICITY
Col. **David Glantz**, *"Journal of Slavic Military Studies"*
Dr. **Marlène Laruelle**, *George Washington University*
Dr. **Stephen Shulman**, *Southern Illinois University*
Prof. **Stefan Troebst**, *University of Leipzig*

POLITICAL ECONOMY & PUBLIC POLICY
Dr. **Andreas Goldthau**, *Central European University*
Dr. **Robert Kravchuk**, *University of North Carolina*
Dr. **David Lane**, *University of Cambridge*
Dr. **Carol Leonard**, *Higher School of Economics, Moscow*
Dr. **Maria Popova**, *McGill University, Montreal*

FOREIGN POLICY & INTERNATIONAL AFFAIRS
Dr. **Peter Duncan**, *University College London*
Prof. **Andreas Heinemann-Grüder**, *University of Bonn*
Prof. **Gerhard Mangott**, *University of Innsbruck*
Dr. **Diana Schmidt-Pfister**, *University of Konstanz*
Dr. **Lisbeth Tarlow**, *Harvard University, Cambridge*
Dr. **Christian Wipperfürth**, *N-Ost Network, Berlin*
Dr. **William Zimmerman**, *University of Michigan*

HISTORY, CULTURE & THOUGHT
Dr. **Catherine Andreyev**, *University of Oxford*
Prof. **Mark Bassin**, *Södertörn University*
Prof. **Karsten Brüggemann**, *Tallinn University*
Dr. **Alexander Etkind**, *University of Cambridge*
Dr. **Gasan Gusejnov**, *Moscow State University*
Prof. **Leonid Luks**, *Catholic University of Eichstaett*
Dr. **Olga Malinova**, *Russian Academy of Sciences*
Dr. **Richard Mole**, *University College London*
Prof. **Andrei Rogatchevski**, *University of Tromsø*
Dr. **Mark Tauger**, *West Virginia University*

ADVISORY BOARD*

Prof. **Dominique Arel**, *University of Ottawa*
Prof. **Jörg Baberowski**, *Humboldt University of Berlin*
Prof. **Margarita Balmaceda**, *Seton Hall University*
Dr. **John Barber**, *University of Cambridge*
Prof. **Timm Beichelt**, *European University Viadrina*
Dr. **Katrin Boeckh**, *University of Munich*
Prof. em. **Archie Brown**, *University of Oxford*
Dr. **Vyacheslav Bryukhovetsky**, *Kyiv-Mohyla Academy*
Prof. **Timothy Colton**, *Harvard University, Cambridge*
Prof. **Paul D'Anieri**, *University of Florida*
Dr. **Heike Dörrenbächer**, *Friedrich Naumann Foundation*
Dr. **John Dunlop**, *Hoover Institution, Stanford, California*
Dr. **Sabine Fischer**, *SWP, Berlin*
Dr. **Geir Flikke**, *NUPI, Oslo*
Prof. **David Galbreath**, *University of Aberdeen*
Prof. **Alexander Galkin**, *Russian Academy of Sciences*
Prof. **Frank Golczewski**, *University of Hamburg*
Dr. **Nikolas Gvosdev**, *Naval War College, Newport, RI*
Prof. **Mark von Hagen**, *Arizona State University*
Dr. **Guido Hausmann**, *University of Munich*
Prof. **Dale Herspring**, *Kansas State University*
Dr. **Stefani Hoffman**, *Hebrew University of Jerusalem*
Prof. **Mikhail Ilyin**, *MGIMO (U) MID RF, Moscow*
Prof. **Vladimir Kantor**, *Higher School of Economics*
Dr. **Ivan Katchanovski**, *University of Ottawa*
Prof. em. **Andrzej Korbonski**, *University of California*
Dr. **Iris Kempe**, *"Caucasus Analytical Digest"*
Prof. **Herbert Küpper**, *Institut für Ostrecht Regensburg*
Dr. **Rainer Lindner**, *CEEER, Berlin*
Dr. **Vladimir Malakhov**, *Russian Academy of Sciences*

Dr. **Luke March**, *University of Edinburgh*
Prof. **Michael McFaul**, *Stanford University, Palo Alto*
Prof. **Birgit Menzel**, *University of Mainz-Germersheim*
Prof. **Valery Mikhailenko**, *The Urals State University*
Prof. **Emil Pain**, *Higher School of Economics, Moscow*
Dr. **Oleg Podvintsev**, *Russian Academy of Sciences*
Prof. **Olga Popova**, *St. Petersburg State University*
Dr. **Alex Pravda**, *University of Oxford*
Dr. **Erik van Ree**, *University of Amsterdam*
Dr. **Joachim Rogall**, *Robert Bosch Foundation Stuttgart*
Prof. **Peter Rutland**, *Wesleyan University, Middletown*
Dr. **Marat Salikov**, *The Urals State Law Academy*
Dr. **Gwendolyn Sasse**, *University of Oxford*
Prof. **Jutta Scherrer**, *EHESS, Paris*
Prof. **Robert Service**, *University of Oxford*
Mr. **James Sherr**, *RIIA Chatham House London*
Dr. **Oxana Shevel**, *Tufts University, Medford*
Prof. **Eberhard Schneider**, *University of Siegen*
Prof. **Olexander Shnyrkov**, *Shevchenko University, Kyiv*
Prof. **Hans-Henning Schröder**, *SWP, Berlin*
Prof. **Yuri Shapoval**, *Ukrainian Academy of Sciences*
Prof. **Viktor Shnirelman**, *Russian Academy of Sciences*
Dr. **Lisa Sundstrom**, *University of British Columbia*
Dr. **Philip Walters**, *"Religion, State and Society", Oxford*
Prof. **Zenon Wasyliw**, *Ithaca College, New York State*
Dr. **Lucan Way**, *University of Toronto*
Dr. **Markus Wehner**, *"Frankfurter Allgemeine Zeitung"*
Dr. **Andrew Wilson**, *University College London*
Prof. **Jan Zielonka**, *University of Oxford*
Prof. **Andrei Zorin**, *University of Oxford*

---

* While the Editorial Committee and Advisory Board support the General Editor in the choice and improvement of manuscripts for publication, responsibility for remaining errors and misinterpretations in the series' volumes lies with the books' authors.

Soviet and Post-Soviet Politics and Society (SPPS)
ISSN 1614-3515

Founded in 2004 and refereed since 2007, SPPS makes available affordable English-, German-, and Russian-language studies on the history of the countries of the former Soviet bloc from the late Tsarist period to today. It publishes between 5 and 20 volumes per year and focuses on issues in transitions to and from democracy such as economic crisis, identity formation, civil society development, and constitutional reform in CEE and the NIS. SPPS also aims to highlight so far understudied themes in East European studies such as right-wing radicalism, religious life, higher education, or human rights protection. The authors and titles of all previously published volumes are listed at the end of this book. For a full description of the series and reviews of its books, see

www.ibidem-verlag.de/red/spps.

Editorial correspondence & manuscripts should be sent to: Dr. Andreas Umland, Institute for Euro-Atlantic Cooperation, vul. Volodymyrska 42, off. 21, UA-01030 Kyiv, Ukraine

Business correspondence & review copy requests should be sent to: *ibidem* Press, Leuschnerstr. 40, 30457 Hannover, Germany; tel.: +49 511 2622200; fax: +49 511 2622201; spps@ibidem.eu.

Authors, reviewers, referees, and editors for (as well as all other persons sympathetic to) SPPS are invited to join its networks at www.facebook.com/group.php?gid=52638198614
www.linkedin.com/groups?about=&gid=103012
www.xing.com/net/spps-ibidem-verlag/

Recent Volumes

197 Alla Leukavets
The Integration Policies of Belarus and Ukraine vis-à-vis the EU and Russia
A Comparative Case Study Through the Prism of a Two-Level Game Approach
ISBN 978-3-8382-1247-0

198 Oksana Kim
The Development and Challenges of Russian Corporate Governance I
The Roles and Functions of Boards of Directors
With a foreword by Sheila M. Puffer
ISBN 978-3-8382-1287-6

199 Thomas D. Grant
International Law and the Post-Soviet Space I
Essays on Chechnya and the Baltic States
With a foreword by Stephen M. Schwebel
ISBN 978-3-8382-1279-1

200 Thomas D. Grant
International Law and the Post-Soviet Space II
Essays on Ukraine, Intervention, and Non-Proliferation
ISBN 978-3-8382-1280-7

201 Slavomír Michálek, Michal Štefanský
The Age of Fear
The Cold War and Its Influence on Czechoslovakia 1945–1968
ISBN 978-3-8382-1285-2

202 Iulia-Sabina Joja
Romania's Strategic Culture 1990–2014
Continuity and Change in a Post-Communist Country's Evolution of National Interests and Security Policies
With a foreword by Heiko Biehl
ISBN 978-3-8382-1286-9

203 Andrei Rogatchevski, Yngvar B. Steinholt, Arve Hansen, David-Emil Wickström
War of Songs
Popular Music and Recent Russia-Ukraine Relations
With a foreword by Artemy Troitsky
ISBN 978-3-8382-1173-2

204 Maria Lipman (ed.)
Russian Voices on Post-Crimea Russia
An Almanac of Counterpoint Essays from 2015–2018
ISBN 978-3-8382-1251-7

205 Ksenia Maksimovtsova
Language Conflicts in Contemporary Estonia, Latvia, and Ukraine
A Comparative Exploration of Discourses in Post-Soviet Russian-Language Digital Media
With a foreword by Ammon Cheskin
ISBN 978-3-8382-1282-1

Contents

Foreword: Gone Down in History. By Andrea Pető 9

1. Preface 11

2. Introduction 13
   2.1. Overview of the book 13
   2.2. The context of the CEE region 17
   2.3. Central Eastern Europe as matter of research 22

3. Structure 27

4. Theoretical background 29
   4.1. Political parties 30
       4.1.1. The role of political parties 30
       4.1.2. Europeanization 33
           4.1.2.1. Perspective of democratization 33
           4.1.2.2. Party systems 35
   4.2. European political space 37
   4.3. Analytical framework 45

5. Operationalizing of research and research questions 49

6. Limits of research 51

7. Nationalism, national identity, and policy of national identity .. 53
   7.1. National identity — overview of existing research 54
   7.2. Applied concept of national identity in
        Central East Europe after 1990 58
   7.3. Policy of national identity 60
       7.3.1. The European Union 61
       7.3.2. Values 62
       7.3.3. Minorities 62
       7.3.4. World 63

8. **Methodology and Research Procedure** 67
    8.1. Grounded theory 69
        8.1.1. How to identify parties' nationalist emphasis? 70
            8.1.1.1. The Manifesto Project methodology 72
            8.1.1.2. The Grounded Theory methodology 74
            8.1.1.3. Comparison of the implemented methods 76
    8.2. Operationalization of the behavior of political parties in the European arena 79
        8.2.1. Data and the technical attributes of the analysis 80
        8.2.2. Favouring nation, less for the EU? 80

9. **Results** 83
    9.1. National identity in political competition 83
        9.1.1. Parties covered for analysis and issues selected in the Czech Republic, Poland, and Slovakia 86
        9.1.2. The Czech Republic: Introduction into party system and national identity 88
            9.1.2.1. Czech Social Democratic Party (Česká strana sociálně demokratická, ČSSD) 97
            9.1.2.2. Civic Democratic Party, (Občanská demokratická strana, ODS) 100
            9.1.2.3. Christian and Democratic Union-Czechoslovak People´s Party (Křesťanská a demokratická unie-Československá strana lidová, KDU-ČSL) 103
            9.1.2.4. Communist party of Bohemia and Moravia (Komunistická strana Čech a Moravy, KSČM) 105
            9.1.2.5. Tradition Responsibility Prosperity 09 (Tradice, Odpovědnost, Prosperita 09, TOP 09) ... 107
            9.1.2.6. Action of Dissatisfied Citizens 2011, (Akce nespokojených občanů, ANO 2011) 109
            9.1.2.7. Tomio Okamura's Dawn of Direct Democracy (Hnutí úsvit přímé demokracie Tomia Okamury) 110

9.1.2.8.	Greens (Strana zelených, SZ)	111
9.1.2.9.	Public Affairs (Věci veřejné, VV)	113
9.1.3.	Poland: Introduction into the party system and national identity	114
9.1.3.1.	Civic Platform (Platforma Obywatelska, PO)	124
9.1.3.2.	Law and Justice (Prawo i Sprawiedliwość, PiS)	126
9.1.3.3.	Alliance of the Democratic Left (Sojusz Lewicy Demokratycznej, SLD)	129
9.1.3.4.	Polish People's Party (Polske Stronictwo Ludowe, PSL)	131
9.1.3.5.	The League of Polish Families (Liga Polskich Rodzin, LPR)	133
9.1.3.6.	Self-defense of Polish Republic (Samoobrona Rzeczpospolitej Polskiej, SRP)	135
9.1.3.7.	Your Movement (Twoj Ruch, TR)	137
9.1.4.	Slovakia: Introduction into party system and national identity	138
9.1.4.1.	Direction-Social democracy (Smer-Sociálna demokracia, Smer-SD)	145
9.1.4.2.	Christian-Democratic Movement (Krestansko-demokraticke hnuti, KDH)	148
9.1.4.3.	Slovak Democratic and Christian Union-Democratic Party (Slovenská demokratická a kresťanská únia-Demokratická strana, SDKÚ-DS)	151
9.1.4.4.	Freedom and Solidarity (Sloboda a Spravodlist, SaS)	153
9.1.4.5.	Most-Híd (Bridge, Most-Híd)	156
9.1.4.6.	Ordinary People (Obyčajní ľudia, OĽaNO)	157
9.1.4.7.	Slovak National Party (Slovenská národná strana-SNS)	159
9.1.4.8.	People's Party — Movement for a Democratic Slovakia (Ľudová strana — Hnutie za demokratické Slovensko ĽS-HZDS)	162

10. Conclusions 165
    10.1. Czech Republic 167
    10.2. Slovakia 173
    10.3. Poland 178
    10.4. Comparison 183
    10.5. Effects of participation of political parties in
          the European political space 184
11. Appendix A 191
12. Appendix B: The Grounded Theory Codebook 193
13. Appendix C 223
14. List of Tables 225
15. List of Abbreviations 227
16. References 229

Foreword
Gone Down in History

By Andrea Pető

A joke holds that political scientists are the only ones who take party programs seriously, and if there is a grain of truth in every joke then Michal Vit's book is a true work of political science. The volume focuses on party programs in Central Europe in the period between 2004 and 2013, that is from the enlargement of the European Union until the moment illiberalism gained ground in most Eastern European countries. The analyzed decade was indeed a game changer in the history of the Czech Republic, Poland and Slovakia, the states in Vit's focus, as well as for the whole region. These countries joined the EU when it was still described as an organization based on the "sharing and pooling of the member states' sovereignty", i.e. an organization that leaves the national identity of member states unperturbed while offering great economic prosperity. But the reality was different. Many Central European citizens became losers in the European integration processes, while the development funding that poured into the new member states with little oversight was used for the building of an anti-EU political culture the EU seems to be powerless to oppose.

Based on party programs, the volume examines the effects and interconnections of supra-national European law and national-level policy making practices, all the while remaining aware that the states are no longer the only and perhaps not even among the primary actors of the international system. The volume focuses on the learning process through which parties that had previously deployed a national framework have managed to change their programs when their respective countries have gained state membership of the EU.

In the cases of the Czech Republic, Poland and Slovakia the author expects the party programs to influence national identity through socialization processes. Michal Vit's questions are of vital importance: how does the international terrain affect the way individual parties envision national identity?; how does EU membership affect the formation of national identity?; and lastly, why did certain parties change their views on national identity while others didn't? The book attempts to offer responses within the framework of constructivist grounded theory and via the concept of Europeanisation. Vit takes Stefano Bartolini's 2005 concept further and uses it to explain the unforeseen phenomenon of rising support for parties that defined themselves in a "nationalism positive" way against the processes of Europeanisation.

Europeanisation, as a model of integration based on the primacy of liberal values, was the dominant model during the Eastern enlargement of the EU. Ironically, as the EU establishment was working to popularize "nationalism negative" identity constructions and the expansion of a liberal Europeanisation model in Central Europe, "nationalism positive" parties got into power (or at least were readying themselves for power by mainstreaming anti-EU discourses and politics). The decade under examination here – between 2004 and 2013 – therefore not only changed the system of political values but the modus operandi of parties too. Michal Vit's book therefore offers an insight into a key period of the region's history. What the future holds for us is unknown, but not because of political scientists.

Andrea Pető
Budapest, 2019

1. Preface

In the course of my work on this book I was repeatedly confronted with the issue of national identity and how it relates to political parties, thanks primarily to the project National Identity in Central East Europe, which I have had the opportunity to coordinate under the aegis of the EUROPEUM Institute for European Policy. This long-term cooperation raised many concrete questions concerning the issue of national identity as taken up by specific political parties and other political representatives – including questions about Slovak Prime Minister Robert Fico's relationship to Slovak history, about the migration issues raised by Czech MP, Tomio Okamura, and the conservative revival in Poland. Despite their apparent dissimilarity, these topics display similar patterns that can be unveiled through a rigorous analysis of political parties' manifestos. Comprehension of these patterns would not, however, be complete without an understanding of their contexts: ongoing globalisation and the related decline of the importance of a nation state's boundaries in the context of European integration. Therefore election manifestos are a very valuable source of data through which to analyse these influences, both at domestic and international level.[1]

Unintentionally, issues of national identity became the centre of attention during the migrant crisis of 2015 and 2016, which coincided with the conclusion of the CEE states' first decade as EU members. This has been happening despite the original expectation that with their increased involvement in European politics, individual political parties would become more homogenous in the sense of sharing the interests of the European political environment (Bartollini 2005 and Scully 2005). In the course of researching the Czech, Slovak and Polish political parties' relationship with national identity, essential questions that had been rather marginal at the time of

---

[1] The election manifestos mirror the social and political context in particular time captured by individual political party. In addition to that, they are also results of intra-party debates when it comes to definition of policy priorities as well as understanding of terms such identity. Said that, the understanding is developing in time and reffers to cerating time and context.

these countries' accession to the EU emerged relatively quickly and unexpectedly.

The starting point of this work is a phenomenon expected by academics in the field of European integration and operating in the social constructivist framework, namely that the European political space is fundamentally an environment supportive of integration, allowing for the socializating of new actors that in the process adopt its norms. This study thus works on the following assumption: that political parties, which intentionally and purposefully engage in the European political space through election (in terms of being elected) or appointment of their representatives into offices in European institutions will, over time, acquire the tendency to adopt attitudes prevalent in the European political space; and that there is a direct and positive relationship between the number of purposefully gained functions and the tendency to adopt norms conducive to deeper integration. At the same time, it may be expected that this phenomenon would also be reflected in a softer approach by political parties to issues of national identity as manifested in their political programs, for example.

The fundamental question that arises therefore is whether it is still possible to understand the European political space as an environment conducive to deeper integration in a normative sense. This work considers such an environment as norm-creating in a sense of supporting deeper EU integration. The researched decade therefore allows us to analyse how the European political space influenced one specific policy shaped by political parties: national identity. Coincidentally, at the very end of the period, the European political space is experiencing a rise of divergent tendencies in regard to EU integration. This development, which in the context of European integration presents a legitimate critique, significantly shifts the normative understanding of the European political space. In the same vein, this work aims to introduce a deeper understanding of the relationship between the European political space and divergent tendencies on a national level.

2. Introduction

2.1. Overview of the book

The ten-year time frame (2004–2013) is sufficiently long to record changes in election manifestos and, at the same time, to understand the effects of any external influences stemming from the parties' participation in the political environment at the EU level. In this context, the book focuses on changing perception of national identity over the first decade of membership for the three CEE countries in the EU. In this time, each country experienced three general elections for which its political parties published election manifestos. The year 2004 is perceived as a time when enthusiasm for integration was at its greatest and, coincidently, offered a new opportunity for political parties to broaden their influence to include the European level also. This necessarily involves the parties' adoption of norms shared in the European political environment, which support the EU integration process, and carries the risk of a possible clash between understandings of national identity—between those who stress a developing national identity and those who accept the norms of the European political space.

The book focuses on three countries of the Central East Europe (or CEE) region, which share similar experience of their past development (detailed focus is to be found in the section 3 dedicated to operationalizing of research as well as setting individual research questions). All three countries have partaken in swift integration towards Western European communities as a "return to Europe". This required not only an economic transformation, but also acceptance of Western European norms into their political and social praxis. Since the accession to the EU in 2004, the substance of attitudes towards the EU has changed. Instead of a policy goal of foreign policy, membership became a new normality and political parties had to accommodate to this new context. The thesis approaches the situation from a theoretical perspective focusing on the role of political parties in liberal democracies.It explores how their behaviour was influenced by the European environment. At the same time, it investigates how they coped with possible misconceptions of their understanding of national identity and how these (mis)fits interplay when being part of the European political environment. The thesis also means to define the understanding of national identity. For the purpose of this research, as well as to arrive at a complex understanding of national identity, the policy of national identity is introduced. To address the above-mentioned issues, this work uses an analytical framework, which analyses how the shaping and transmission of norms in the European political space influences changes in policies at a national level., Attention is paid to the influence of European political space on perception of national identity in the context of European politics and the acceptance of influence of European politics by political parties at a national level.[2]

In the time period after 2004, political parties are constantly influenced by the European political space only when they identify with their wider European environment, as well as the effects that follow from this identification. In other words, the process of socialisation takes place only when the actors have an interest in taking part in the formation of Europe. This presents a question: How do the parties that do not identify with the political environment, and that refuse its influence, react to it?[3] This question may also be approached from a different angle: How do political parties deal with the issue of deepening globalisation, increasing interdependence and the decreasing role of the nation-state under circumstances that are characterised by the nation-state remaining the basic legitimating unit? In a liberal democracy, it is expected that the question of national identity is a complex process, involving a broad palate of influences on the political party..[4] This means that the European and national contexts are set to converge. For this reason, an

---

[2] The European political space is understood as the EU institutions and Europarties. Active participation is understood as an appointment to the executive function or the election of a party member within the institution to the executive function.

[3] The most prominent case is Polish party PiS.

[4] In this sense understood as a democratic political system based on institutional check and balances

analytical framework for exploring these developments is used to analyse this process.

When discussing national identity, the potentially problematic nature of the term itself cannot go unaddressed. This work should not be considered as either a critique or defence of the term "national identity." As such, the work cannot escape the intricate relationship between the way of knowing "national identity" and the term's definition. This work introduces a research framework that allows the analysis of national identity without normative connotation. At the same time, it does not claim to offer the reader a neutral and objective way of exploring the issue of national identity. Based on the author's conscientious and careful consideration of the definition of national identity, this work aims to bring a contribution to the wider academic debate, which avoids leaning towards one concrete definition of national identity or another. The reason behind this is not to alleviate the complexity of the issue for the researcher but rather to treat it as a methodological challenge. Even though the main methodological tool used in this research is a fundamentally constructivist method of grounded theory,[5] the goal is not to present a neutral academic insight into the topic of party politics and national identity, as that is — due to its nature — almost impossible.

In the course of my work on this topic, a question arose regarding people and how they shape this European environment. This question became particularly relevant after the victory of PiS (Prawo i Sprawiedliwość/Law and Justice, PiS) in the Polish parliamentary election of 2015. This put a new perspective on the

---

5   The term itself is an object of extensive normative and methodological clashes. This work attempts to avoid these by defining four major policy areas in which the issue of national identity manifests itself the most often; based on these four areas I define the term "policy of national identity". By taking this approach, it is to some extent possible to avoid the criticism arising from not employing one of the many definitions of (national) identity. At the same time, this approach allows the researcher to overcome the division in how national identity is understood in Western and Eastern Europe, particularly through the use of a code book. The evaluation of more than ten years of CEE countries' EU membership enables us to make the conclusion that these states should not be, from the perspective of the development of national identity, considered frozen.

relationship between the European political space and the national one—and whether their interaction can be considered inadvertent or intentional.

However, the developments towards the end of 2015 demonstrated that overcoming this issue methodologically might be much easier compared to social and political reality. The migration crisis of 2015 also highlighted the ways in which this work may be beneficial to the wider public; the analytical framework employed in the political sphere allows for the analysis of issues related to migration and migrants using a framework that is identical when applied to the states of Eastern, Central and Western Europe. It is becoming clear that new political movements included in this research tend to thematize the same issues as parties in Western Europe. What is, however, even more interesting is that in doing so they use similar formulations to those that can be detected in election programs. It could be argued that in this regard, certain divisions in the conceptions of national identity have been overcome. In the course of work on the evaluation of analytical results, it was necessary to determine which codes support the building of national identity and which refuse this term. The list of codes classified according to this division is given in the Appendix A, together with the codebook that explains individual codes.

Through this process, this work provides an insight into how and to what degree the European political space is attractive for national level political parties and what this means for their participation in it, as well as their socialisation into this environment and the related adoption of attitudes corresponding to it. This approach involves an understanding of the European political space as one that is conducive to further EU integration. The approach involves analysis of election manifestos issued on the occasion of an upcoming Parliamentary election. Manifestos of three consecutive parliamentary elections serve as the main source of data.

One has to also consider the rise of political movements, which use issues related to national identity as one of their main priorities, such as TR (Twoj Ruch/Your Movement, TR), KNP (Kongres Nowej Prawycy/Congress of the New Right, KNP) in Poland, or Úsvit (Úsvit přímé demokracie Tomia Okamury/Dawn of

Direct Democracy, led by Tomio Okamura, Úsvit) in the Czech republic. In regard to the above-mentioned parties, one should pay attention to the fact that the environment of national party systems can be penetrated by external influence, in this case by the participation of parties at a European level. Therefore, the conducted research offers a complex picture of not only the development of national identity in Central East Europe, but also of the influence of external impulses on political parties. In other words, how parties are able to respond to the demand of the public for policies related to national identity.

In a national context, the analysis covers parliamentary political parties that have had political representation at both national and also European level. Election manifestos published on the occasion of the three parliamentary elections, in the period from 2004 till 2013 in each country, have been used as the main source of data for the analysis. The descriptions of three selected issues related to the issue of national identity serve to set the context for the issue of national identity in each country.

In the context of this work, the perception of national identity is understood as the policy of individual parties which reflect national identity. At the general level, this work focuses on how a certain specific policy area, at a national level, is influenced under circumstances whereby the European political environment is understood as a forum in which policies are created and/or realised by individual party representative. A party representative's nomination or election to office in a European institution – part of the defined European political space – is then considered to be the party's deliberate activity in this political space.

2.2. The context of the CEE region

With their entrance into the EU, countries in the CEE regions reached a so-called Return to Europe.[6] While this moment is often

---

6 All three countries (the Czech Republic, Polandand Slovakia) belong in geographic terms to Central (East) Europe. At the same time, this geographic aspect may be considered as limited by a lack of clarity with regard to the notion of

perceived as having only now brought political and economic success, a great part of getting closer to Europe began only after 2004. For direct actors, entrance into the EU meant the aim of getting closer to the so-called old EU countries. However, the year 2004 was merely the beginning of the much more difficult process of accepting the norms and functions of the EU and of the European political arena (Pridham 2005, Bandej et. al. 2015).

"Central Europe." Where exactly can we find its borders? Are the cultural or historical frontiers salient? In addition to the fact that 'Central Europe' is a rather fluid concept, this idea also has the function of refusing the label of "Eastern Europe". Overall, what we can observe is a case of delimitation vis-a-vis the outside. The transformation post 1989 results into two points: firstly all three countries aimed to be part of Western Europe after 1989 and therefore incorporated the norms of the Western communities with this aim. Secondly, all three countries aimed to cultivate their Central-Europeanness as a phenomenon delineated primarily not in geographic terms, but as a cultural space between the East and the West. At its center is a continuing discussion and negotiations over mutual influence and the adoption of culture and social norms — not only inside the V4 region but also from outside. Through consolidation of Central-Europeanness the aim is not only to achieve certain neutrality in the context of advancing globalization, but also to take advantage of it in cementing a shared awareness. In the context of the EU integration project it is often called into question the regional consciousness is being artificially solidified without necessarily provoking aggressive criticism.

From this perspective these states represent an example of building Central-Europeanness but at the same time they prove eager to be integrated into the EU hand in hand with accepting the norms of the European political space. After 1989 each of the three countries experienced a rise in ethic nationalism that has been left out of mainstream politics — with the exception of Slovakia. Not much attention is paid to developments after 2004 — can these countries be analyzed without dividing them from Western Europe? To what extent have these countries different patterns of party politics as well as the perception of national identity? Therefore, the most interesting perspective to be researched in the particular case of the three countries is the rapidity of changes that these states experienced in the context of shaping their Central-Europeanness. These elements make them interesting cases for further analysis, as the immigration crisis showed in 2015. There is another characteristic that makes these named states interesting from the perspective of national identity research, namely the rapidity of changes of their governing parties promoting a conservative or liberal understanding of national identity. Based on scholarly literature, it has to be mentioned that this work tries to overlap an approach of seeing the CEE region as a special one and at the same time to propose an analytical framework for national identity research. In this context, the argumentation of Jan Rovný is followed in terms analyzing the cleavage order of individual party systems in both the CEE region and Western Europe (Rovný 2012a, 2015).

The transformation of individual states after 1990 has also meant that the current impact of trans-nationalisation is much greater, because states were not directly involved in the beginning of mutual post-war integration. This is demonstrated for instance by Hloušek and Chytilek (2007: 7) and Birch (2007: 11), who discuss the effect of accepting EU norms via *aquis communitaere* as proof of the will to be part of Western structures (meaning the EU and NATO). Nevertheless, after their entry into the EU, these conditions became the same for both the old and the new states of the EU (Kriesi et al. 2006: 922).

The accession was perceived predominantly to be opening new opportunities for societies as well as for political parties (Cibulka 2012: 33, Szpala 2015, Strážay 2015). Speaking about individual case studies, governments in the Czech Republic, Poland and Slovakia each conducted a referendum on joining the EU in 2003. All three states followed a similar path – and the results oscillated between 71 and 77 % in favor of entering the EU (Strážay 2015: 35, Szpala 2015: 66). In this context, one has to consider the high, positive expectations of the public and of political parties to support their country's accession. This meant that raising relevant opposition was not only undertaken by less relevant political bodies, but also among government representatives such as ODS (the leading government party between 2006 and 2009) and PiS (between 2005 and 2007). The context of the Slovak accession to the EU is particularly interesting. The political commitment to join the EU came in 1998 with the formation of the so-called "anti-Mečiar" pro-EU government. This resulted in the rapid adoption of aquis communiteare as well as important free market-oriented reforms. It would not have been possible without a strong, shared political and social engagement (Strážay 2015). Another important characteristic of entry into the EU was the fact that, despite the existence of opposition, positive perception of and support for the EU in these in individual countries had reached unprecedented heights.

In the decade after 2004 there was a drop in these positive perceptions and a shift toward a daily struggle with European matters. Parties and societies experience the impact of growing trans-nationalization on their own and they assess these implications in regard to their electorate (Werner-Müller 2016). The result of this process is not always a positive acceptance of the trans-nationalization process or effective participation in the European political space. This is demonstrated, for instance, in research published by Klingemann (2014: 123) showing that the perception of democracy as a positive value in Central East European societies did not rise significantly in the period between 1999 and 2009. Therefore, it is expected that the impact of trans-nationalization on societies of the CEE region, as well as their political parties, may result in significant changes of political competition.[7]

Constant evolution of the external environment — such as the EU — is reflected among other things in the form of deepening of EU integration in its federalized understanding. The main factor remains the ever-increasing degree of interconnectedness of individual EU member states and their regions. There is an ever-growing intensity of influence from transnational companies, where the unit of sovereign states as the basic category plays an increasingly minor role (Beck 2007, Mau and Mewes 2012, Kaupi 2013). Nevertheless, politics is still a national affair (de Vries 2007, Krouwel 2004). In this context, it is necessary to take into account the manner in which such a development is reflected by political parties.[8] Looking at the

---

[7] From a broader perspective, entry into the EU represented the end of the development of national and nationalistic tendencies, which emerged after the fall of the USSR in individual countries. This issue was intensely dealt with, for example, by George Schöpflin (2000) who approached the post-communist countries like he would a group of states which after 1990 saw the opportunity of building a new national, ethnically influenced, identity. This argument primarily applies to countries of the former Soviet Union and is less applicable to the Czech Republic, Poland, and Slovakia. It cannot be ignored that the fall of communism kicked some nationally tuned tendencies which had been kept under wraps by the communist regime (Breurilly 1993, Walsch 2015, Wegs and Landrech 2002: 334).

[8] The argument is based on the assumption that dimensional differences of the EU party systems were overcome. This also applies to the issue of national identity. The researched states accept similar concepts of insight into the perception of national identity by political parties, which is of course true of mainstream parties. This especially includes the situation where CEE parties face similar issues connected with national identity (such as immigration) as Western European states such as immigration. An entirely typical example is the issue of refugees from the Middle East and Africa. It follows that political parties will be

timeline after the 2004, it is evident that boosting social and political expectations during a pro-EU campaign leads to opposite consequence. Namely, the shaping of a new national identity narrative as a new member state, whilst coping with negative aspects of free market, such as the economic and debt crisis and the migration crisis. The historian Philipp Ther (2015: 318) argues that over the past decade, the CEE region has struggled to find its role in a globalized Europe.[9] This flux is often translated into politics coloured with a national identity when seeking the easiest political solutions.[10] Therefore issues related to national identity — not just in the CEE region — become increasingly significant and help create new political divisions (Krastev, Leonard 2014, Hanley 2015).[11]

There has been a gradual growth of socialization towards party activities in the European political arena , along with a growing presumption that party positions are reflected in party programs and activities. To this extent it is not perceived merely as a sector worthy of being thematized in a political struggle, but rather as a complex transformation of the political and social functioning of society and the states. This issue has been the focus of extensive academic attention (Haughton 2009, Pridham 2002, 2005, van Kessel 2015). Generally speaking the issue centres around the relationship between external environment and political party-interaction between European political space and individual parties using party members as agents of policy change.

---

exposed to a much wider range of questions regarding national identity rather than "only" concerning themselves with issues of consolidating national consciousness.

9   Following this argumentation, Ivan Krastev (2016) points out that values of liberal democracy have not penetrated all layers of CEE societies properly and therefore political leaders orient themselves in the current complex situation only with difficulty.

10 As confirmed by the representatives of several parties during field research, these issues are very easily used when mobilizing voters.

11 For more about the question of rise of new identity narrative that contradicts norms of European political space in the CEE region see (Krastev, Leonard 2014, Zalan 2016).

2.3. Central Eastern Europe as matter of research

The CEE region has been widely researched over the past decade when it comes to transferring EU norms to the context of individual countries. Furthermore, a significant body of research has paid attention to the rise of nationalistic tendencies during the early transformation period — as was the case of Poland and Slovakia. Haughton eds. (2011), Lewis, Mansfredová eds. (2006), and Klingemann, Fuchs, Klingemann, Zielonka eds. (2006) have produced extensive analysis of the impact of Europeanization on the party systems of CEE countries, each with a focus on ‚particular events and point in time, and on the impact of participation on EU policy-making. More detailed research has been carried out in individual states of the CEE region, for example Poland: Deegan-Krause, Haughton (2014), Poland—Szczerbiak (2012), Kasprowicz (2014), the Czech Republic—Hloušek, Kopeček (2011), Hanley (2008), and Slovakia Haughton, Rybář (2008). One should also mention scholars focusing on the CEE region as a unique research topic experiencing different development than that which has been researched in Western democracies. For example, Daniel Bochesler (2010) or Maria Spirova (2007) researched the effects of nationalization on electoral systems. Only a very limited scope of research — speaking about the CEE region as a whole — sets a broader framework for the interaction of norms at a national and supranational level on the perception of political parties, see for example, Whitefield and Rohrscheider (2012). This is also the case for research published by Freyburg and Richter (2010) on the role of national identity within the EU integration process of the Western Balkan states.

Based on various studies (Haughton 2010, Webb, White 2007), it has been proven that selected CEE countries differ in terms of the question of dominance of topics or dimensionality. It is therefore not surprising that the area of socio-economics is dominant in the Czech Republic. In the case of Poland and Slovakia, there is less emphasis on the socio-economic dimension and instead a focus on the city versus countryside[12] (Hloušek 2005, Kopeček 2005). This does not mean that in all states, the same dominating dimension affects policy.

In this context Rovný (2012, 2015) points out that the definitions of otherness represent the view of Western academics from the perspective of Western political party systems as well as the quest for aproximity with those systems. Furthermore, it is necessary to consider the fact that political party systems in the CEE countries were often shaped on the basis of cleavages without a deeper regard either for historical or broader social context. Key elements of the CEE party systems were defined by Herbert Kitschelt (1992: 14) as follows: there is an emphasis on the individualization of society with a lesser emphasis on traditional concepts of the social and class layers of post-communist regimes. In terms of policy, it is the dominance of social liberalism versus particularism/ social conservatism/ authoritarianism, and market versus state allocation of resources. On the other hand, studies published following Herbert Kitschelt have stressed the need to focus on the specifics of individual countries and pointed out the unreliability of area comparisons (Evans, Whitefield 1993).

As shown, for example, by research published by Jan Rovný (2012, 2015: 11), there is a blurring of the differences between the relevance of selected policies on the left-right political spectrum in

---

12 At this point it is necessary to also mention the broad elements which shape the political concept of the CEE region based on shared characteristics which reinforce the argument of mutual closeness; this is an element of views about Central Europeanism, not primarily in geographic categories, but also as a cultural space between the East and West. This has resulted in constant discussion about the mutual influence and acceptance of culture and social norms, not only within the V4 but also externally. The effort to consolidate Central European aims to achieve some sort of neutrality on advancing globalization, but also to use its resources to strengthen this awareness. This awareness also strengthens a third element: affiliation with the communist legacy. The role of this element underlines the fact that this is a generally negative connotation of legacy. The legacy of the past is bound to the element of the commemorated Austro-Hungarian link – a nostalgic legacy that is growing stronger in the center of the V4 region, i.e. in those places which were direct parts of the Austrian influence. The legacy is kept alive by existing architectural monuments, built up by interconnected infrastructures, and among other things, by a shared gastronomical heritage.

the old and new EU countries. Based on research aimed at the policy of dimensionality, Rovný (2015: 6) reached the conclusion that "some of these copy the West with the economic left taking social liberal positions, while the economic right adopts social conservatism." Strikingly, the variance in these competition patterns does not reflect the explanations highlighted in the literature. These competition patterns do not coincide with different communist regime types, communist successor party strategies or transition paths. Research by Gaxie and Hubé (2013: 178–179), which is focused on the perception of European integration by political and socio-economic national elites, concludes that between eastern and western member states there is almost no difference in stance toward the EU, and in turn what actually dominate the ideological base. Therefore, economic questions are beginning to prevail, while ethnic ones are being side-lined. In other words, a shift is developing in the examination of the CEE region in comparison to Western European states, without the context and peculiarity of individual CEE states having to be extensively specified.

The bulk of recently published literature pays attention to the development of the CEE region in regard to trends in party systems (Haughton 2014, Klíma 2015, Hanley 2015) in a context of interaction with EU norms. Similarly to the attention to the early transformation period, the issue of nationalism is researched again. Despite significant attention to divergent political and social tendencies of the CEE region with Western EU states, comprehensive research focusing on this development is missing. In this context, Ágh (2016: 78) analyses the "second wave" of the Europeanization of the CEE, as a result of significant negative effects of participating in the European political space, due to a declined attractiveness of the EU-supporting narrative.[13] Research undertaken by Whitenfield and Rohrschneider (2015: 15, 26) shows the erosion of permissive consensus in the case of support for the EU in the CEE region. They prove that this development in the region follows the similar path

---

13 Rupnik and Zielonka call this process a "democratic regression" (2012: 7). Both Rupnik and Zielonka as well as Ágh see the main challange to strenghten civil society in order to act as a counter element to business and political elite.

of Western party systems by picking up the European issue. This puts the region into a different research perspective in terms of Europeanization research, as e.g. Rovný (2015) shows. Following a similar logic, Haugton and Deegan-Krause (2015) place the rapid changes in the party systems of CEE states into the broader context of the external (European) environment in line with eroding support of traditional parties as key defenders of a European consensus. In a similar way, Vachudova (2005: 524) points out that the leverage of the EU is declining as it loses attractiveness in the CEE region.

3. Structure

This thesis is divided into five main parts. The first chapter introduces the theoretical background and describes the complexity of the topic being researched. To get a complex picture about the influence of the European political space on political parties on national level, the context as well as the substance of the party system in each individual state has to be considered. Therefore, the first part is dedicated to framing the trans-national context that influences individual states and their responses of this influence. This part deals with the question of swift integration with the EU and the opening of space for national parties to participate in European politics. Through their participation, political parties become aware of the fact that EU membership also means a diminished role for borders and having to react more often to external influences that they are not able to affect. It introduces the theoretical background in regard to European political space, namely to perception of the political space as a normative arena as well as a window of opportunity.

The second part is dedicated to the elements that constitute the policy of national identity. These elements combine both a long and short-term strategy. In broader terms, they aim to set a background for constituting any policy field. The use of such an approach in this research intends to combine sources dealing with aspects shaping policies and literature relevant for national identity. Every policy is constituted in a certain context — domestic as well as external. For the purpose of this work, the domestic context has been set as a past experience, which enables parties to put their election manifestos into the accurate social context they act in. The external environment has been set as influencing the shaping of policy but with less visible impact on individual outputs — as the European integration, in other words as the European political space. Both elements are intended to shape the environment for the individual actions of a political party.

The third part of this work is dedicated to describing the research methodology and procedure. Emphasis is placed on a theoretical background for the research procedure, as well as a comparison of both quantitative and qualitative methods used for evaluation of results. For this purpose, the research procedure is framed by theories of constructivism used in social science research.

The fourth part aims to explore the results of data analysis, focusing on individual states, and comparing them as well. Based on the introduced context this part focuses on changes within the election manifestos of all parliamentary political parties. This is done by quantifying the changes in election manifestos using both negative and positive codes for nationalism. This provides space for a comparison of individual election manifestos within individual countries and also allows one to see the development over time during the past three general elections. The second part of the analysis puts the results of evaluation of election manifestos into a context of parties' participation in the European political space. It analyses the influence of the European political space on individual parties in the researched period. The fifth and final part is dedicated to conclusions and focuses on the most relevant results of research connected to the influence of the European space on political parties.

4. Theoretical background

This work contributes to existing research from the following perspectives. Firstly, the work explores how parties accepted the European political space between 2004 and 2013. It focuses on the extension of influence from perspective of the European political space and its attractiveness for political parties to accommodate its ements into party manifestos. To do so, the work employs a theoretical background relevant for Europeanization and the role of political parties when transferring norms from the European to a national level. Secondly, this work contributes to a deeper understanding of the European political space and its influence both on political parties and the CEE region – meaning the Czech Republic, Poland and Slovakia. Based on above-mentioned, the work applies an analytical framework focusing on the influence of the European political space on the perception of policy of national identity in election manifestos. It also conceptualizes the issue of national identity as used by political parties. This issue is defined as a scope of issues used by parties regardless of their purpose (nationalistic as well as liberal parties). This open definition – the work sets the general framework – offers a tool for research of the perception of national identity and its development. Approaching the national identity as a policy field, the work sets the term *policy of national identity*. Bearing this in mind, the meaning of national identity is changing from party to party, and from manifesto to manifesto. From this point of view, the work aims to research the perception of national identity instead of a definition of national identity.[14]

---

14   In literature as well as in the academic environment, the terms nationalizing and national identity are widely used without specific definition. To avoid any misinterpretations, this work follows this definition: nationalizing in terms of developing political actions in order to strengthen national consciousness as well as actively developing a particular national myth. In this case, this term is approached from a normative perspective. The term national identity, in contrast to the previous term, is understood without normative connotations. and is expanded on/filled out by issues relevant to national identity, case by case as it is defined by each political party.

4.1. Political parties

4.1.1. The role of political parties

Political parties are undoubtedly one of the most important actors in society. Political parties communicate the interests and demands of the public and of interest groups to government. The broad definition of the function of political parties can be summarized as follows: 1) the integration and mobilization of citizens; 2) the articulation and aggregation of interests; 3) the formulation of public policy; 4) the recruitment of political leaders; and 5) the organization of parliament and government (Norris 2005). Kriesi et al (2006: 150) points out that the public has the possibility to constantly mobilize their interests towards political parties. At the same time, parties set the agenda on what topics are discussed and direct attention towards particular political aims or decisions (Kriesi 2006: 151). In this context, parties frame certain issues in a manner that is tailored to the public. Processing of these issues is the key common area of focus for both citizen and political party (Kriesi 2006: 151). Therefore, political parties are a relevant component in the process of shaping the perceptions of historical and cultural factors that play an important role in constituting a nation's identity (Jarausch and Lindenberger 2007).[15] As Benoit and Laver (2006:1) mention, a justification for representative democracy is to promote certain issues to the wider electorate. These issues represent positions of public and into certain extent, these issues represent public positions. The role of political parties is especially important in those societies which have undergone repeated processes of transition—from authoritarian regimes to liberal democracy (Bornschier 2009).

The role of political parties in liberal democracies is to transmit the interests and demands of society to correspond with a given social context. In other words, parties shape their manifestos based on their previous experience and also the political and social context. In this sense, the electoral process is a mechanism for identifying preferences from voters to political parties (McDonald, Budge

---

15 See the part on political parties and election manifestos.

2005:4). Pierson (2000, 2004) argues that historical knowledge is a key source of insight into the nature of the social world (2004: 2). Pierson claims that real social processes have a distinctly temporal dimension and therefore we cannot separate historical knowledge from theories produced by social sciences (2004: 5). For this purpose, one can use the path dependence theory to strengthen the role of history. The works of the prominent constructivist scholar Alexander Wendt are related to path dependence theory. His research emphasizes the effect of cultural and political identity on foreign policy and how states act in international relations in general.[16] This generally explains utilization of history and the past experience of parties in their actions as a relevant factor for constituting policy.[17]

To put the significance of the political and social context into a vocabulary of political competition, one can employ the cleavage framework – and in particular, the Rokkanean cleavage analytical framework. Rokkan focused on the set of party system specific cleavage order; he found the role of "national cleavage" relevant for the positioning of political parties towards the issue of nationality. Although his main concerns were the specific processes of democratization and nation building, his most significant contribution is a definition of widely applicable cleavages in a party system. One can adopt Rokkan's analytical concept because it emphasizes the connection between territorial boundary-building strategies and the cleavage theory. Rokkan uses the term cleavage structure as a conceptual link between a social structure and political system, and between structuring and boundary-building (Flora 1999: 35).

---

16 Pierson (2000: 263) defines four categories which are significant for the political life of parties regarding their "returns" and "path dependency" to their own past experience. Multiple equilibria: under a set of initial conditions conducive to increasing returns, a number of general outcomes are possible. Contingency: small events, if they occur, can have large consequences. A critical role for timing and sequencing: in increasing returns processes, when an event occurs, may be crucial; the earlier part of a sequence matters more than the later ones.Inertia: Once an increasing returns process is established, positive feedback may lead to a single equilibrium that will in turn be resistant to change.

17 In regard to research on political parties' perception of national identity, a national history may inspire self-sacrificing love. This, together with kinship expressions like motherland, home, or natural ties with the territory constitute the narrative "nation" ties between person and nation (Anderson 2005: 141, 205).

In the post-war period, the emphasis on quality of life, the environment, democracy, and human rights rose significantly. Inglehart claims there has been a culture shift evidenced by the rise of new social movements (e.g. peace movements), and the growth of post-materialist parties (e.g. Greens). This went hand-in-hand, Rokkan contends, with the diminishing role of a traditional left working class and the rise of new left political parties who tended to accept post-materialist values in their manifestos as well (Inglehart 1989). Therefore, a new cleavage in party systems has emerged, between materialism and post-materialism. Inglehart argues that there is evidence of a shift towards post-materialism, away from religious values, and towards a redefinition of the right/left continuum. At the same time the party system has been faced with pressure to appeal to a new generation, which in turn has also driven the trend towards post-materialism (Inglehart 1989). In this sense, the rise of post-materialistic values has occurred alongside the process of trans-nationalization of boundaries and the generally decreasing role of nation states discussed above. Further research by Inglehart (2007) shows that the changing perception of values in Western democracies has significantly reshaped the party system. As already mentioned, the response of a political system based on nation states is problematic. Echoing Rokkan's ideas on the impact of historical experience on nation states, one has to add the popular phrase history matters. Taking into account Rokkan's concept, the analysis cannot be separated from historical circumstances that shaped the—in this case—the country party system.

Since the parties have to cope with a wider arena of activities than only the national one, this opens a discussion of how the broader context is incorporated into parties' manifestos. Looking at the issue from a different point of view, it indicates the possibility of creating a transnational cleavage in individual party systems. There has been a rise in national identity colored politics across Europe in the past few years. Issues such as the migration crisis (2015/2016), the British referendum concerning the UK leaving the EU, or the concept of illiberal democracy by Viktor Orbán in 2014 are framed by a rhetoric stressing thee national sovereignty and aiming to decrease freedom of cross-border exchange. Using

Rokkan's approach, the issue of trans-nationalization has become a critical juncture in terms of an emerging political cleavage (Inglehart 2007: 133). This means that the post-materialistic cleavage becomes increasingly relevant to the issues mentioned above and the agenda of political competition.

4.1.2. Europeanization

The previous section was dedicated to the contextual mechanisms of individual party systems when policy priorities emerge. Despite the fact that policy priorities are relevant to the national level, the influence of the EU as a norm-creating structure has to be considered. Although policies are primarily created at a national level, the wider EU context plays a crucial role considering the influx of contracts and structure as well as new ideas shaping society. The study of the Europeanization of political parties has introduced a wide scope of volumes of investigation of EU integration and its influence on the national party system from the perspective of a) the EU as a normative transforming power in terms of the democratization of post-communist states, b) the effects on national party systems both of policy and institutional change, and c) individual case studies experiencing the impact of transformation. Each individual analysis is highly relevant for an understanding of institutional change in post-communist countries. The following overview focuses on political parties of the CEE region from an institutional and policy perspective.

4.1.2.1. Perspective of democratization

Speaking about the CEE region, the literature focusing on the development of communist regimes into liberal democracies is connected with the process of EU accession. It deals mainly with the international dimension and the domestic context of democratization. Pridham (1996: 2) defines democratization as an overall process of regime change from start to completion, i.e. from the end of the previous authoritarian regime to the stabilisation and rooting of new democracies. Pridham contends that countries which experienced the democratization process followed the narrative of liberal democracy as constituted in the case of Western countries.

Following that narrative served as a device for undertaking the process of democratization (Whitehead 2002: 36–37). Adhering to a similar line, Kubicek (2003: 10) gives an account of the context of democratization of CEE countries and EU integration while describing the conditions for transformation. He pays attention to the fact that democratization goes hand in hand with an enlarging space of certain (EU) norms.– in other words, to fill up the vacuum left after the removal of the norms and praxis of authoritarian regimes. In a similar vein, Sedelmeier argues that setting up developing conditions for the Eastern enlargement of the EU was a sign of the EU's responsibility towards the CEE region (2009: 102).

This corresponds with the argument that the setting of conditions also brought an element of normative pressure on political parties and institutions. The fall of communism in Central-East Europe was accompanied by an emphasis on the narrative of the EU as a democratic community. This was done to frame the relations of the EU towards the CEE countries, as well as to bolster resistance to communism in those countries. In doing so, the democratizing nature of the CEE region's transformation was supported as the key element (Fuchs, Klingemann 2011: 26). Many scholars argue that for successful democratization, cultural similarities have to exist. However, these can vary when it comes to the level of a shared (political) culture (Fuchs 1999, Fuchs, Klingemann 2006: 27). Fuchs, Klingemann (2006: 28) define four factors determining the density of the democratization process: a) the quality of the political process as a realization of collective goals, b) the cultural level as a support for fundamental democratic values, c) the structural level in terms of dedicating support to the state as a democratic system, d) the process level as a realization of political objectives by producing collectively binding decisions.

In this context, the EU has acted as a strong transformative power, enabling CEE countries the process of democratic transition. At the same time, CEE countries proved capable of being influenced by liberal democracy as defined by the EU. Furthermore, values of liberal democracy are constantly developing within the EU environment, i.e. the environment CEE countries are part of.

4.1.2.2. Party systems

The wide scope of Europeanization literature offers various perspectives on the impact on parties acting in the European political space. Ladrech (2012) argues that performance on the European level has rarely had any significant impact on the activities of national organizations (2012: 185).[18] At the same time, changes to party politics may happen during election campaigns and – less commonly – in the arena of real policy or institutional practice. Therefore, most policy changes rely on the institutional changes of an individual party, on domestic factors and less on external (EU) factors. In this regard Börzel (2009: 15) points out that Europeanization can be conceived of as a two-fold process. It involves the evolution at the European level of a distinct governance system, a new set of political structures and processes, which interact with the established ones of the member states. Hence, Europeanization entails a "bottom-up" and a "top-down" dimension.

The common denominator of Europeanization literature is the significant rise of elements influencing the national party system, as well as the functions of individual political parties. A significant number of studies of the Europeanization of political parties deal with policy and institutional (polity) change of policy-policy level (European versus national), as well as polity-polity level (institutional change of the parties). Tanja Börzel (2009: 16) summarizes the main scopes of research: a) domestic systems of interest intermediation, b) territorial politics, c) national bureaucracies, d) administrative structures, e) regulatory structures, f) the relationship between executive and legislature, g) electoral and party politics, h) judicial structures, i) macro-economic institutions, and j) national identities. The research implies that institutional changes in polity dimension or the existence of a transnational polity dimension as such implies changes in the fields of policy (Knill 2001). This conceptual dimension of a party's Europeanization also include

---

18 This mechanism has been matter of theoretical research for example by Mair (2000) or more specifically when it comes to CEE region by von dem Berge and Poguntke (2012)

intergovernmental bargaining or non/governmental party status (Sitter 2003, Haughton 2009, Dimitri 2012).

One set of studies focuses on the demarcation line between parties opposing integration and partisan actors supporting integration (Taggart 1998; Taggart and Szczerbiak 2003, Topaloff 2012). The approach to the research of EU-integration and partisan responses can be understood as a product of divergent opposition strategies (Sitter 2003). Sitter (2003) offers a different perspective, arguing that government participation is generally incompatible with the pursuit of party-based Euroscepticism. Participating in a government coalition constrains the articulation of (natural) Eurosceptical positions.[19] Another line of research provides insight into EU-integration-based party responses and conceives these as an outcome of ideological compatibilities and incompatibilities between parties' preferences (e.g. Hooghe et al. 2002).

Considering the perspectives described above, the approach of accommodation developed by Thomas Risse and Tanja Börzel (Börzel 2005; Börzel and Risse 2002, 2010) shows the expected influence of EU membership. They argue (Börzel, Risse 2011) that the key element of Europeanization is that Europeanization must be "inconvenient," i.e. there must be some degree of "misfit" or incompatibility between European-level processes, policies and institutions, on the one hand, and domestic-level processes, policies and institutions, on the other. This degree of fit or misfit leads to adaptational pressures, which constitute a necessary but not sufficient condition for expecting domestic change. The second condition is that various facilitating factors respond to the adaptational pressures, thus inducing the change. However, this does not necessarily mean that the parties will maintain EU-friendly policy; as the effect on the Europeanization of political parties shows (Dimitri 2012).

---

19 Dimitri (2012: 36) assumes that party-based Euroscepticism is seen by the electorate as being incompatible with governmental credibility. This can be considered as the influence of EU integration has differentiated government-opposition positions, impacting political parties and their policies. If one takes into consideration the general presumption that experience in government leads to a weakening of Eurosceptic positioning, the analytical emphasis will be given on changes in content of parties' policies.

Risse and Börzel's theories help to tackle the wider context of the environment that is based upon both the effect of confronting with a norm and the result of bargaining.[20]

This leads to two different frameworks for the Europeanization of political parties, from Whitenfield and Rohrscheider. Whitefield (2006) argues that the EU has an impact on political parties in terms of dynamic representation—changing the structure of party organization. At the same time, both scholars expect institutional and policy stability due to the fact that voters do not expect such changes where they are not directly involved. Speaking about CEE countries and the effect of Europeanization, Poguntke (2010) expects variations among individual countries. As Haughton (2011: 7) mentions, the change of party policies varies case by case and the penetration of EU-related issues does not take place to a broader extent. In this context, a policy of national identity is a cross-dimensional policy that may prove to have a broader, indirect impact of the EU on party politics.

4.2. European political space

Regarding the deepening process of European Integration as well as the deepening globalization of societies across nation states, nation-based party systems must react to this new state. Political parties have to deal with the growing transnational dimension in their policy as they respond to a lessening of their direct influence, but the basic architecture of nation-based party systems remains

---

[20] Considering the literature on Europeanization, it may be approached from the perspective of rational choice and/or sociological institutionalism. The first argues that the EU enabled domestic changes as a result of inducing changes in opportunity structures for (domestic) actors (as newly-created conditions demanded domestic change). In other words, parties will tend to have changes in policy if they see practical benefits and new funding opportunities. The second approach focuses on the changed behaviour of actors as the result of a change in norms, practices, and ideas (in terms of identification with the new structures). Tanja Börzel (2011: 25) points to the rational choice and sociological institutionalist approaches having two underlying logics of Europeanization — the logic of consequentialism and the logic of appropriateness.

unchanged.[21] However, a rise in the trans-nationalization of political parties challenges party systems bounded by nations. This in spite of the fact that parties still gain their legitimacy at national elections.[22] The most important arena therefore remains the national one.

---

21 Sarcinelli (2009: 124–5) argues that political communication creates the legitimization structure as well. In this respect, from an institutional perspective, communication enables inner and outer legitimacy (Sarcinelli 2009: 127) Ruderin offers two types of representation: descriptive, referring to the demographic characteristic of the state and bringing some interesting insight on researched issues. The higher the level of descriptive representation, the more stable the system. However, this claim is based on a normative presumption that a representative should mirror the population (Ruedin 2013:14). In this sense, mobilization without group identification is possible. The second type of representation is substantive, focusing for example on the dynamics of spatial voting and aiming to define the conflict dimension of politics (in a certain state). If one employs the Weberian approach, communication is a power tool in a politician's hands and also an element of political leadership. Therefore, the level of personalisation between politicians and the electorate grows significantly, especially at election time. As argued above, representatives (here operationalized as political parties) influence and shape the arenas of acting; nonetheless, representative democracy is based on the presumption that parties act for the people. Therefore, elections provide widely accepted claims to legitimacy since the relationship between representative and citizens is reinforced during an election campaign. In Weberian understanding, the relationship between representative and citizen can be legitimized only if those giving up power accept it as such. In empirical research Dider Ruedin shows that issues of national identity as well as nationalism (focused on national minorities) are still relevant in some party systems. Therefore, one should consider the role of policy dimension properly.

22 Although political parties act in an environment that is transnational in terms of policy as well as polity, still, they gain their legitimacy primarily on a national level. Therefore, the consequences for a national party system in terms of the structure of policy competition, has to be considered. Parties reflect this fact by incorporating these issues into their manifestos and policies etc. Thanks to this, parties create — rationally and emotionally — new spaces of belonging that are incorporated into their policies; and create a foreign policy for the state when in government. An investigation of party ideology shows differences in content between parties, but does not explain deeper party motivation. The issue of trans-nationalization may become a critical juncture in terms of emerging a political cleavage. In this context, the Rokkanean Cleavage Analytical Framework must be mentioned. Rokkan focused on the set of party system specific cleavage order; Rokkan found the role of "national cleavage" relevant for the positioning of political parties towards the element of nationality. Although Rokkan focused on party systems in the process of democratization and nation-building, his most significant contribution to party system analysis is a definition of widely applicable cleavages in the party system. One can adopt Rokkan's

However, in spite of the amount of political activity realized beyond the national state (e.g. within the EU) and the organisation of parties into transnational political parties, they have a significant lack of legitimacy outside the national level. Nonetheless, parties cope with issues that are essentially transnational ones.

Writing from a normative perspective, Mau, Mewes (2012) and Zürn (1998) suggest that closed national states are threatened with decreasing control over territory and society, and that no new political party system has been effectively developed.[23] In this sense, many scholars advocate for the introduction of an EU-wide common electoral system for the European Parliament election, or else a significant redefinition of the role of the European Council (see e.g. Werner Müller 2015). By that logic, the European political space would have a role in each national party system regardless of whether parties intend to participate. The argument rests on the proposition that European political parties as well as political groups in the European Parliament represent the transnational influence on parties in a practical way.[24] Speaking about the role of political parties, this process can be "seen as a new critical juncture, which is likely to result in the formation of new structural cleavages, both within and between national contexts" (Kriesi et al. 2006: 922). Referring to the impact on political

---

    analytical concept because it emphasizes the connection of territorial boundary-building strategies and the cleavage theory. Rokkan uses the term cleavage structure as a conceptual link between social structure and political system, and between structuring and boundary-building (Flora 1999: 35).

23 One can argue that even though some new deliberative mechanism within the EU has been implemented (such as the Convention on Negotiation of the European Constitution), effective execution is missing.

24 Regarding the growth in transnational exchange, Castells (2010, 333) argues that the deconstruction of nation states brings significant growth in regionalism. In an extreme case, the territories are able to mobilize for a renegotiation of their nation-state contract, or be an active player in the global system, e.g. the case of Catalonia. Castells (2010, 334) claims that civil society is the key element for responding to a plurality of identities forwarding to the nation-state. Concerning the topic of national identity and nationalism issues in analysed countries, it is highly important to mention this fact. One has to take into consideration how far the parties reflect this changing environment and how their communications channels, for example their election manifestos, are influenced. This process can also cause divergence in connection with trans-nationalization, leading to a growth of national perceptions and (re)nationalizing of their profiles by using this process in negative connotations.

competition, Kriesi goes on to argue that "the lowering and unbundling of national boundaries renders them politically more salient. As they are weakened and reassessed, their political importance increases. Generally, we expect losers of the globalization process to seek to protect themselves through protectionist measures and through an emphasis on the maintenance of national boundaries and independence. Winners, by contrast, who benefit from the increased competition, should support the opening up of the national boundaries and the process of international integration." (Kriesi et al. 2006: 923)

On the same subject, Paasi (2001) argues that the decreasing role of the national state, together with movements towards an increased role for the regions, causes a significant redefinition of subnational units in Europe. Still, political parties frame the concrete region/state in order to divide and control space and people (Paasi 2009, 15).[25]

The European political space is an environment consisting of two main elements. Firstly, the space beyond the national arena enables parties to expand their field of influence. In this respect, it is in the long-term interest for parties to promote the national interest in Europe, which can thus be perceived as an arena for promoting the interests of political parties. Following this logic, political parties have to identify their short- and long-term goals within the European political space in order to effectively participate in the European political arena (Moravscik, Vachudova 2003: 52).[26] Secondly, there is an

---

25 According to this logic, states are still the main constituent unit for political parties to secure their influence and power. Therefore the nationally colour labels are being offered to political subjects to secure the state against erosion. However, political parties also use national labels to erode the state, e.g. Catalan flags everywhere or Scottish language signage to take two pertinent examples. Catalunya and Scotland are nations by most definitions, but they are not states.

26 A common part of the political discourse of the CEE states was the normative perception of the region as different or "more frozen" than the old member states of the EU. According to this, they experienced swift change from being concerned only with national issues to being influenced by the European arena (Pridham 2005). The key characteristics of the difference are summarized by Lewis (2000: 24) as follows: "the weak links of many new parties with well-defined social groups and the increasingly professional approach taken to the critical task of winning elections suggest the growing association of east European parties with variants of the catch-all and electoral professional party.:" Political parties of the CEE region that joined in 2004 already existing political

influence of the European space on political parties in terms of policy change. The influence of the European space on national political parties and their institutional setting as well as policy setting has been widely researched by Checkel (2007), Schimmelfennig, Engert, and Knobel (2006) while the effect of membership of parties in the European Parliament in terms of institutional or policy change has been researched by Scully 2005.[27]

When it comes to the issue of motivation for parties to participate in the European political space, a rational-consequentialist approach provides frameworks for further analysis. According to this method, parties are motivated to participate in the European arena to maximize their utility (Müller 2004. 403). Müller argues that "the logic of consequences would dominate in a sequence that starts with the actors applying the logic of consequences to the framework-setting conditions and then moving to rule-following which is presumably meant to be useful — because it is saving time and transaction costs — on detail." Müller (2004: 402) also argues, following March and Olson's argument (1998), that the logic of consequences is applied, if a bargain produces a higher utility when the normative environment is weak and preferences are clear. Accordingly, it worth asking whether the European political space is best understood as an environment with set rules or with rather vague definitions. Considering the fact that the European political space consists of several

---

space on the European level and did not take part in its initiation in the past. Therefore, their influence as well as their bargaining power has been significantly smaller than is the case for parties from older member states (Moravscik, Vachudova 2003: 52).

[27] The research referred to here concluded that despite an emphasis on the socialization effect of the European Parliament, the key element remains at a national level — the responsibility to the national party to be re-elected. Lots of attention was paid also to the effects of Euroscepticism and policy changes in the case of individual parties and the party system as such. In the context of CEE parties, they were the subject of research interest in terms of accommodation within the European space during the EU accession process and shortly after the accession. Focusing on three CEE states which are already members of the EU, we cover the time period from when they were enjoying membership at the beginning and the consecutive shift towards "business as usual". In this regard, it is important to mention the wider context. The longer a country is a member of the EU, the greater the penetration by EU and transnational issues of individual policy areas, leading to a decline in the role of borders.

institutions as well as various levels of decision-making, the environment can be hardly defined as constituted by strictly given rules. The European space is perceived as an environment with a meta-commitment — supporting deeper EU integration — but the rules for individual actors involved are rather vague.

This evaluation of the European political space was shaped during its constitution; meaning that internal rules and practises are set by participating actors with emphasis on institutional knowledge. If one considers the fact that the main movers of deeper integration are participants as such in individual EU institutions, as well as Europarties,[28] the arena is very normative in terms of supporting further steps towards integration. To secure its continuity, the arena has to be norms-setting – able to socialize new actors, as well as convince actors to see the arena as an opportunity. Considering the fact that the arena has been able to absorb new actors and elements after the 2004 EU enlargement, one can assume that the socialization factor dominates. The motivation of participating parties in the European arena is therefore an interest that is shared with different national parties. This interest can be motivated by policy change, or by personalized interest e.g. to be elected into European party positions. From the perspective of rational choice theorists, the European arena is a space where parties can promote and push their interests without any costs to their national election responsibility. In Weberian logic, the parties maximize their gains without interference from nationally based responsibility (Carter and Poguntke 2010, 300).[29]

The second dimension relating to policy change is, for purposes of this research, approached from the perspective of the socialization of parties in the European political space. The process of socialization can be defined from various viewpoints. The common denominator

---

28 Europarties are understood as an organized grouping of political parties.
29 Another point of view on the structure of the European arena is the perspective of theorists dealing with the functions of international institutions. Barbara Koremenos, Charles Lipson a Duncan Snidal (2001) developed the concept of The Rational Design of International Institutions where they set five conditions for the analysis of principals in international institutions: a) form of membership, b) scope of activities/responsibility, c) level of centralization of decision-making process, d) mechanisms of internal control, e) functional flexibility.

for the definition follows the constructivist approach, which emphasises the adoption of rules and norms into national institutions and their context. Jeffery Checkel defines socialization as a process of inducting actors into the norms and rules of a given community. Its outcome is sustained compliance based on the internalization of these new norms. In adopting community rules, socialization implies that an agent switches from following a logic of consequences to a logic of appropriateness; this adoption is sustained over time and is quite independent from a particular structure of material incentives or sanctions (Checkel 2007: 5-6). In this case, the definition focuses on the way in which member states aim to adopt the norms of the (European) community in terms of educating and socializing themselves in that community. To the same point, Checkel adds that this is a bottom-down process in which they accommodate norms as "the right thing to do" (Checkel 2007: 5).[30]

It is assumed that through this process, the interests and identities of the socialized will change (Olson 2002: 921). Again, if one rephrases the party intention, it can look like European integration refers to our ideology and policy goals; therefore we accommodate our policies according to the European political arena.

Speaking about policy change as an effect of socialization, three dimensions have to be considered. First, the arena of socialization: the effect of the European arena on the national level in terms of penetration by norms, ideas and habits. Secondly, the effects of norms uploaded by individual parties to the wider arena. Paciorek-Herrmann (2012) defines this process as a "doing" and "socialization", where she distinguishes between the arena and practices of a

---

30   FSchimmelfennig, Engert and Knobel (2006) make further definitions. In their perspective, there are two main approaches to socialization: a rationalist theory and a constructivist. Rationalist theories of international institutions had largely neglected international socialization as a relevant process in international politics or conceptualized international socialization as a power-driven process in an anarchical environment, devoid of any institutionalized normative content and downplaying international organizations as relevant socialization agencies. By contrast, the new constructivist research agenda emphasized the importance of international and transnational organizations, and theorized international socialization as a process driven by logics of 'appropriateness' and 'arguing' and leading to the internalization of international norms.

(changing) environment. Thirdly, a strong emphasis is placed on the change of the arena itself (environment) through a new assemblage of players (parties) after the enlargement of the EU in 2004 and 2007. Paciorek-Herrmann argues that attention should be paid to this process in terms of the "analytical emphasis on the reflexive, practical process and the *socialization* (...) to analyse the effects of the process". This enables one to analyse the arena from the bottom up and from a horizontal perspective. In other words, the European arena is not considered to be static, but a constantly developing environment. Therefore, the practice of policy-making, in terms of routinized manner, results in changes of norms (Paciorek-Herrmann 2012, 2).

This argumentation uses a horizontal approach to the European political environment and perceives the arena as a space for top-down and bottom-up processes at the same time. It means that we do not stick to one process with any preference. In this understanding, the arena is assumed to be both a space of shared interest, as well as a space for policy making. Following Paciorek-Herrmann's argumentation, socialization is constantly executed through praxis. Therefore, norms are considered as standards [31] of players (i.e. political parties), as the institutionalized interests of players, and (their) identity (i.e. policy priorities) as a concept upon which the interests (influencing policy) rely.

The European arena is understood as a quasi-institutionalized space where actors push their interests and influence certain policy outcomes. This space is based on a broad institutionalized structure — the institutions of the EU, the European political parties and interactions among them. The meaning of the space is shaped by a normative perception of the pro-integration approach. At the same time, this opens up an opportunity for politicizing the space and for participation of anti-integration parties and movements. According to rational choice theory, such a composition creates a space where its members maximize their profit by influencing policy outcomes, by the setting of the structure of the space, and by personal representation. The effects of socialization on individual actors by the normative pro-integration

---

31 Katzenstein (1996: 5) understands norms as collective expectations for the proper behavior of actors with a given identity.

environment cannot be omitted. All of these elements create a complex European and national arena of mutual interests and divergent goals.

The normative substance of EU institutions can be shown in the case of those who create the normative environment in terms of support for EU integration. Generally speaking, those who perceive the EU institution as a positive thing and develop an EU-supportive environment are the most relevant movers and shapers within the normative EU-supporting environment. Those who think of it negatively – and oppose EU integration – do not implement their activities to any significant extent. This is the case for the Council of Regions and the activities of its members from individual countries. If representatives of regions perceive the Council of Regions as a window of opportunity, they participate in meetings and actively develop networks with other representatives. On the other hand, representatives with the opposite view do not participate in meetings.

The European arena is defined as normative in terms of being supportive of integration by definition. This can be seen, for example, in the appointment of new commissioners, where being a supporter of European integration is one of the conditions. Therefore, it is expected that parties that participate in the European level of politics will share positive attitudes to the EU. In other words, these parties will participate on a European level to a greater extent than nationalistic parties.

4.3. Analytical framework

The behaviour of political parties on the national or European level has been widely analyzed, but there are few empirical studies of the way that functioning political parties such as the EP interact regarding participation in the European political arena (Landrech 200, 2012, Radaelli 2003, 2015). In addition to this, there is a lack of systematic analysis of whether there is consistency between the behavior of parties within the EU structures and the emphasis of their policies addressed to voters in their home countries. As Ladrech (2012:185) points out, there is only limited evidence of influence on policy through participation of parties' representatives in the European political space, like transnational parties or EU institutions. Radaelli (2003:42) argues that an absence of pressure weakens the

EU policy model, despite various sociological explanations of the influence of norms. Therefore, representatives of political parties in EU bodies or transnational formations serve primarily to reduce the degree of uncertainty between national and European levels (Ladrech 2012: 186). That said, the policy of national identity is a cross-dimensional policy issue that is very often connoted by emotions and immediate feelings. Stefano Bartollini (2005) contributes to this debate on the influence of the European political parties on parties at a national level in terms of institutional and policy changes. He perceives the European environment as supporting a deeper EU integration, which means creating a federalized form of the EU. Bartollini's concept provides a good introduction into the relationship between both the EU and the national level. To do so, Bartollini uses Weberian logic to define forms of shaping statehood, which is also the case for the EU as such, in its ultimate goal. He argues that the Weberian definition emphasizes the features of bounded space, of an internally organized community, and of external strategies of demarcation through signals of possession or through physical defence against intruders. The Weberian formulation establishes a link between the strategies of demarcation of the external boundaries of the geographical space, on one hand, and the differentiation of roles in the internal organization of the population occupying the space, on the other (Bartollini 2005: 1).[32]

These ideas about the interplay between external relations and internal boundaries provide a useful way of thinking about the mutual relationship between national and European levels of politics. Again, one has to note that the ultimate goal of the EU is to provide

---

[32] This issue can be approached from a utilitarian perspective, namely as a choice of strategy choice for an individual party. In this regard, Jan Rovný (2012: 20) offers a well developed definition of party strategy. He points out that the choice of party strategy is determined by varying party involvement in political issue dimensions. The well-studied fact that political parties are endowed with varying core constituencies, ideological heritages, and organizational structures has an important implication. Rovný (2015: 7) develops his argumentation further focusing on the relation between structure and policy priority. He says that (one) should focus on the interplay between strategic action and its structural limitations — whether these limitations stem from social divides, institutional imperatives, organizational characteristics, or political issue frames.

a structure corresponding to statehood, and that perception of norms will necessarily correspond with this goal.

Regardless of ideological orientation, all parties have tended to use the development of international contacts and activities as a means of greater justifying their policies. This has led generally to an increase in each individual party's international contacts and socialization within the European arena.[33]

The individual elements of the model are understood as follows:

First, the influence on a party through its participation in the European arena is captured by the identification of the number of changes in the thematisation of the issue of national identity in their election programs. References relating to the issue of national identity, whether positive or negative, cannot be understood as a mere quantification of positive or negative developments related to the nation, but rather as the expression of the number of changes, or turns, in election manifestos. Such expression is an auxiliary factor for, first, expressing a country-specific context and, second, a manner in which the individual political parties react to this development. Since this quantification expresses changes in the thematisation of the issue, the first election in a given time period needs to be treated as the starting point and as such is not included in the analysis. The use of categories or codes such as "nationalism positive" and "nationalism negative" should allow for a greater plasticity in understanding the development of the parties' perception of national identity and related issues. On the other hand, a numerical expression would enable one to capture a greater number of changes.[34]

Secondly, fragmentation is understood as the number of political parties that have in the observed period become parliamentary

---

33 The attractiveness has declined in the past period; therefore across Europe we can observe a rise of formations opposing EU integration. This can be attributed to the decline of attractiveness of the European arena for all political parties and therefore some parties refuse to participate there and be influenced by the European environment.
34 Yet these are imperative for understanding how political parties understand social context. The manner in which positive and negative codes for nationalism were distinguished and applied is captured in the relevant chapter.

parties divided by the change in the number of parties (compared to the previous electoral period as is show later).[35]

Thirdly, the European arena is composed of the entire institutional structure of the EU, European political parties, and other platforms on a European level where individual representatives can be nominated or elected on behalf of their party. The key factor for considering the position as relevant is the momentum of being elected by the plenary, the committee of the institution, or being nominated by the party to a position; the quorum is applied. In support of above, the quantification of the European integration element is taken to be the number of positions represented by individual party members within the European political space. The parties are treated equally in regard to their electoral gains in the general election, as well as to the number of members. Looking at individual cases, there is no direct link or influence between the size of the party and its the gains within individual institutions of the EU.

---

[35] Considering the small number of cases in this book, this definition may be considered as an auxiliary descriptively-analytical factor used for the purpose of the perception of national identity and the representation of parties in the European political arena. In evaluating individual cases, it is necessary to tackle the question of how the party system reacts to (increasing) voter demand for parties thematising national identity (such as those that actively use nationalist election manifestos). The answer may be twofold. On the one hand, we may observe the general tendency of codes representing the support for nationalism to rise. On the other hand, it is possible that the relevance of a movement that (primarily) thematizes national identity and related issues (and thus has a high occurrence of nationalism-related codes) increases.

5. Operationalizing of research and research questions

The research is based on the presumption that political parties shape their understanding of national identity. Therefore, there is nothing fixed or given in terms of a definition of national identity. For the purpose of this research, the grounded theory method was employed to identify an individual party's understanding. In the process of analysing all election manifestos for parliamentary parties, individual codes have emerged. During this research procedure, the term policy of national identity has emerged. To observe the development of changes in the understanding of national identity, focus was given to the number of changes within each election manifesto of each party.

The European political space is understood as a set of institutions within the EU. Active participation within this structure is defined as an election or the nomination of a party's representative to the institutions. The crucial point of the research is to explore the relationship between the participation of an individual party in the European political space to ascertain if this translates into a decrease of the use of codes understood as nationalism positive. In other words, codes aimed at actively developing a national identity.

The study combines qualitative research using the grounded theory method for analysing election manifestos and quantitative research for analysing the numbers of changes within election manifestos and the number of representatives within elected or nominated positions. Since the use of such quantitative methods in social research does not aim to explore an absolute correlation, the study shows trends rather than fixed results. For this purpose, the interpretation of results is the most important part of this work. Here, the environment is perceived in a normative way supporting deeper European integration.

Using the theoretical background mentioned above, the research aims to answer the following questions:

1. How is the perception of national identity among the political parties changing while they are participants in the European political space?
2. How does the length of membership in the EU translate into parties' perceptions of national identity?
3. How does this affect constituting policies relevant to national identity?
4. Why do some parties change their understanding of national identity while others resist any significant influence?

6. Limits of research

The research has to cope with two main challenges. The first is connected to the methods used, ‚namely quantitative methods in the issue relating to national identity. This issue is, by definition, both complex as well as fluid. Given the fact that using quantitative research methods can explain general trends as well as individual deviations, the complex explanation of outputs has to be given in its proper context. This means that despite results showing trends of development, the results have to be properly explained. In this regard, some elements can be simplified by the analysis of data, but a broader knowledge explains these simplifications. This is the case with ODS or PiS. Both parties have participated extensively in the European political space since 2004, but their perception of national identity has remained unchanged or even shifted towards a more nationalist rhetoric. Each has a different motivation for its policies, but a quantitative analysis does not have to necessarily discover these policy roots. Therefore, detailed knowledge of individual cases (parties) is needed.

The second challenge is the definition of the European political space as the environment supporting European integration. One must bear in mind that the composition of the European environment by political parties is a matter of continual change and that this environment can lose its normative Europeanness. This trend can be observed in the case of the Hungarian party Fidesz as well as the Polish party PiS. Neither considers the European environment as relevant for their policies. This means that, a priori, they reject any influence created by that environment. Therefore, the causal relationship between the European political space and political parties at a local level cannot reach the same substance as other parties have. In this regard, the European space would have been understood in terms of an international institution lacking norms that create aims, which is not the case here. In addition to this, in the past it was almost unthinkable to consider the European political space as not supporting deeper European integration. However, recent development shows how this limited perspective can bias a researcher's perspective. This consequently implies that the European political space can change more quickly than expected. Hand in hand with this, one also has take into consideration the varieties and different perspectives of individual actors when it comes to a proper definition of the European arena. As mentioned in the case of the definition of a policy of national identity, the up thrust of this research is to propose frames that can later be used towards precise further research outputs or to serve as the subject of further definition. If individual actors in a given environment perceive that it might be losing its attractiveness, there can arise the probability that parties will become increasingly utilitarian. Despite a possible decrease, one cannot ignore the fact that political parties execute utilitarian action unexpectedly. This can depend on inter-party development that is hard to include in research if it does not appear in the election manifesto.

Lastly, the research has to cope with several limitations. Even if the work aims to propose a research frame instead of a strict definition, the grounded theory method can be subject to biased research outputs. For example, if a researcher is unable to put aside their own normative assumptions, or if their a priori knowledge about a certain topic does not allow them to approach the researched topic with sufficient distance. This can also be the case with political parties that view the constituent elements of national identity from different perspectives and might omit some relevant shaping factors when framing their policy of national identity. This can be, for instance, the case of ČSSD or KDU-ČSL, which both have a long tradition they have come to perceive as their own identity.

7. Nationalism, national identity, and policy of national identity

In the following section, definitions of different relevant approaches to national identity are introduced. The aim is to provide an overview of the main trends in various disciplines that examine the topic. Since the topic is very complex, and crosses many disciplines, a single, unified definition is almost impossible. Therefore, based on the overview of relevant approaches, this chapter concludes with the definition of policy of national identity used in this research.

The issue of national identity is a very complex one, and research aiming to analyse even a part of a complex issue poses a significant intellectual and academic challenge. The reason for that is hidden in the substance of the words national and identity.[36] Both concepts are challenged from various perspectives — philosophy, sociology, political science, language science or historiography — and each discipline has academic relevancy. In the following part, I will introduce the most relevant approaches toward the study of national identity. In addition to this, I will introduce the concept used in this work — a policy of national identity. This concept builds on several others mentioned in academic literature but has not been elaborated upon as a research tool for analysing issues relevant to national identity. The chapter introduces concepts from sociology and political science to establish a framework for a policy of national identity which is then used to operationalize national identity in political parties' manifestos.

---

[36] The term of national identity is similar to the term populism. In this sense, Sean Hanley (2014) mentioned struggles while doing research on populism and political parties: (...) a notoriously slippery term — and one often used in a loose, disparaging sense to describe demagogic promise-making by unsavoury extremist outsiders.

7.1. National identity — overview of existing research

The term 'national identity' poses difficulties for many scholars, since it is very often bounded with nationalism and its role in nation-building processes (Gellner 2009), modernisation of nations (Hroch 2003, 2009), and experience with nationalism in the 20th century. The constructivist approach – represented, for example, by Anderson – constituted a major change in research on national identity. He argued that societies are to be distinguished not by their 'falsity-genuineness', but by the style in which they are imagined (2006: 6). This paradigmatic shift opened space for more complex research into questions of identity in specific bounded territories – a fact that allows scholars to investigate these phenomena with a higher emphasis on "what is behind". In fact, terms such as 'national identity' or 'spaces of belonging' are very fluid and have been associated to many different concepts (e.g. Jörrisen, Zirfas 2010)

The current discussion of the use of the term 'nationalism' focuses on its critical use as a social and research issue. However, it is difficult to distinguish a clear line between nationalism and national identity, and their use in the political process (e.g. in the case of elections). Therefore, national identity is emphasized as a political tool that can be instrumentalised in a specific territory. Bell (2003: 69) finds four basic features for the study of nationalism regardless of different conceptual approaches: the construction of stories about identity, origins, history and community. He continues explaining how the representation systems (in this understanding, political parties) are bound to a process of national identity formation: (…) to mould a national identity — a sense of unity with others belonging to the same nation — it is necessary to have an understanding of oneself as located in a temporally extended narrative, and in order to be able to locate one as such, nationalist discourse must be able to represent the unfolding of time in such a way that the nation assumes a privileged and valorized role. (Bell 2003: 70)[37]

According to the widely used constructivist definition, the term (national) identity is understood as a representation of necessary myths to constitute a national community. Therefore, the self is defined in relation to a specific other (e.g. Diez 2004, Rumelili 2004, or Tulments 2012). As Castells (2010: 7) argues, people identify themselves primarily with their locality. Territorial identity is a fundamental anchor of belonging that has not been lost despite the on-going process of trans-nationalization and globalization. Castells adds that ethnicity has always been a basic attribute of self-identification. To concepts of self/otherness, Castells (2010: xxv) suggests that creating the perception of otherness is based not only on historical practice, but because people are reminded every day that they are others themselves. He also explains the processes of identity construction, for example on the basis of a cultural attribute, or a related set of cultural attributes, that is given priority over other sources of meaning (Castells 2010: xxvi).

Benedict Anderson has proposed the most widely accepted concept of nation and its construction. Anderson claims that the terms nation and national identity are imagined and, therefore, the sense of belonging to a nation-state — together with boundary

---

[37] The literature offers varied explanations and interpretations of the term national identity, and of how political parties shape societies regardless of whether or not it is their intent. Morley (2001: 425–426) argues that belonging and (national) identity can be understood similarly in symbolic terms. He applies this finding to the local, national and transnational communities in which people think of themselves as being "at home" (2001: 426). Morley finds that within each society are some elements that give rise to a sense of belonging and that do not necessarily divide groups between self and others e.g. the weather forecasts in Britain or Sweden have a strict emphasis on national territory but are not primarily aimed at nationalising society. In this understanding, the role of political parties does not necessarily mean that their aim is to nationalise the society. For a better understanding of current processes of shaping national identities, one should consider how political parties create spaces of belonging. I focus on this particular dimension to avoid using too narrow an understanding of (spatial) boundaries of identity. One should avoid getting stuck in a classical understanding of the boundaries of individual national party systems because the concept of a space of belonging transcends national party systems and takes into account overlapping space in all policy fields stressed by the parties.

terms, such as sovereignty, community and religious plurality – is the result of perception (Anderson 2006: 5-6). John Breuilly develops this argument further. He (1993: 62) defines three elements of pursuing a national ideology. First, the actors' notion of the nation as a unique (national) community that can be restored to its natural and authentic state. Second, there is an idea of the nation as a society, which should have its own state. The historical aspect of the nation is significant for justifying the existence of the community. Finally, the nation is thought of as body of citizens and self-determination is justified in terms of universal political principles.[38]

Ernst Gellner, from a slightly different perspective, (2009: 17) argues that nationalism – operationalizing identity – is a natural part of the modern state because the concept is based on analyses of Western countries. At the same time, the modernization process brings the erosion of territorial and social stability. In this respect, the ideology of national identity has to define itself against cosmopolitanism, liberalism, and economic progress, and against Marxism (Grew 2003: 211).[39]

According to Deutsch (1954: 35), each society uses specific methods of communication, sets of rules, and specific codes to mobilise the members of society. Deutsch argues that the more effective the political communication, the more successful the political unit and the more predictable the interaction between the ruling elite and society becomes. Deutsch also considers society-bounded communication as a tool that strengthens each society. Among the many definitions of 'nation' and 'nationalism', a particularly useful one is provided by Walker Connor (1978: 154). His argument can

---

38 Breuilly (1993: 62) also claims that the nationalistic ideology is part of political competition and can be easily used as a demand to justify or answer to the relation between state and society. Many scholars treat 'national' as a part of an aggregation of party priorities in the political process; in which the parties represent their particular goals.

39 According to this process, nationalistic movements find their justification because fragmentation and individualization create a gap between the individual and society (Eriksen 2010: 173). Nationalistic movements react against cosmopolitanism and globalization. In this context, Eriksen (2010) also claims that nationalism occurs in situations where a disconnect between society and individuals arises. From this point of view, it is questionable how one should deal with populist nationalism as used in politics and society.

be seen neither as traditional (according to unifying features), nor as constructivist and thus individual, imagined understanding. The main feature of national identity is a belief in common descent. In Connors' view, objective criteria like culture and religion are insufficient to define which group constitutes a nation (Triandafyllidou 1998: 597).[40] With regard to the aforementioned functional dimension of political parties, again, Karl W. Deutsch (1954: 39) must be mentioned at this point. In his functional understanding of national identity, he states that peoples are held together "from within" by this communicative efficiency. The more effective a system of social communication is, the more separate it becomes from those groups that it cannot incorporate: unable to bear promiscuity, it must choose marriage or divorce (Deutsch 1966: 97–98). Deutsch's definition implies that the members of a nation are able to communicate more easily than outsiders and share more with each other than with individuals from another society.[41]

---

[40] However, Triandafyllidou (1998) simplifies the term national identity arguing that elements like culture, religion or language are important not only to the degree that they reinforce the nation's identity but because they differentiate the in-group from the out-group and thus justify and make real this divided view of the world.

[41] In this respect, the role of communication is a significant element. Political systems are bounded by the territory in which they operate. Therefore, political communication between parties and society is limited to a nation/territory and the state is also important as a research unit. However, the rise of European political parties, European integration and a growing level of transnational (political) exchange, forces each national political system to respond, whereas national party systems remain unchanged. On the other hand, if one considers Deutsch's role of communication as significant; the static understanding of political communication is no longer untenable. As I argue below, a growing level of trans-nationalisation and external influences on states causes growing mobility and cognition of a "world beyond borders". The higher the level of awareness of the external environment there is, the higher the level of communication with other communities. If one considers that the researched countries are members of the EU, the rise of external influences as well as the rise of mobility and increasing communication with citizens of other states must cause at least a redefinition of Deutsch' concept — moving from the state unit towards the European level. The rational definition of nation argues that the key elements that construct unity are the economic benefits — when the level of economic exchange among members of the same nation is higher than the level of external exchange. Therefore the main force unifying individuals is the search for

The influence of social context that shape parties' perception of national identity was approached already from a different perspective. Thomas Risse (2000, 2002, and 2007) paid attention to the developing of national identity in the context of deepening European integration, whereas Hans Maull (1990) conducted research of strategic culture whereby he focused on the impact of the domestic social context on foreign policy. The impact of national identity perception on political parties has also been covered from the perspective of populist tendencies. Decker (2007) and Lochoki (2012) focus on the use of nationally relevant policies on accommodation of this environment by parliamentary parties.

7.2. Applied concept of national identity in Central East Europe after 1990

Concepts of national identity were used for the research of Easter European states during the 1990s (Taggart 1996, 2002, Hobsbwam 1996). Only a few of those researches in the past twenty years considered the rapid development in these countries within its broader context of a globalized world (Schöpflin 2000, Brubaker 1996, Guibernau 2000). They focused either on comparison of phenomena with Western countries or on structural changes of political and party systems in former Soviet bloc countries (Brubaker 1996, Eriksen 2010). As Ther (2012: 26) points out, after 1990 East and Central European countries became engaged in a new debate about the shape of nationalism. Contrary to the West European use of ius soli, East European states focused their societal narrative in an ius sanguinis way. Historiography deals with the phenomena of national identity in many cases, with reference to national uprisings in the 19th century within former monarchies (see e.g. Ther 2006, Troebst, Hroch 2009). Despite substantial differences between definitions of and attitudes towards nationalism in West and East European states, there was a common quest for centralism within newly created states in both regions (Ther 2012: 36). The question of

---

common (economic) gains. This approach refers to Deutsch's concept in sharing the main argument of nation unity: easier/better exchange and communication that justify the common organisational unit, the state.

"identity policy" may lack an antithesis. Schöpflin (2000: 15) claims that there is no such "non-identity politics". There are no political actors without identities and this has an influence on how we engage in politics.[42] These acts create potential problems, with a peoples' identification functioning as political dynamite. This element was highlighted in the early 1990s, when economic struggles drew attention to the unfeasibility of communism in societies that were on the verge of transforming into market economies.

When discussing national identity, the perspective of populist policy analysis can also be employed. As Canovan (2002: 26) argues, the general quest for democratisation of politics has a contradictory effect on populist political parties. Populist parties stress the following issues in the party system: sovereignty, majority against minority and popular unity against multiplicity. Populist parties use these topics to affect the basic political environment like unity, belonging to certain social systems etc. (Canovan 2002: 33). Therefore, these parties incorporate such topics into their strategy (e.g. in election campaign). Canovan (2002: 38) exemplifies their acting as follows: the terms people, sovereignty, and majority rule.[43] Taggart also argues similarly. He claims that populist parties transform the cultural leitmotif into either a fully-fledged political movement or political ideology (Taggart 2002: 66). This move is then a basis for mobilization that is framed by their language of frustration that is translated into political action and/or political ideology. It can be illustrated as stressing the collective and sovereignty over pluralism and individuality (Taggart 2002: 74, 77).[44]

---

42 In this context Paasi (2009) offers a suitable general definition of national identity as well. He finds two basic elements; first, territorialisation or spatialization of the community, which points to the construction and reproduction of territoriality in cultural, environmental, security or other discourses; second, temporization of the community—that is narratives and memories of the past, images of the present and (often) utopias of the future.

43 Papandopoulos (2002: 53) to this point adds that this responsiveness refers to the substantial content of policy choices, whilst accountability is related to the availability of adequate instruments that enable voters to respond in the election.

44 For a detailed definition of populism and its use by political parties see e.g. Canovan (1999). Focusing on parties' mobilization, Oakeshott (1975) distinguishes three main conflicting strands within modern political parties: enterprise

7.3. Policy of national identity

Through work by the above-mentioned scholars, we can arrive at some sort of definition of the use of the term national identity from the perspective of social science, and of how this term is used in political discourses. The concept of the policy of national identity comes from two perspectives—national identity is operationalized as an analytical concept for further research; and national identity matters as a unit for a citizen's identification (Bechofer, McCrone 2009: 3-4). Translated into parties' activities, national identity is exercised by 'doing' (Bechofer, McCrone 2009: 8).[45] In terms of political parties 'doing' national identity is achieved by the use of an election manifesto as a tool. The overview shows the different analytical attempts to set up a definition of national identity. However, this research aims to focus on symptoms that have not yet been put into one framework. Therefore the approach used in this research proposes an open definition of national identity, in a broader contextual framework, instead of a strict definition. Before going into an evaluation of outputs, the way of constituting the policy of national identity will be introduced. The policy of national areas is not contained in one or two specific policy fields such as tax or health policy. In most of the cases, the codes (memos) are scattered throughout entire manifestos. However, these policies may also contain national identity-colored statement that is relevant to the research. Keeping in mind that national identity in relevant parts of

---

association, civil association, and the politics of faith that entails mobilization of popular enthusiasm behind an enterprise (Canovan 1999: 8). In this logic, Oakeshott considers the rationality of politics to be very questionable, because of these emotion-based desires. Therefore, one should consider political strategies involving identity/belonging as a significant feature. The parties use their tactics to emotionally mobilize the electorate; this understanding can be applied to the parties as a level of emotional mobilisation that varies from very low (e.g. liberal parties) to very high (nationalistic and populist parties).

45 Becghofer and McCrone in regard to national identity research point out that: Identity, including national identity, is not the preserve of any single social science discipline; it is plainly a political, sociological, cultural and psychological phenomenon, and more. Inevitably, and usefully, sociologists, social anthropologists, social psychologists and political scientists bring different perspectives to bear. Accordingly, our team was drawn deliberately from different disciplines, using a variety of methods and approaches (Bechofer, McCrone 2009: 8).

a manifesto might be present in different variations; one should pay attention to each part of the manifesto. The proposed setting of a policy of national identity offers a framework for further analysis of individual manifestations of national identity. In this context, national identity is understood as a term developed and framed by shapers — political parties. It is believed that political parties are part of the framing process of a society and therefore contribute to the construction of social reality. This can be demonstrated for example through the case of the immigration crisis between 2015 and 2016. The framing of this issue by individual parties in regard to other areas of national identity shows the penetration of immigration into party priorities. For example, if a party, hand in hand with refusing immigration quotas starts to support the preservation of its national culture and/or lessen its support for EU integration, then shifts the context towards broad support of nationalizing policies. Therefore, the approach to national identity allows one to research the broad context of party policies in regard to a specific topic such as immigration (Lasheras 2016).

The term policy of national identity can be constituted by the policy areas listed below – described through individual codes in the Appendix. These help to structure our understanding..

7.3.1. The European Union

This area covers issues relating to how the EU is perceived within election manifestos. The purpose of the party is to enhance the party's attitude towards issues relating to the EU. The most crucial point is the party's position towards deeper integration of the EU. In other words, the party's commitment to the European idea. This example shows the complexity of the whole issue. Usually, the manifesto does not contain a statement supporting or rejecting deeper integration. It might be collected from various mentions such as support for joining the monetary union or explicit mentions of nationally sensitive policy such as integration of tax policy. The domain of the EU consists of declaratory statements towards European integration as such, as well as mentions in various policy fields. It also shows how EU affairs penetrate each national context at both policy and polity level; and the extent to which issues relating to the EU are politicized.

7.3.2. Values

This area covers party statements that touch on the fluidly defined area of the *values* of the society. In addition to this, it is important to pay attention to how the party understands its role in shaping and communicating those values. In other words, to what extent the party understands its role as a generator of particular values or as a cultivator. Although this area might be perceived as unclear, the emphasis on the party's role in a system that shapes values brings a new perspective to the analysis. In addition to this, the context of an individual country plays a crucial role; e.g. whether there are any national minorities in the country and how they are asked to participate in a society's value system.

There is also a focus on the party's perception of culture and cultural heritage and the role it assigns to culture: whether culture plays any role in national identity consciousness or if culture is perceived as a civic service. One must distinguish the role which culture should play: that of actively developing national culture and national feelings; or cultivating certain traditions and cultural heritage. One of the most important aspects here is the role of language: does the party consider this to be a sign to be protected in its standard form or left to natural development. In addition to those mentioned above, attention should also be paid to the attitude towards the culture of national minorities.

7.3.3. Minorities

This area covers various topics connected with different kinds of minorities. Although the main focus here is on national minorities, the area also covers immigration policy and gender minorities. Attention is paid to the level of their recognition by the majority society, i.e. political parties. Does the party support the right to self-determination and supports developing a minority's sense of belonging? To what extent does it stress their integration into majority society/culture? At the same time, how does the party distinguish between traditional national minorities and newly formed minorities of immigrants from different cultural and political spaces such as Africa or Near East? By putting this into a wider context of other dimensions, the framework enables us to achieve a better understanding of a very specific party policy.

7.3.4. World

This section focuses on the perception of complex international and regional affairs outside of the EU. Questions are asked regarding a party's ideas about cooperation with any particular country or geographical area. In addition to this, attention is paid to the role of values claimed by a party in its foreign policy; particularly in the case of the promotion of human rights. The second main area of focus is the party's relation to globalization and capitalism and its response to the development of the external environment. Finally, this section covers the proposed reaction of a party to a possible external threat.

Table 1: Overview of codes

	EU	Values	Minorities	World
1	Support of deeper integration	Support of new emancipation movements, open society	Inclusiveness	Support of the EU
2	Support of the EU but not deeper integration	Nationalism negative	Protection of minorities	Openness towards world
3	Strong in the EU	Pluralism	Dialogue with minority	International solidarity
4	Europe of nations	Individualism and freedom as a values	Limited immigration	Pushing for human rights in foreign policy
5	Against the EU, leaving possible	Human rights as a value	Limited rights for minorities	Western orientation
6		Culture as a value	Against immigration	Central European identity
7		National culture as a part of identity	Against minority rights	positive connotation of Germany
8		Traditional values		negative perception of EU

9		Support of national culture	positive connotation of RU
10		support of national identity building	perceived foreign economic threat
11		Soil as proof of nation	stressing sovereignty
12		Christian values	Pacifism
13		Nation is threatened	Slavs positive
14			negative towards neighbouring country
15			West orientation negative
16			otherness as a threat
17			militarization

Source: Code book, author

8. Methodology and Research Procedure

For a better understanding of this work, a methodological point has to be mentioned: the issue of national identity, or rather its framing, cannot be researched and understood without setting appropriate ontological and epistemological viewpoints. Since the purpose of this research is not to advocate a primordial or post-modern definition of national identity or follow a scholarly defined term for national identity, it is necessary to find a common denominator of this "non definition". In this respect, national identity is not inherently understood per se, but as a process that political parties use to frame national identity. In other words, they use — as will be shown later — a policy of national identity.

The constitution of policy cannot be done without regard to the careful perception of the mood in society to a party's perception of a certain policy. The party experience is therefore understood as the result of a combination of public demand for certain policies that may lead to policy change; the social context based on historical development; and the role of individual representatives of the party and their own narrative. This continual learning process can be understood as the result of policy development or event change. The departure point for this dimension is the role of collected features that shape the environment — in this case a nationally-based political system. For this purpose, one can assume that the state's context is a result of events that shape the society continually.[46]

---

46 The basic presumption consists in the role of the path experienced by an individual state (named according to the path dependency theory developed by Paul Pierson). This approach describes the basic elements needed for (substantial) change within the state and its consequent influence on the nation; if one considers this influence in regard to the nation-based political system. The concept of path dependency understands the upcoming events as dependent on previous events/experience; where the element of history plays a crucial role. Further development is not understood as linear, but as the result of increasing returns (Pierson 2000, 2004). For Pierson, the crucial element of this development is the timing of further development. In his understanding, even a minor change may cause significant effects, if timing is appropriate (Pierson 2000).

Therefore, the starting point of this research lies in constructivist ontology. In this understanding, objects and subjects are given meanings through language, and this language creates a reality. As Guzzini pointed out in regard to social constructivism, its purpose is to create a social reality (2000: 147). Following this logic, the human social world is based on the construction of human interactions, and based on the previous claim, such a social world cannot be studied independently by definition since the researcher is part of his/her social context that influences the perception of social reality while also shaping it (Braun 2008: 18). Therefore, the social world, understood as national identity here, is constantly fluid, because it corresponds with a broader context of how perception is shaped. This element is even clearer, when one considers the election manifesto as a tool for shaping a particular imagination of national identity. In this respect, the issue of national identity, as it is used in this work, is understood as something that is framed by movers, i.e. political parties. It is also understood as something that has a broader framing impact, since it is designed to evoke unifying feelings among society. The point is directly connected to the understanding of power as an element that transforms a constructed national identity into a political tool that can be used. For this purpose, national identity and its framing by political parties is analysed by grounded theory as an inductive methodology for evaluating the data. The research carried out in line with grounded theory should generate a mid-range theory. However, the purpose of this research is not to generate theory, but to propose an analytical

---

In the case of political party analysis, this approach refers to the constructivist approach (e.g. Gellner, Hroch) focusing on the historical understanding of a researched state. Both Gellner and Hroch perceive a community's features dependent on a particular context and therefore given to some extent. Those features are, for example, geographically bounded cultural features shaped within a country's historically specific context. In this regard, one should consider the specific features of nation-building, such as national revival events and the reflection of these movements by political parties as well as the origin of the (national) states. For this purpose, election manifestos offer an excellent comparable source. The significant advantage of election manifestos is the developed methodology that aims to establish comparable date for analysis.

tool for researching how political parties shape our understanding of national identity.

8.1. Grounded theory

The grounded theory is based on analysis of any kind of data (text, voice record etc.) while generating memos later grouped under the codes.[47] Using this method, the researcher has to consider the meanings of any data sources analyzed. This gives him/her a very good opportunity to explore hidden meanings though oscillation between deduction and induction while analyzing the data (Glaser, Straus 1967, Braun 2008). The researcher cannot easily erase their a priori knowledge about the researched issues. However, the researcher should avoid a priori judgements and should open up a space for further re-evaluation of any data gained. Therefore, the first phase of research should be open to any interpretation (Braun 2008: 29).

The memos are inductively devised during the continuous analysis of manifestos and when a new one is established, all of the previously analysed texts are re-evaluated to establish whether the new code should be applied to them. After the first analyst has finished their task, the whole process is repeated a few times by other analysts. The only difference is that there is always only one person analysing the manifestos at any time, and they are also re-evaluating not only the data, but the whole structure of codes and policy fields. The aim of these multiple revisions is to limit subjective, unconscious bias an – as far as possible – to objectify the structures of the codes. In this respect, as Braun (2008: 28) points out, a "researcher constructs terms based on the studied material which are then gradually transformed into categories and concepts on a higher level of generalisation and abstraction". This is done hand in hand with constant comparison of data emerging from the analysis. As Glaser (2002) points out, the method requires the ability to adopt and adapt the method and the field of data. From his

---

47 For more details on grounded theory see e.g. (Glaser and Strauss 1967; Gynnild and Martin 2011; Kelle 2005; Simmons 2010).

perspective, using grounded theory expects a researcher to be capable of conceptualizing a manifestos' content and to have the capacity to process some degree of confusion included in the texts.

The Grounded Theory offers a relatively high level of conceptual freedom and enables researchers to consider a wide scope of meaning during their collection and analysis (Glaser 2002, 12). On the other side, the method must be precisely developed for a particular research (and topic) and this requires a large amount of effort on the part of the analytical team to eliminate any type of confusion and misinterpretation from definitions in their coding scheme. It must be set, according to the coding methodology that was developed.

For the purpose of this research, a strict body of data was chosen — election manifestos for the past three general elections in three countries in the time period 2004–2013. This delimitation helps to overcome any significant problems associated with using grounded theory. Data sources can be unlimited as long as the issue is not saturated. If the individual codes are saturated within an individual election manifesto, then research has to define the precise name of the code. In addition to this, individual codes and research procedure can easily be double-checked.

8.1.1. How to identify parties' nationalist emphasis?

According to McDonald and Mendes (2001, 91), one can simply and consistently expect that "parties compete by emphasizing policy areas they believe give them electoral advantage and by glossing over or ignoring those areas that they deem to help their rivals." Political science has a few methodological approaches for mapping these tendencies and for inserting parties into the political space accordingly, but none of them is flawless. Every one disposes of specific pros and cons that make the measuring of parties' positions within the policy space and towards a variety of issues quite problematic (for further details see Benoit and Laver 2006; Havlík 2008).

Nevertheless, the political text offers itself as one of the main resources in an effort to gain information about political parties and their attitudes (Benoit and Laver 2006, 64). Even if election manifestos are not the main elements shaping the pre-electoral discourse (Klingemann et al. 2006, 8), they offer political parties more or less unlimited space for expressing their attitude to various topics and issues. Political parties are solely responsible for the content of manifestos, which are issued by councils of elected party elites or legally ratified by party conventions. Thus, they can be understood as authoritative statements of party preferences, and as representative of the whole party (Budge, Robertson, and Hearl 1987, 14; Klingemann, Hofferbert, and Budge 1994, 21) and (Alonso et al. 2012: 7). Furthermore, the manifestos are issued at regular intervals, which means both that programmatic changes over parties' lifetimes (Alonso et al. 2012: 7) and programmatic differences at a particular point in time within specific countries can be observed (König, Marbach, and Osnabrugge 2013, 1). Moreover, its indisputable advantage in comparison to other information resources and means of mapping of the political space is sustainability, which brings the researchers an opportunity to read and reanalyse the text at any time in the future and to revaluate the conclusions.

For the purpose of this research, election manifestos offer an excellent source of data. The manifestos are the results of a party's perception of relevant issues to be politicized and their projection of public demand. Due to the fact that manifestos are not elaborated by a single person, one can assume that there was a party discussion before approving the manifesto. In regards to the issue of election manifesto and national identity, there might even be a functioning connection. Focusing on the election manifesto enables one to overcome these obstacles by its substance. To sum up this discussion, this work follows argumentation of Laver and Garry (2000, 620) who argue, "Party manifestos are strategic documents written by politically sophisticated party elites with many different objectives in mind." This leaves considerable scope for debate about whether party manifestos reflect the 'real' positions of the parties that publish them. In our view this debate is ultimately fruitless, however, since the 'real' policy position of a political actor is a fundamentally elusive, even metaphysical, notion."

The categorization of codes into "nationalism positive" and "nationalism negative" involves the necessary step of determining which codes belong to which category. I am aware that there is a high normative change involved in this decision, yet I consider the benefits of this approach, particularly the possibility of a systematic analysis of the development in the perception of national identity, to outweigh its shortcomings. The analysis could be conducted on the basis of the evaluation of parties' categorization into individual codes. However, the nationalism positive and negative categories, and particularly the recording of parties' shifts from one to another, enable scholars to capture the developments in the nationally-coloured rhetoric. Rather than denoting any sort of evaluation on the part of the author (national identity as presented by a political party being perceived positively or negatively), this categorisation denotes particular qualities characteristic of one approach to national identity over another. The sole aim of this approach is, thus, to explore the development of the political parties´ perception of national identity.

8.1.1.1. *The Manifesto Project methodology*

The following chapter is devoted to introducing the manner of evaluation of national identity and related issues in manifestos created for the purpose of parliamentary elections. To a large extent it is preoccupied with the Manifesto Project that aims to collect and analyse a wide spectrum of parties' election manifestos. The advantage of this project is, first, the comparability of the collected data across countries and, second, a time-tested methodology for analysing manifestos. This framework is very useful in situations where the object of research is a specific policy area (most often corresponding to a specific part of the manifesto). However, under circumstances where the studied issue is scattered among various parts of the programme and manifests itself less subtly in metaphors, for example, the Manifesto Project may be considered a useful auxiliary framework rather than the main data tool. This is also the case due to the fact that the Manifesto Project covers the issue of national identity only tangentially, with only a few codes covering it, which reduces the possibility of using the data and the methodology of this project in this work.

The second applied method is the creation of a code book, using grounded theory. This approach contains benefits that are absent from the Manifesto Project. On the one hand, its validity depends on the quality of the work performed by researchers responsible for coding the manifestos. Its main advantage lies in the possibility to focus on a specific issue-area — in the case of this publication, the perception of national identity — and to bring attention to small details. This allows researchers to include peculiarities that would, in the case of standardized approaches, remain unexposed in the analysis. Its main disadvantage, on the other hand, is its limited validity, a matter related to the quality of the code book and its focus on a certain geographical area. The possibility to apply the framework used in this work therefore further depends on the validity of the code book and the extent to which its structure allows the addition of other codes.

The Manifesto Project,[48] (Budge et al. 2001; Klingemann et al. 2006) has developed a high quality of coding methodology, including a long tradition of codebooks and the training of coders in the skill of analysing the manifestos (see Volkens et al. 2015b).

In order to obtain the information about parties' positions on European integration, transnational cooperation, and national identity topics we used the average of a relative share of four categories[49] in parties' manifestos from the Manifesto Project dataset (Volkens et al. 2015a) positively associated with transnational cooperation and negatively with national way of life. For refusal of international integration and emphasis on a national way of life we applied four opposite categories.[50] We ended up with two different variables. Positive variables included the averages of relative shares of the above mentioned categories that had assigned to each of the parties for every election the degree of inclination towards

---

48 Formerly also known as Manifesto Research Group (MRG) and Comparative Manifestos Project (CMP).
49 101: Foreign Special Relationships: Positive; 107: Internationalism: Positive; 108: European Community/Union: Positive; 602: National Way of Life: Negative
50 102: Foreign Special Relationships: Negative; 109: Internationalism: Negative; 110: European Community/Union: Negative; 601: National Way of Life: Positive

international cooperation rather than support of national culture. The negative one contained the opposite tendencies observed in parties' manifestos and identified by trained coders – such as refusing the term "nation", or refusing any kind of education towards national pride.

Although the research methodology follows a precise research procedure, the author is aware of problems with reliability when working with political space, party positioning, and human coders (e.g. Benoit and Laver 2007; Laver and Garry 2000; Laver et al. 2003; Mikhaylov, Laver, and Benoit 2012). To avoid misinterpretations, another way of measuring the saliency of and emphasis on European integration or national identity was implemented. The success in capturing these trends relies on the specific advantages or disadvantages of various methods of mapping the political space.[51]

8.1.1.2. *The Grounded Theory methodology*

All concerned manifestos were analysed in MAXQDA, a quantitative data analysis software programme that was subsequently also used to create the above-mentioned code book. This approach allowed for a quick comparability among individual manifestos and memos. In the first phase of the process, approximately 700 memos were drafted, which were subsequently grouped into 56 codes on the basis of their thematic similarity. At this stage of the process, two other researchers were consulted, who checked these groupings based on their knowledge of the manifestos included in the analysis. Using the memos as the primary input, codes were created by taking advantage of thematic correspondence. After validation

---

[51] A different approach for how to measure party positions is the expert survey method. As Bakker et al 2012 on behalf of the Chapel Hill expert survey trend file, 1999–2010 argues, they allow researchers to obtain positions for a large number of parties irrespective of their size, parliamentary status, whether they have a manifesto or not, and independent from the electoral cycle. There also exists research on roll-call data analysis, voter placements, or the positioning of individual members of parliaments (König et al 2012). In the past decade, there is a significant rise of popularity of online projects aimed at quantifying party positions with voters preferences — such as projects conducted by the German Federal Agency for Civic Education or the Austrian network netPOL. However, these projects have primarily an advocacy role to engage the public with political life.

conducted with the other researchers, forty final codes were arrived at. Finally, based on a mutual agreement, thematically related codes were clustered together.[52]

Due to the process of its creation, the code book used in this work captures the specific social and political context of Poland, Slovakia and the Czech Republic especially, as it relates to national identity. Its use in another context, such as Hungary, presents two challenges. The first is related to the specific relationship between the context and the election programme: specifically, the manner in which similar topics are framed differently in election programmes. The use of this code book in another social context, even though it might be geographically close, should be done conscientiously, taking into account the existing codes. The second challenge arises from the fact that every use of this code book, provided the code book is done well, means the validation of the method used and potentially also increased accuracy of the codes in the context in which it was primarily created. The normative decision to categorize individual codes as either nationalism positive or nationalism negative was done by, and as such is the sole responsibility of, the author of this work. The individual codes and their categorization, as well as explanatory memos are included in the code book, where the reader may consult it (Němčok, Vít 2016).

As mentioned above, the number of codes that eventually arose from the analysis of the manifestos far exceeds the number of codes related to national identity that were used for the purpose of this research, and that are considered in the Manifesto Project coding schema. The code book presented in this work thus allows for capturing a much greater plasticity in the analysis of matters related to the political parties' perception of national identity. The complexity of policy of national identity presumes that the researcher will be able to cope with the complexity of data needed for research. This qualitative method of social science research, developed by

---

52 The code book's final shape is the result of more than three years of work; it was also applied in the context of the National Identity in CEE analytical project that was realized in the EUROPEUM Institute for European Policy. To find out more about the National Identity in CEE project, please visit ceeidentity.eu

Glaser and Strauss (1967), forces the researcher to analyse the data without any a priori biases.

The election manifestos coding structure carried out by the analytical team, led by one of the authors, contains more than 700 memos discussing national identity issues, European integration or international cooperation. These memos are aggregated under 56 codes that constitute four policy fields: (1.) the European Union, (2.) values, (3.) minorities, and (4.) world.[53] In most of the cases, the memos that gave rise to the establishment or application of particular codes are scattered throughout all of the manifestos, which means that the code works for the whole body.

Assigning simple codes does not allow us to compare the degree of emphasis that political parties put on the topics we are interested in. That is why particular codes are grouped into positive and negative categories[54]. The mathematical background of the Pearson correlation coefficient, implemented in the later correlation analysis, indicates the relative share of positive and negative categories assigned to the particular political party manifestos (Němčok, Vít 2016).

8.1.1.3. Comparison of the implemented methods

Both of the implemented methods are based on human coders going case-by-case through electoral manifestos issued by political parties whose relevance depended on their presence in the parliament. The main thing differentiating the techniques from one another is the way in which they approach the categories. While the Manifesto Project has deductively given a set of categories/codes that were used by coders during the analysis of manifestos, coders using the Grounded Theory were conjunctively responsible for the inductively established set of categories allocated to the party manifesto for a particular election. The second difference lies in their

---

[53] The whole coding book resulting from the application of Grounded Theory can be found in the Appendix.

[54] The positive category brings together 16 codes representing positive attitudes towards transnational cooperation with negative connotations towards national identity. The negative category groups 17 codes manifesting the opposite attitudes. The complete codes and division into categories can be found in Appendix B.

theoretical background. The methodology for the Manifesto Project is based on the issues of salience theory (Budge et al. 2001, 12), since it is focused on a portion of particular categories within the manifestos, and is sometimes referred to as quantitative content analysis. Meanwhile, the Grounded Theory method is closer to the Issue Ownership Theory (Bélanger and Meguid 2008; van der Brug 2004) and represents a qualitative approach that doesn't say much about portions or shares, but allows us to attach more specific labels to parties, better reflecting the system context and topics of the research.

As Němčkok and Vít (2016) showed in previous research, both methods can be used for getting better and more reliable explanations. As Table 2 shows, in this case the two policy mapping methods are measuring similar tendencies but not the same things, since the correlation coefficients for positive-positive as well as negative-negative relationships gain positive values. Even though the value for positive-positive relationship is not very high ($r = 0{,}149$), at least the positive value confirms that the prevailing tendencies are more or less similar for both methods. The positive-negative coefficients confirm the same thing. The only value contradicting the assumptions is $r = 0{,}121$ for Grounded theory negative vs. Manifesto Project positive. But since it is the only one, and – moreover – quite close to zero, it is not considered to disprove the reliability of the implemented methods, merely as a note of caution for subsequent interpretations.

Table 2: Pearson correlation coefficients for the various methods of measuring the party policy positions

	Grounded Theory positive	Grounded Theory negative	Manifesto Project positive	Manifesto Project negative
Grounded Theory positive	1	-0,249	0,149	-0,370
Grounded Theory negative	-0,249	1	0,121	0,784
Manifesto Project positive	0,149	0,121	1	-0,172
Manifesto Project negative	-0,370	0,784	-0,172	1

N = 45
Notes: The analysis is conducted on the level of political parties in a particular election.
The positive categories represent support for international cooperation, European integration and refusal of a national way of life. The negative categories represent the opposite.
The variables Grounded Theory positive/negative are calculated as a relative share of all categories included in the codebook assigned to a particular political party classified positively or negatively with transnational cooperation and national way of life consistently with the above-mentioned definitions.
The Manifesto Project positive is the average share of categories 101, 107, 108, 602 of the Manifesto Project Codebook (Volkens et al. 2015b). The Manifesto Project negative is the average share of categories 102, 109, 110, 601 of the same codebook.
Source: Němčok, Vít 2016; part of the calculations based on the (Volkens et al. 2015a)

Even though the correlation analysis did not reveal mutual validation for reliability of both implemented methods, it does not constitute a problem for the research design. The kind of objective criterion that would allow one normatively to decide whether one of the methods is more reliable than the other is missing. On the contrary, by having two methods for mapping political parties' policy preferences, this arranges the researchers' ability to capture parties' positive or negative emphasis towards transnational cooperation and nationalism (Nemčok, Vít 2016).

8.2. Operationalization of the behavior of political parties in the European arena

Based on theoretical assumptions, it is argued that the European arena is a normative environment in terms of supporting deeper integration. Therefore, the arena will be represented by actors and movers who will follow the path towards deeper integration and their representations will thus be higher than is the case with Eurosceptical or Euro-pessimist parties. This corresponds with the logic of constructivist scholars who consider the normative dimension of European institutions as one of the most relevant (Checkel 2007, Wendt 1999, Börzel 2011).

In this respect, it is expected that only political parties who support European integration participate within the structures of European Union.[55] To check this, the numbers of positions occupied by the representatives of particular subjects during the national elections were counted.[56] The size of individual national party systems follows the logic of research conducted by Nemčok and Vít (2016). They pointed out that "we are aware of the fact that the size of Czech, Polish, and Slovak delegations vary in a way that cannot be controlled in any of the methods for mapping the policy preferences. In order to eliminate spurious correlations caused by variable delegation size from our analysis, we weighted the number of occupied positions by political subjects' nominees by dividing it by the amount of MEPs reserved for a particular country." This solution helps to stress the compatibility of data for the purpose of comparison of individual states.

---

55 However, for example UKIP is a problematic case for evaluation since the party is since the 1994 in the European Parliament and does not prove any significant softening of the anti-EU rhetoric.

56 A list of all selected positions we have been working with can be found in the Appendix B.

80 IDENTITY FORMATION

8.2.1. Data and the technical attributes of the analysis

As mentioned earlier, our analysis was conducted on the three states — the Czech Republic, Poland, and Slovakia. As it was understood, the whole interval since their EU accession in 2004, which led to three elections to the lower parliamentary chamber in each and every country.

The data are organized by the level of political parties participating in the electoral competition, while only the parties that gained a mandate in the previous or current election were included. The very same condition is used by the Manifesto Project when considering the relevance of political subjects. This criterion is important, but leads to a very low number of parties on which to conduct research. Since applying the correlation analysis, in order to increase the number of observations we did the analysis for whole countries and not just for particular elections. All of the data are therefore organized according to the elections within the selected countries, while their behavior in the European arena is operationalized by the weighted number of their nominees occupying political positions calculated for the day on which elections are held.

8.2.2. Favouring nation, less for the EU?

When looking at the outcomes shown in table below, we can observe that the coefficients reveal either the verification of our theoretical expectations, or no relationship between the variables. The moderately strong correlation in the case of the Czech Republic (when using Grounded Theory positive categories) and in the cases of the Czech Republic and Poland (when using the Manifesto Project positive categories) confirm that those parties who are more integrated into the structures of the European Union are less liable to engage in strong protection of the national identity (that is incompatible with the transnational cooperation) during political campaigns in their nation states. The same thing is confirmed but from the opposite side in the case of negative categories. Again, the moderately strong negative correlation for Slovakia (when using Grounded theory negative categories) and for the Czech Republic and Slovakia (when using Manifesto Project negative categories) means that those political parties strongly promoting the national identity and thereby refusing further international cooperation and European integration are, at the same time, less integrated into the structures of the European Union.

Values in the last column, working with all of the cases, reveal for each and every implemented method more or less the same strength of the relationship—slightly above r = 0,12. The direction of all of them once again confirms our expectations and trends outlined in the paragraph above.

Table 3: Pearson correlation coefficients for the political parties' emphasis on transnational cooperation and national identity and weighted number of occupied positions within the EU structures by its nominees

	The Czech Republic	Slovakia	Poland	Total
Grounded Theory positive	0,370	-0,010	-0,029	0,123
Grounded Theory negative	0,051	-0,262	-0,018	-0,124
Manifesto Project positive	0,280	0,082	0,286	0,128
Manifesto Project negative	-0,201	-0,152	-0,004	-0,137
	N = 17	N = 17	N = 11	N = 45

Note: Second variable included in the correlation analysis is the weighted number of occupied positions in the EU structures.
Source: Vít, Nemčok 2016; part of the calculations based on the (Volkens et al. 2015a)

The rest of the coefficients reveal no relationship. That may be caused by the low number of observations; by the presence of parties that slightly deviate from each counts (e.g. ODS in the Czech

Republic, Smer-SD in Slovakia or PiS in Poland); or by parties having shifted their positions and thereby confused the research design—despite the fact that they participate in European politics. These parties demonstrate long-term participation in European politics in terms of presence in the institutions incorporated into our research design. All parties named develop their statements relating to national identity in language that is more nationalistic, even though they are involved in European-level institutions. Therefore, one can see divergence in the environment that is supportive of deeper integration, namely parties that sustain or even strengthen nationally coloured politics.

9. Results

9.1. National identity in political competition

The following section focuses on three issues relating to national identity from the perspective of parliamentary political parties in an individual country. These issues cover the most relevant topics in regard to national identity in political and social discourse and its reflection/use by political parties. This serves for a better understanding of the context of individual states in regard to the outputs of political parties in election manifestos for general elections. Issues in individual states serve as an introduction to the context for the evaluation of data used for the analysis. The introduction to each country does not cover the entire complexity of arguments used by parties but rather provides an overview of arguments relating to individual issues.

The starting point for this evaluation is the fact that at the beginning of the observed period there was a decrease in the relevance of topics related to an extreme form of national identity and the harmonization of institutional conditions within the realms of party systems (Kupka et al. 2009: 23). This means that all parties were exposed to the same influences within EU institutions and European political parties/Europarties. In that common milieu of political parties influenced by the European political space, it is important to set the context for individual countries. In particular, we pay attention to the development of a policy of national identity by individual political parties within the researched period. Before focusing on individual parties, the context of national identity in political competition has to be mentioned as well as the development of a policy of national identity in election manifestos. At the same time, there is an increase in the number of newly founded parties (meaning those entering Parliament) who are operationalizing national identity. Across the region, a common feature of these new movements is observable, namely their short lifespan (with the exception of Slovakia).

Table 4: Overview of new parties' using national identity in general elections

Country	General election/name of movement	General election/name of movement	General election/name of movement
The Czech Republic	2006/-	2010/Public Affairs	2013/Úsvit
Slovakia	2006/-	2010/-	2012/OL
Poland	2005/-	2007/-	2011/TR

Source: Author

As stated by Jan Rovný (2012), new parties that challenge traditional parties, from the perspective of issues used, are trying to create political space for the establishment of secondary themes. Traditional parties that work with socio-economic themes try to ignore those themes raised by new movements, thereby inhibiting the space for their establishment and the possibility of losing votes to the new movements (Haughton 2013). This argument is interesting since it offers two perspectives that explain the growth and decline of influence of the above-mentioned movements. The first is the fact that themes linked to national identity are relevant, but they are not the main ones expressing the political concerns of individual states. The second factor is that these movements lack the deeper political background sufficient to stand as challengers to traditional parties in areas other than just (in this case) those related to national identity. It is, thus, a logical consequence that over time, these parties are substantively exhausted and lose their attractiveness from the voters' point of view. Hanley and Sikk (2013: 22) make an interesting point regarding the rise of new political parties with their finding that in the CEE, anti-establishment reform parties more often broke through in economic good times than bad. In general terms, this is also a significant contribution to the scope of literature that deals with populism and nationalistic parties in the CEE region. It shows the demand for a kind of a story that is in these cases promoted by new parties and often touches the issue of national identity.

In each country covered by the analysis, traditional parties were challenged by new movements. In the case of Poland, PiS formed a national-conservative coalition with LPR and SRP after the elections in 2005. Following the succession of the PO government in 2007, the moderation of these national tendencies in the political system occurred in Poland. None of the observed countries registered a significant increase in national tendencies following the onset of the economic crisis in 2008. On the Polish political scene, a considerably larger thematization of national identity occurred. This was, however, not directed toward the otherwise stable coalition government of PO and PSL. After the election defeat of LPR and SRP in 2007, the political party Ruch Palikota, which received 11 % in the following election in the year 2011, thematized national identity and even questioned its existence, as well promoting a negative definition of the church, patriotism, and the relationship of the individual and the state on the basis of critical historicized emotions. The subsequent gradual decline of the movement was replaced by the success of the national conservative movement of KNP led by Janusz Korwin Mike in the election to the European parliament in 2014. Both the establishment and the downfall of the movement (Ruch Palikota), which are defined negatively toward (traditional) national identity, or conversely emphasize it, show the increasingly strong demand for these themes in Polish society The issues analyzed in this research are as follows:

In the case of the Czech Republic between 2012 and 2013, a phenomenon emerged—Tomio Okamura who formed the Úsvit movement for the 2013 parliamentary elections, and whose political campaign was concerned with the question of socially excluded localities with an emphasis on the Roma population. The party gained 7.3% in the elections and continued to intensively pursue the thematization of the Roma issue in parliament. The party also intensively focused on the negative effects of globalization, the EU and even occasionally supported conspiracy theories until its demise. In the first half of 2015, the movement fell apart due to disputes about party finances.

Slovak politics are also characterized by the demand for nationally-colored themes. In the observed period, the dominance of Smer-SD occurred – a party which occasionally used national identity in the political struggle. It is also related to the fact that SNS and SMK, parties representing the Hungarian minority and Slovak majority respectively, did not enter parliament in the 2010 and 2012 elections. Concurrently, the right-wing scene has become very heterogeneous, as can be seen from the viewpoint of a number of parties such as SaS, OL, Most-Híd. In the 2010 election, the Most-Híd party, who aimed to link the Slovak majority with the Hungarian minority through politics, were elected. Somewhat surprisingly, the nationalist movement of Marian Kotleba succeeded in the regional election in 2013 (Kocúr, Mesežnikov 2015: 136). Although it was only a regional election for the district governor of the Bánsko-Bystrický region, this success created space for the implementation of policies representing extreme positions on the question of national identity.

9.1.1. Parties covered for analysis and issues selected in the Czech Republic, Poland, and Slovakia

The parties analysed below are divided into two sections. First, the following section serves as an introduction to the development of policies by individual political parties that are relevant to issues of national identity. Close attention is paid to political parties who were in parliament during the researched period 2004–2013. Each country's party system is introduced by describing the basic context of the development of the party system. However, the analysis of the influence of the European political space on the perception of national identity at a national level covers parties having representation on both levels at the same time. In this way, one can observe changes of policy that took place when the parties were interacting with Europe. It should be underlined that the analysis focuses on changes beyond one election period. Therefore, it focuses on parties that are present within the party system of individual countries for a longer period. In the setting of the context for the evaluation of results, parties that have been in parliament only for one period are relevant and are not to be covered by the analysis since they do not have representatives in the European politics.

Secondly, the introduction of each party system also comprises an overview of the development by political parties of a policy of national identity. In addition to this, three issues relating to national identity (as reflected in election manifestos) are used to set out each country's context. The purpose of such a complex introduction is to identify any cover of relevant issues of public debate in the various election manifestos used in each election over the researched period. These issues have been selected based on the following parameters. First, issues representing a mixture of domestic relevancy (Roma issues in the Czech Republic and Slovakia; the role of the Church in Poland), international relevancy (role of the European integration in the party systems), and foreign (neighbouring) issues aiming to capture the perception of influence in domestic politics (Sudeten Germans in the Czech Republic, Smolensk disaster in Poland, and myths shaping the history of Slovakia). In this sense, the different dynamics of each issue can be analyzed in terms of relevancy and the level of emphasis given. Secondly, all selected issues that proved to be relevant for the public and political agenda over the whole time period researched and are, to different extents, thematized in the election manifestos of researched parties. The general definition of issues also allows one to include various niche topics relevant for a short time.

Table 5: Overview of national identity relevant issues

Country			
The Czech Republic	Sudeten Germans	Roma minority	Economic dimension of integration
Poland	Role of Church	Smolensk catastrophe	European integration
Slovakia	Shaping historical myth	European integration	Roma minority

Source: Author

Although it would be desirable to present the context in the researched countries in a comparable way, the dimensionality and relevancy of topics relevant for national identity makes this hardly possible. Therefore, the following section presents the relevant issues for national identity in each country, but a scale of relevancy of these issues in contrast to other policies is not presented. The overview of individual parties relevant in individual countries is developed based on election manifestos. It serves to set the context of individual states properly based on the development of parties that have been the subject of analysis

In the following section, the development of policy related to national identity in the case of individual parliamentary political parties is introduced. After an introduction into each country's party system, each parliament party is subjected to analysis. The profiles of individual parties have the following structure — brief introduction of the party and overview of the most relevant elements of policy related to national identity in the election manifestos of the past three general elections. In addition to this, when analyzing individual manifestos, codes corresponding to the code book, are used to symbolize the party's development.

9.1.2. The Czech Republic: Introduction into party system and national identity

The main scope of topics dominating the interests of the party system relates to a socio-economic cleavage (Havlík, Voda 2014). As research published by Voda (2015) shows, there is a stronger preference of libertarian/authoritarian axis as well as a significant role of values in voter's preferences in the CEE region (Voda 2015). Looking on the election manifestos of parties competing in the 2006 and 2010 general elections to the Czech parliament, the dominance of socio-economic issues is evident (Hloušek, Procházková 2013:126). Issues relating to national identity have never been a mainstream topic within Czech politics (Kopecký 2006: 126-127, Eibl 2010: 94-95). As Hloušek, Kopeček (2008: 547), claim, a significant factor of the 2006 general election was the deepening importance of socio-economic cleavage and confirmation of a strongly entrenched right-left division in Czech politics. However, after the 2013 general election the structure of the cleavage order in Czech politics has changed, with a weakening of the importance of socio-economic cleavage (Eibl 2013: 50–51). This trend goes hand in hand with the rise of new populist movements across Europe. After the 2013 election, it is evident that both the party system and the issues represented have changed, making it difficult to establish a new party grouping that would become a relevant actor in terms of policy niche. This is a significant development since the 2010 election (Hloušek 2005: 451; Rohrschneider, Whitefield 2010: 63; Havlík et. al. 2014: 286). This shift has been represented by two new political movements entering into parliament and a significant erosion of support for ODS as well as ČSSD (Havlík 2014: 48).[57] The election in 2010 has shown a beginning in electoral volatility within the centre and to the right of the ideological spectrum (Pink, Valterová 2010, Hanley et al. 2008, Hanley 2011). This trend was confirmed in the 2013 general election (Hanley, Sikk 2013, Havlík et. al 284; 148). As demonstrated by a wide body of research, the rise of EU related issues in election manifestos of parliamentary parties has happened only rarely in comparison to the 2002 general election (Hloušek, Pšeja 2009: 115, Procházková, Hloušek 2013: 127, Cibulka 2013: 49).

Three relevant issues — Sudeten Germans, the Roma minority, and EU integration — resonated in the time period 2005–2013. However, issues of national identity do not represent the most influential cleavage in Czech politics; Sudeten German issues were used heavily only during the presidential campaign. The relevancy of national identity in its extreme form in terms of far-right wing parties in Czech politics has not affected the political mainstream, as can be seen in the significant electoral success of mainstream parties such as DS/DSSS (Černoch et al. 2011: 76). Although parties such as Úsvit, KSČM, or DSSS have used the national identity card in their manifestations, its use does not cause a significant rise in the emphasis on national identity in general (Vít 2014). The following part describes the development of the perception of national identity in policy as well as the above-mentioned issues, as reflected in election manifestos.

---

57 In case of ODS, it can be seen as the result of long-term policy tensions such as EU integration (see Vodička 2005: 162)

Table 6: Overview of Czech parties covered and their election gains

Party	Profile	2006/seats	2010/seats	2013/seats	Government coalition
ČSSD	Left	35.38/81	22.08/56	20.45/50	2013–2017
ODS	Conservative right	32.32/74	20.22/53	7.72/16	2006–2009; 2010–2013
KDU-ČSL	Centre right	7.22/13		6.78/14	2006–2009
KSČM	Communist	12.81/26	11.27/26	14.91/33	-
TOP 09	Liberal right	-	16.7/41	11.99/26	2010–2013
ANO 2011	Centre	-	-	18.65/47	2013–2017
VV	Centre-right	-	10.88/24	-	2010–2013
Úsvit	-	-	-	6.88/14	-
Zelení	Left	6.29/6	-	-	–2009

Source: Volby.cz

The decline of issues relating to national identity in the past decade can be demonstrated by the example of the absence of any openly xenophobic political party in parliament from 1992 to 1998. Following the argumentation developed in previous sections, it is expected that the density of policies coloured by national identity in the election manifestos would decrease with involvement in Europe. To get a complex picture of how national identity is reflected in election manifestos, an overview of three relevant issues is also introduced. Bearing in mind that selection of three issues was done according to their relevancy in social and political discussion over the researched period, their reflection in individual election manifestos is rather low. It is evident that despite the relevancy of these issues in public debate, their impact to reshape a party's policy is rather weak since these issues are not thought to be sufficiently relevant to be mentioned in election manifestos. However, issues relating to European integration are reflected with stronger emphasis due to the multidimensionality of this topic in Czech politics — from the general role of EU integration to individual policies and their impact on national level.

Table 7: Overview of parties' positions on selected issues

Party	Election	Sudeten Germans	Roma minority	Economic dimension of EU integration	Change
ČSSD	2006	Good relations with neighbours	Integration of Roma families, social justice	Strengthening political and social dimension	-
	2010	No specific mention	Against social exclusion, no Roma specific	Joining EUR	Softening openness
	2013	Good relations with neighbour	No specific mention	Joining EUR only if bringing benefits	Softening openness
ODS	2006	No specific mention	No specific mention	Fiscal and social sovereignty	-
	2010	No specific mention	No specific mention	Strengthening intergovernmental cooperation; Joining EUR only if bringing benefits	No change
	2013	Good relations with neighbours, special emphasis on Germany	No specific mention	Against Joining EUR	Nationalizing

KDU-ČSL	2006	No specific mention	No specific mention	EU as set of values, no specific mention	-
	2010	Good relations with neighbours, special emphasis on Germany	No specific mention	Joining EUR, political union	Stressing openness
	2013	Good relations with neighbours, special emphasis on Germany	No specific mention	Joining EUR in the "right time"	No change
KSČM	2006	Against Sudeten Germans' representation in Prague	Support Roma identity	Joining EUR only if bringing benefits	-
	2010	Against Sudeten Germans' to interfere into Czech politics	No specific mention	No specific mention	Nationalizing
	2013	Against Germans' to interfere into Czech politics	No specific mention	No specific mention	No change

IDENTITY FORMATION

TOP 09	2010	No specific mention	No specific mention	Joining EUR, political union	-
	2013	No specific mention	No specific mention	Joining EUR, political union	No change
ANO 2011	2013	No specific mention	No specific mention	No specific mention	-
Úsvit	2013	No specific mention	No specific mention, against forced inclusion	Joining EUR only if bringing benefits	-
Greens	2006	No specific mention	Inclusion of excluded groups into society	Joining EUR, political union	-
	2010	No specific mention	Inclusion of excluded groups into society	Joining EUR, political union	No change
Public Affairs	2010	No specific mention	Against misusing social system	Joining EUR only if bringing benefits	-

Source: Election manifestos, author

Shortly after EU accession in 2004, negotiations for new treaty reforms started. EU integration issues were an important cleavage during the 2007–2009 centre-right coalition (ODS, KDU-ČSL, Green Party). The issue of deeper EU integration was concluded by the approval of the Lisbon Treaty in November 2009. Internal argument within the ODS did not cause it to form a possible "European cleavage" in Czech domestic policy. However, the newly formed centre-right party TOP 09 (formed in 2009) built up its profile based on strong support for the EU. In contrast, ODS increasingly started to define itself as a defender of Czech national interests in Europe (Hanley 2004: 526–527; Millard 2004: 146–147). Therefore, the European discussion was between supporters of President Klaus and the anti-Klaus wing (Černoch et al. 2011: 22).[58] Despite this, EU related issues did not become particularly significant. It is also evident from the overview that parties' policies tended to converge, especially when it came to the EU.

Another issue of the early post accession period that is relevant to national identity was the US radar system and its possible location in the Czech Republic in the time period of 2008–2009. As with the approval of the Lisbon Treaty, this foreign policy issue became one of the most substantial issues for public discussion for some time. The debate about the US radar system was much more emotional than that of the Lisbon Treaty. This also led to arguments about sovereignty by ČSSD and KSČM as well as a significant questioning of transatlantic relations by the biggest opposition party, ČSSD. The division between right and left parties was significant for subsequent public and political controversy (Vít 2016: 275). ODS and KDU-ČSL, as promoters of the transatlantic coalition, supported the installation of the American radar system. The Green Party (SZ) was split, with some members adopting a pragmatic approach and others, as pacifists, principally against the military (Hloušek, Kopeček 2010: 185). ČSSD opposed the radar system because they preferred to strengthen military cooperation at a European level rather than form a transatlantic coalition. There were

---

58   For a detailed analysis of Klaus's role in Czech politics see Kopeček 2012. His role in forming the European politics of ODS can be found here: 2012: 226–228.

internal tensions within ČSSD concerning the US radar, but there are unanswered questions, about whether their opposition to the system was primarily to earn domestic gains or because of a European orientation (Husák et al. 2011: 22).

The economic crisis, followed by Czech government budgetary cuts between 2008 and 2011, increased the sensibility of external influence, as well as the image depicting a specific segment of society as guilty for weak economic performance (Gabal 2015). During the governing period of the center-right coalition (ODS, TOP 09, VV/LIDEM), Roma people in particular were pictured as misusing the social system (Klukavská, Zagibová 2013: 303). This rising negative perception of the Roma reached its climax on a summer night in 2013 in the midst of the election campaigns. Several riots were organized, the biggest of which occurred in July 2013 in České Budějovice and in Duchcov, North Bohemia. A new feature of these riots is that they were attended primarily by so-called ordinary people, not by far-right extremists.[59] Those attending proclaimed their non-affiliation to any extremist faction. Surprisingly, these riots were not discussed during the 2013 election campaigns of the mainstream political parties. Only Úsvit used this card during the campaign, picturing Roma people as those who misuse the social system.[60] The riots increased sensitivity over the role of Roma people in society but did not lead to a significant rise in extremist movements.

However, during the 2013 election campaign there were attempts to touch upon two issues relevant for national identity: the EU, and the perception of the Roma minority in broader terms. Although the EU was discussed as a divisive issue for the parties, none of the mainstream parties (except Úsvit) strictly opposed the integration process. On the other side, there is evidence of a lack of a clear consensus on European integration. New movements (Úsvit and ANO 2011) — not anchored in European politics — did not elaborate on their EU policy with details. Especially in the case of the Úsvit movement, the uncertainty of the manifesto is evident. In a

---

59   For further details about this issue eg. jeseniky.ceeidentity.eu
60   Workers Party of Social Justice/Dělnická strana sociální spravedlnosti, DSSS

similar way, the European policy of KSČM remained ambiguous.[61] Nonetheless, overall, EU policy does not dominate the political discourse in Czech politics and the election campaign confirms this fact. In regard to the anti-Roma riots that took place in the summer of 2013, the parties failed to respond to this issue in their election manifestos.[62] This is interesting with regard to the leftist parties who, with the exception of the Greens, probably decided not to "speak with the voice of the excluded" for tactical reasons. Only one party out of all those in parliament, namely Úsvit, focused on blaming Roma people for misusing the social system, and strictly opposed immigration.[63]

9.1.2.1. Czech Social Democratic Party (Česká strana sociálně demokratická, ČSSD)

The Czech Social Democratic Party was established during 1990 and quickly became the strongest left-wing party. From 1998 to 2002, the party formed a minority government with the support of ODS, and in the period from 2002 to 2006 there was the emergence of a ČSSD minimum majority (101 votes out 200 members of the Chamber of Deputies) centre-left cabinet with the conservative KDU-ČSL party and liberal US-DEU party. The first cabinet is commonly understood to have come about because of the strong role of Miloš Zeman, the chairman of the party. In the period 2002 to 2006 the party had to change its leader three times. Jiří Paroubek saved the party from a deep crisis, but his new leadership did not bring about an election victory in either the 2006, 2009 or 2010 elections (Černoch et al. 2011: 42). After the 2010 election defeat, Paroubek resigned the chairman's position. He was replaced by Bohuslav Sobotka, representing the liberal wing of the party, oriented to Western Europe.

---

61   As many scholars argue, KSČM's position is de facto in isolation from the main flow of Czech policy (Vodička 2010: 292).
62   Only the Greens reflected this event both in their election manifesto and in official party channels. TOP 09, the Greens, and ANO were the only parties that mentioned social inclusion explicitly.
63   The movement struggled with internal tension in March 2015 before splitting into two separate parties. Tomio Okamura, former leader of the Úsvit movement, founded a new party Strana za přímou demokracii/Party of Direct Democracy (SPD) using similar language against immigrants and Roma people.

Table 8: Overview of development of policy of national identity of ČSSD

2006	2010	2013
1. 3 Strong in the EU	1. 1 Support of deeper integration	1. 1 Support of deeper integration
2. 8 support of national identity building	2. 1. 1 Nationalism negative	1. 3 Strong in the EU
4. 2 Openness towards world	2. 1 Pluralism	2. 3 Human rights as a value
	2. 3 Human rights as a value	2. 4 Culture as a value
	3. 4 Limited immigration	4. 3 Western orientation

Source: Election manifestos[64]

Looking at the development of the perception of national identity in the past three election manifestos, there is evidence of a shift towards a softening of national character on several levels. However, the 2010 election manifesto stressed nation-friendly policies such as limited immigration or support for developing national culture. Both the 2006 and 2010 election manifestos offer contradictory data on national identity. On the one side, the protection of human rights is stressed, also in the case of the Roma minority. On the other side, they proposed limits to immigration — such as preferring immigration from South-Eastern Europe. In addition to this, both election manifestos stress the positive role of national culture within society. The 2013 election manifesto shows a significant move towards weakening of national character policies. References to the preferences for any particular group of citizens are significantly softened. The element of culture is also used in a much-softened way (ceeidentity.eu 2016a).

In all three elections, the role of EU integration plays a significant role. From a long-term perspective, the party shaped its policy to become one of the most EU-supporting political parties

---

[64] Analysis based on the 2006, 2010, and 2013 election manifestos.

According to Sobotka, leader of the party, continuing integration is a logical reaction in order for Europe to maintain its position in the current world. At the same time, he argued, it was of crucial importance to adhere to the principle of subsidiarity. At the same time also, the accession of the Czech Republic to the eurozone was decided in the referendum about EU accession in 2003, which gave the government and parliament the task of setting the date for accepting the common currency, the Euro, once the optimal conditions were met. In Sobotka's opinion, the common currency will be beneficial for the Czech economy. This demonstrates both a multidimensionality to the party's position towards the EU, enhanced by its acceptance of the external environment through groups such as the PES group in the EP. In addition to this, the party aims to be perceived as supporting the European mainstream policy of social democratic parties. Therefore the party does not stress in its manifestos the national interests and it pushes the quest for broader reform of the EU when referring to its democratic deficit. From a different perspective, it shows that the party considers the European political space to be relevant when shaping its policies (ceeidentity.eu 2016a).

It has to also be mentioned that the party suffered a significant decline in support between 2006 and 2013, despite winning the election in 2010 and 2013. Hand in hand with a decrease in support, the party experienced a change of leader. The successor of Jiří Paroubek, Bohuslav Sobotka, represents the liberal wing within the party and perceives the need to develop ties with political allies at the European level, with an emphasis on Germany. In contrast to Sobotka, Jiří Paroubek represented the conservative wing of the party whose stronghold is mainly in the northern parts of Bohemia (Blažek 2014). This may also explain the shift in the 2010 election manifesto to a more friendly towards the nationalizing of party politics.

9.1.2.2. Civic Democratic Party, (Občanská demokratická strana, ODS)

The Civic Democratic Party was the dominant conservative formation in the Czech Republic. The beginning of its political activity dates to the early 1990s with the fragmentation of OF. Václav Klaus led the conservative stream inside the OF. ODS was the most successful political party in the elections of 1991, 1992 and 1996, and Václav Klaus became the prime minister three times. Václav Klaus was replaced in November 2002 by the less charismatic and ideologically moderate Mirek Topolánek. Substantial ideological change did not follow this change of party leader. The shifting of European policy towards pragmatism was adhered to by the Czech EU-Presidency in 2009, which can be understood as a peak of EU-education or rather the "Europeanisation" of ODS (Černoch et al. 2011: 36). This was followed by significant tensions within the party when the party leadership showed its approval for the Lisbon Treaty. Despite the fact that the party participated in its approval, the 2010 election manifesto shows a turning point in its EU policy.

Table 9: Overview of development of policy of national identity of ODS

2006	2010	2013
1. 3 Strong in the EU	1. 3 Strong in the EU	1. 3 Strong in the EU
2. 4 Culture as a value	1. 4 Europe of nations	2. 1 Pluralism
4. 1 Support of the EU	2. 2 Individualism and freedom as a values	2. 6 Traditional values
4. 3 Western orientation	2. 3 Human rights as a value	3. 4 Limited immigration
	2. 4 Culture as a value	4. 3 Western orientation
	3. 2 Protection of minorities	4. 6 negative perception of EU
	3. 4 Limited immigration	4. 8 perceived foreign economic threat
	4. 3 Western orientation	
	4. 8 perceived foreign economic threat	

Source: Election manifestos[65]

The case of ODS shows how rapidly this party – the most significant player in shaping the transformation period – changed its perception of national identity. Analysing the 2006 election manifesto, it shows a rise of national friendly perceptions. In this light, one can observe a strong commitment to orientation towards the West and the EU in international politics. However, ODS never supported the supra-national basis of the EU. The party understands the EU as a space of shared benefits instead of a deep socially and politically integrated Union. At the same time, the 2006 election result was a climax in public support for the party, shaping the legacy of the conservative-liberal ideological camp in Czech politics. The 2010

---

65   Analysis based on the 2006, 2010, and 2013 election manifestos.

election was followed by rising tensions within the party, which resulted – among other things – in a noticeable strengthening of its perception of national identity. This is observable on several levels. First, the perception of the EU towards the ground of national states has been strengthened. At the same time, on the EU level, the party left the EPP group after the 2009 European Parliament election as a result of a growing clash over the substance of EU integration. Interestingly, the party started to shape its policy against international openness as a result of the economic crisis and the EU debt crisis. Hand in hand with this shift, the party started to call for restrictions against immigrants and foreigners coming to the Czech Republic. At the same time, the manifesto stressed liberal policies such as equality and pluralism etc. Therefore, the 2010 election manifesto is the halfway point in the transformation of party policies. 2013 marks a clear shift from a policy supporting the EU to one that resisted against the social dimension of EU integration, as well as supported policies that strengthened so called *traditional* values. This nationalizing shift stands in contrast with a significantly reduced emphasis on individual freedom in comparison to both the 2006 and 2010 election manifestos (ceeidentity.eu 2016b).

During the researched period the party experienced a significant loss of voters followed by two changes of party leadership. This change had its consequences for the election manifestos. Focusing on those issues relevant to national identity, the changing perception of which went hand in hand with structural changes within the party and the search for a new ideological stronghold (Kopecký 2014). As with ČSSD, the reaction of the party upon losing support of the electorate is followed by changes in the understanding of values, which then affect policies.

9.1.2.3. Christian and Democratic Union-Czechoslovak People´s Party (Křesťanská a demokratická unie-Československá strana lidová, KDU-ČSL)

KDU-ČSL originally represented Christian and traditional conservative values as stated above, but since the 1990s it has profiled itself as a non-confessional party for all people even if most of its members are still connected to the Church (Černoch et al. 2011: 53). The party has participated in both centre-right and left-wing government coalitions in the past 25 years, profiling itself as a centrist party. This has resulted in party tensions between its own left and right wings, which caused a separation of part of KDU-ČSL into a new liberal-oriented movement. In 2009 one of the former leaders of the party, Miroslav Kalousek, split from the party and founded the more conservative and right-wing party TOP 09, which drained substantial numbers of members from KDU-ČSL. In the subsequent 2010 general election, TOP 09 won 16.7 % of the vote and KDU-ČSL received only 4.29 %, thus, failing to reach even the threshold of 5 % required to enter the Lower house of the Czech parliament. After 2013, the party experienced a comeback to the parliament under its ideologically moderate chairman Pavel Bělobrádek.

Table 10: Overview of development of policy of national identity of KDU-ČSL

2006	2010	2013
1. 3 Strong in the EU	1. 1 Support of deeper integration	2. 1 Support of deeper integration
2. 1 Support of new emancipation movements, open society	2. 1 Support of new emancipation movements, open society	2. 4 Culture as a value
2. 10 Christian values	2. 1 Pluralism	2. 6 Traditional values
4. 3 Western orientation	2. 3 Human rights as a value	3. 3 Dialogue with minority
	3. 1 Inclusiveness	3. 4 Limited immigration
	3. 2 Protection of minorities	4. 3 Western orientation
	3. 4 Limited immigration	
	4. 8 perceived foreign economic threat	

Source: Election manifestos[66]

Looking at the election manifestos of the Christian Democrats, a pattern similar to ODS emerges. The party oscillates between a more conservative and liberal understanding of national identity. In contrast to ODS, however, Christian Democrats have moved from a rather conservative perception of national identity towards a liberal one. The 2006 election manifesto stressed Christian values, as well as the national interest when it came to the EU. In contrast to this, the 2010 manifesto was penetrated by a liberal understanding of national identity to a much greater extent than that of 2006. The role of individual freedom and pluralism in society increased hand in hand with support for European integration in its supranational substance. In addition to this, the manifesto also stresses the equality of minorities and their protection. The stress on

---

66 Analysis based on the 2006, 2010, and 2013 election manifestos.

individual freedom and its protection goes in sharp contrast with support for conservative Christian values in the 2006 manifesto. Beside this, the 2010 manifesto interprets the EU as an integrated supranational community.

Analysing the 2013 manifesto, the support for EU integration remains the main element to keep continual development of party policy. This can be understood as a result of important role of ties cultivated by the party at the European level. Nevertheless, the 2013 manifesto combines a stress on liberal values, as well as slightly nationalizing the understanding of national identity. This is evident when it comes to support for the rights of minorities, but at the same time the manifesto also supports limits to immigration such as support for particular ethnic/cultural groups. As with the above mentioned ODS, the 2013 election manifesto understands the role of culture and values as significant for social development.

Similarly to ČSSD and ODS, Christian Democrats experienced a change of leadership as well as being out of Parliament between 2010 and 2013. In this context, their policy shift is not surprising. Nor is it surprising that a slight move of the party towards nationalizing friendly policies in 2013 brought the party back to Parliament. Despite this shift, the party continually supports deeper EU integration — which is rather exceptional.

9.1.2.4. *Communist party of Bohemia and Moravia (Komunistická strana Čech a Moravy, KSČM)*

Since 1990, there has been an unwritten agreement between other political parties in the Czech Republic about excluding KSČM from high level policy-decision processes; therefore, the party has been excluded from government coalition participation on the national level. However in reality there are many political contacts and KSČM has already become a legitimate part of the political system in the Czech Republic. Some more radical or reformist wings left the party after the revolution and throughout the 1990s. Nonetheless, the program of the party continues to be based on the Marxist tradition and on communist ideology as such. KSČM tries to escape from the label and historical legacy of communism in Czechoslovakia, particularly from the totalitarian practices connected with

Stalinism and Brezhnevism, and presents itself as a party representing democracy and the interests of regular citizens striving for social change toward socialism in a democratic way (Černoch et al. 2011: 61). The party represents a conservative-left perception of globalization which contradicts with communist internationalism.

Table 11: Overview of development of policy of national identity of KSČM

2006	2010	2013
2. 5 National culture as a part of identity	2. 1 Pluralism	1. 3 Strong in the EU
	2. 4 Culture as a value	2. 1 Pluralism
	4. 8 Perceived foreign economic threat	2. 4 Culture as a value
	4. 10 Pacifism	3. 7 Against minority rights
		4. 8 Perceived foreign economic threat

Source: Election manifestos[67]

Looking at the election manifestos of the KSČM, one can see a trend of gradual strengthening of nationalizing friendly policies. In the 2006 election manifesto, the party placed little emphasis on the relationship with Germany, an important topic when it comes to the issue of Sudeten Germans living in the Czech Republic before 1945. Although the party emphasized this issue at the time of the 2004 EU accession, the election manifesto was not affected by this policy. Nevertheless, the manifesto uses the issue of national identity when stressing the role of national culture. In this context, the party aims to oppose broader globalization and the EU integration process, which could lead to a weakening of national culture.

Interestingly, the 2010 election manifesto—despite deepened EU integration—emphasizes pluralism as one of its core values. At the same time, the manifesto increasingly sharpens its language

---

[67] Analysis based on the 2006, 2010, and 2013 election manifestos.

towards a negative perception of a globalized world as well as participation of the Czech Republic in international organizations such as NATO. In this context, the manifesto shapes its policy of national identity in terms of anti-globalism but also in terms of open society at the same time. Considering the context of the economic crisis, the party similarly to the policy of other left parties frames the economic crisis as a failure of globalized capitalism.

In contrast, the 2013 election manifesto moves policies, relevant for national identity, towards a more conservative understanding than in the 2006 and 2010 manifestos. Beside a negative perception of global capitalism, the manifesto also opposes any involvement of other ethnic or cultural minorities in political and social development. In addition to this, the party frames this policy hand in hand with the need for a strengthening of national culture and history (ceeidentity.eu 2016c).

9.1.2.5. Tradition Responsibility Prosperity 09 (Tradice, Odpovědnost, Prosperita 09, TOP 09)

This conservative party was founded in 2009 through its separation from the KDU-ČSL due to a long-time tension between the conservative and the more liberal wings. The party has gained a lot of popularity thanks to the role of its chairman, Prince Karel Schwarzenberg, who has been nominated as the leading person of the political party. Between 2010 and 2013, the party participated in the government in a centre-right coalition. The party nominated Schwarzenberg to the first direct presidential election in the 2013. The fundamental elements of TOP 09 are the liberty of individuals, the family as a fundamental part of society, common responsibility of individuals to society, shared values of the state, the rule of law, and social solidarity in terms of the free market and public goods (Černoch et al. 2011: 25).

Table 12: Overview of development of policy of national identity of TOP09

2006	2010	2013
	1. 1 Support of deeper integration	2. 1 Support of deeper integration
	3. 2 Protection of minorities	1. 3 Strong in the EU
		2. 3 Human rights as a value
		2. 4 Culture as a value
		4. 3 Western orientation

Source: Election manifestos[68]

The 2010 election manifesto supports the common European currency — the Euro — which is seen as a big transfer of national sovereignty towards a supra-national institution. This commitment marked the political party as the one most supportive of the EU. In this regard, the manifesto also stresses its commitment to policies supporting globalization, such as perceiving human rights as an integral part of foreign policy.

In the following election in 2013, many of the key elements of the 2010 manifesto are softened. Although the manifesto supports deeper EU integration, it also stresses the role of national interests and the influence of the Czech Republic in the EU. It frames support for openness in society by stressing a sense of belonging to the Western community. In contrast to the 2010 manifesto, that of 2013 shows the important role of the Church as a guarantor of continued spiritual and social development. Similarly to other parties, the manifesto perceives the landscape as something of historical value that should be cultivated. In the same way, local traditions should be further developed. The party stresses continuing European integration as an aspiration, and proposes steps for further Czech integration, such as acceding to the European Financial Agreement;

---

[68] Analysis based on the 2006, 2010, and 2013 election manifestos.

deepening the common market; and joining the eurozone. At the same time it also stresses the importance of national interests in the EU and the need to set limits to deeper integration such as considering the crucial role of nation states (ceeidentity.eu 2016d).

9.1.2.6. Action of Dissatisfied Citizens 2011, (Akce nespokojených občanů, ANO 2011)

ANO was founded by Czech billionaire Andrej Babiš as a reaction to what he saw as dissatisfactory political and economic developments in Czech politics. The main reason was the growing level of corruption and a series of scandals involving the centre-right government. Although the movement initially had a leftist profile, during the 2013 election campaign it targeted centre-right middle-class votes. It is rather difficult to categorize the manifesto on a left-right scale or even on a liberal-conservative one. From the content perspective, the manifesto is focused on economical and corruption issues.

Table 13: Overview of development of policy of national identity of ANO2011

2006	2010	2013
		2. 3 Human rights as a value
		4. 3 Western orientation
		4. 8 Perceived foreign economic threat

Source: Election manifestos[69]

The movement declares support for EU integration; however, ANO calls for decreasing VAT in the EU and opposes de facto policies of tax harmonisation. The party supports a higher level of competitiveness in the EU. It does not declare if it means to refuse any extension of EU competences. In foreign policy, the movement speaks in favour of cooperation with NATO allies, the USA, and also the

---

69 Analysis based on the 2013 election manifestos.

V4. Interestingly, ANO also protests against the marginalization of the armed forces. It supports an inclusionary social policy and the positive role of culture in social development (ceeidentity.eu 2016e).

Like the other parties, ANO supports the stability of a food supply produced in the Czech Republic. In this context, the movement wants better conditions for Czech farmers from supermarket companies. To support domestic production, it has expressed the intention to make greater use of domestic energy sources.

9.1.2.7. *Tomio Okamura's Dawn of Direct Democracy (Hnutí úsvit přímé demokracie Tomia Okamury)*

Building up a profile of Tomio Okamura, Czech-Japanese entrepreneur and member of the Senate, is a difficult task. The election manifesto he presented picks up issues that resonate in society without any deeper anchoring to any intellectual basis. Although he speaks publicly about the need for strengthening direct democracy, the manifesto shows many signs of populism. Firstly, it argues that the EU integration process should not include the integration of tax and budgetary competences. The Czech Republic should not transfer further competences to Brussels. Secondly, in economic policy the movement focuses on support for traditional national industry. For that purpose, the Czech energy sources should be used and not exported abroad, or even sold to foreign investors. The manifesto does not mention the immigration and Roma issue that was used by Okamura during the campaign[70].

---

[70] Despite the fact that Úsvit's election manifesto for the 2013 parliament election did not pay attention to the Roma issue, Okamura started the election campaign with this very issue. Among others, Okamura argued that all ethnic minorities should have a right to live in their own state. The Gipsies should wake up their elites ... and to struggle for their own state. The right to self-determination is the right of every nation and therefore the Czech Republic should support this endeavour to create conditions to settle back to their origin country of India (ceeidentity.eu 2014).

Table 14: Overview of development of policy of national identity of Úsvit

2006	2010	2013
		3. 4 Limited immigration
		4. 8 Perceived foreign economic threat

Source: Election manifestos[71]

9.1.2.8. Greens (Strana zelených, SZ)

The party was founded in early 1990 with the purpose of transforming the OF (Občasnké forum/Civic Forum, OF). Their first significant election result was in the 2002 general election, when they gained 2.4 % support. The new party leadership under Martin Bursík positioned SZ closer to the centre and with a pragmatic remit. This change was a successful strategy in the 2006 election when the party gained 6.3% of the vote along with six representatives in the Parliament. The Greens became a member of the centre-right government together with the Christian Democrats and gained 2 ministerial posts. Under new leadership after the 2009 European election, the party did not manage to enter Parliament in either the 2010 or the 2013 general elections.

---

71 Analysis based on the 2013 election manifesto

Table 15: Overview of development of SZ's policy of national identity

2006	2010	2013
1. 1 Support of deeper integration	1. 1 Support of deeper integration	1. 1 Support of deeper integration
2. 1 Support of new emancipation movements, open society	2. 1 Pluralism	2. 1 Support of new emancipation movements, open society
3. 1 Inclusiveness	3. 1 Inclusiveness	

Source: Election manifestos[72]

The 2006 manifesto calls for a stronger emphasis on anti-discrimination in relation to all minorities. This is certainly the case for the Roma minority, who have been disadvantaged for a long time. When it comes to immigration policy, the party wants to make the Czech Republic more open to immigrants and to support them when they are settling in the country. In addition to this, the manifesto claims that education can be used to support tolerance, starting in elementary school. On the issue of equality, the Green Party is primarily concerned with gender equality. Following the issue of human rights, the manifesto supports the strengthening of women's rights and their increased representation in politics. When it comes to European integration, both the 2006 and 2010 manifestos support deeper integration of the EU in the sense of supranational integration of individual policies, such as social policies.

The 2013 manifesto stresses the erosion of social unity and argues, that discrimination against any kind of social group must be removed from political discourse; the goal should be to integrate all minorities into one society and to deal with the issue of parallel societies existing separately rather than together with the main body. In this sense Czech society should strengthen its openness and tolerance. The party manifesto also reflects discussions of

---

[72] Analysis is based on the 2006 and 2010 election manifesto. The 2013 election manifesto was not analyzed due to the fact that the party did not approach the 5 % threshold and remained out of the parliament for a second period.

migration, arguing that this must be perceived as a social issue, not a security one. The party claims that the labour market needs foreigners. Focusing on EU issues, SZ calls for deeper political integration and the establishment of a unified military command. Therefore, the single national armies should be integrated into one.

9.1.2.9. Public Affairs (Věci veřejné, VV)

The first step towards a higher public profile for this party was the European Parliament election in 2009. The first election success took place in 2010. The party gained nearly 11% of the vote, entered Parliament and became a member of the centre-right coalition government led by ODS. The movement was supported by several entrepreneurs affiliated to ODS rather as an investment than as a political movement with a developed party structure. On the one hand, VV declares itself to be a socially sensitive party; on the other VV is very restrictive in its social policy and indirectly uses social policy against excluded minorities. The party did not manage to re-enter Parliament in the 2013 general election.

The 2010 manifesto focuses on preventing the misuse of social assistance. Its European policy does not seem to be a liberal program. The most important point of the program is the emphasis on EU efficiency, liberalised services and efficient use of European funds. The party supports joining the eurozone, but only under the condition that the debate on accepting the Euro would be led by experts instead of politicians. In addition to this, the manifesto proposes a simplified definition of European policy as a "picking gain" of European integration (ceeidentity.eu 2016f).

Table 16: Overview of development of policy of national identity of VV

2006	2010	2013
	1. 1 Support of deeper integration	
	2. 2 Individualism and freedom as a values	
	2. 6 Traditional values	

Source: Election manifestos[73]

9.1.3. Poland: Introduction into the party system and national identity

History and its interpretation play a significant role when it comes to the main elements of Polish politics. Therefore, history is a highly politicized topic in regard to the perception of national identity (Neumann, Pukajlo 2011: 218). Dominika Kasprowicz (2016) summarizes the following key issues when it comes to shaping national community: a tradition of opposing the state; the strong position of the Catholic Church; and the existence of different ideological strongholds. Referring to history and shaping policy decisions based on historical identity is, according to Sczepanik (2012: 66), an aspect of conservative policy in Poland especially during the time of PiS (Prawo i Sprawiedliwość, Law and Justice-PiS) governments. Developments over the past 25 years show a general rise, as well as falls, of movements using national identity: movements such as LPR (League of Polish Families), SRP (Samoobrona Rzeczpospolitej Polskiej, Self-Defence of Polish Republic, SPR), or TR (Twoj Ruch, Your Movement-TR). This can be explained as a backlash against EU and NATO integration by those who feel the need to defend traditional Polish and Christian values. Therefore, nationalistic movements that have participated in Polish politics after 1989 have built their profiles with reference to the interwar uprising of the Polish nation as well as dissatisfaction with post-communist

---

[73] Analysis based on the 2010 election manifestos.

developments (Kupka 2009: 75). Speaking about the transformation period, the framing of contemporary history also plays a crucial role in current politics (Hloušek, Šipulová 2012). In the decade before EU accession, national identity in the rural part of Poland was mobilized using anti-EU language mainly by SRP, which presented themselves as a party defending "losers" of transformation (Dančák 2002: 289). In the first years of transition, the Polish political scene demonstrated a tendency to lean towards the support of national conservative parties—similar to developments in the Czech Republic and Hungary.

A strong anti-communist mood in the society was shaped by the Catholic Church, which traditionally supported the opposition, and has been perceived as the main element of Polish national identity, not only under communism, but also throughout history. This cleavage has had an important impact on the development of the main ideas in their politics. It is the principle cause of disagreement between PiS and PO, in terms of the legacy of the values of the Solidarity Movement. Despite having the same origins, both of the most relevant political formations have cleaved along conservative versus liberal identity lines. PO was founded (along with the PiS) as a result of the demise of conservative-liberal bloc Election Action Solidarity (Akcja Wyborcza Solidarność-AWS). In 2001, ASW promoted classically liberal solutions like: the introduction of a flat tax, the restructuring of public finances, creation of a business environment friendly to entrepreneurs and social policy on a minimal scale (Kasprowicz 2016). In contrast to ASW, PiS started to focus on national identity by using strongly emotional and morally targetted politics, calling for better ethics as well as developing a narrative of unique identity (Wojtas 2012: 170). This was, de facto, the starting point for multiple uses of these issues in political discourse in the researched period.

116 IDENTITY FORMATION

Table 17: Overview of Czech parties covered and their election gains

Party	Profile	2005/seats	2007/seats	2011/seats	Government coalition
PiS	National conservative	27/155	32.11/166	29.89/157	2005-2007
PO	Centre-right	24.3/133	41.51/209	39.18/207	2007-2011
PSL	Conservative right	7/25	8.91/31	8.36/28	2007-2011
SLD	Left	11.3/55	13.15/53	8.24/27	-
LPR	National conservative	8/35	1.30/0	-	2005-2007
SRP	National conservative	11.4/56	1.53/0	0.07/0	2005-2007
TW	Liberal left	-	-	10.02/40	-

Source: wybory.pkw.gov.pl

Such issues have been constantly played up by both parties – although most significantly by politically marginal actors – with a stress placed on openness and a sovereignist understanding of national identity The focus on domestic affairs means that the cleavage between the liberal understanding of national identity and an emphasis on state sovereignty should not be relevant any more. This was the case with the success of the radical right LPR and the populist SRP in 2005, with TR in 2011, and with KNP in the 2014 European election (Baran 2016).

The issue of national identity has been used as an emotional tool in election campaigns mainly in order to stress Polish sovereignty. This has been researched, for example, through the case of SRP by Kinga Wojtas (2012). After the national conservative government led by PiS between 2005 and 2007, EU and foreign-related issues became relevant for the 2007 election campaign in terms, again, of topics to do with national identity, such as Poland's role in the EU integration process (Szcerbiak, Bil 2011: 40). Nevertheless, the impact of the EU on parties' organisation structures was, according to the research published in 2011, rather low (Szcerbiak, Bil 2011: 46). In this regard, PiS present an interesting case – as one of the most important parties to have shown disinterest in established political ties in the EU over the past decade (Szcerbiak, Bil 2011: 46 and Ciancara 2015).

When looking at issues relevant to national identity, the role of external elements is evident. In this regard, the fluidity of this ideological segment arises from Poland's membership in the EU and NATO. The more Poland penetrates into Western structures, the greater the tensions that arise in regard to national identity. When it comes to topics relating to national identity, Polish politics is predictably more concerned with these issues. Therefore, one can observe emphasis on national identity in the cases of PiS, LPR, and SRP during the researched period. PO and PSL moved between liberal and conservative approaches to national identity (Černoch et al. 2011: 148). With TR, SLD represent a liberal understanding of national identity, stressing belonging to the state as a citizen instead of as an ethnic Pole, and framing belonging to the Church as a private rather than state (Černoch et. al. 2011: 157). However, TR have used stronger rhetoric – openly criticizing membership of the Catholic Church (Twoj Ruch 2014).

An analysis published by EUROPEUM (2013), and based on a survey among Polish political parties about issues related to national identity, three basic findings were discovered. First, even though Poland enjoys gains from EU membership, the centre right parties, do not welcome the possibility of a federal structure of the EU (that said, deeper integration is not perceived primarily as a threat). The second distinction among parties is constituted by the stance of education towards patriotism. The parties reflect differently the ongoing process of national identity modernisation[74], and of a so-called modern Poland[75]. The third point is the role of the Catholic Church. Although the role of the Church and education towards national identity plays a crucial role for PiS and to a lesser extent PLS, these issues are considered by Twoj Ruch as the main impediment to the modernisation of Poland. The growing quest for a non-traditional[76] understanding of Polish national identity may likely emerge in a long-term perspective as the key political cleavage. The role of PO is complicated. On one hand, PO understands national identity as given and does not aim to discuss it further; on the other hand PO supports an individualistic understanding of the role of religion in society. Therefore, in the view of PiS, the Church lacks adequate support from PO, while TR is not supportive of the Church at all (EUROPEUM 2014). However, since the 2007 election, PSL formed two government coalitions with the centre-right PO, and its understanding of national identity is very conservative, when speaking about nation and the role of the Catholic Church (Vit 2014a). Liberal topics were left out of the main scope of policies by PO. Hand in hand with this development, it became a key to the success of the other liberal party, TR. Founded by the former PO member Janusz Palikot, TR returned to the question of economic liberalization and was openly anti-clerical. The party also promoted the idea of the secularization of the state and the liberalization of social structures such as marriage for people of the same sex (Kasprowicz 2016).

---

74 To be future oriented and not insist on the "old times".
75 Even if this is not enough for Twoj Ruch intentions, the party stressed the radical liberalization of everything that refers to "old Poland" (Interview with Krzysztof Iszikowski, February 2014).
76 Prof. Jan Hartmann explains this term as a need for the telling of ideas and less about individual historical events (Rozner, Vít 2014).

Table 18: Overview of issues in the election manifestos

Party	Election	Role of Church	Smolensk plane crash	The EU integration	Change
PO	2005	Church active part of society	-	Benefits from integrated EU and general support	-
	2007	Church part of society	-	Benefits from integrated EU and general support	No change
	2011	Not specific mention	Tragedy, no specific framing	Supporting integration and stressing national interests within this process	Stressing national interest
PiS	2005	Church part of society	-	Europe of nation, stressing values of nation	-
	2007	Church as ethic imperative	-	Europe of nations, supporting of internal market integration	Stressing "national ethic"
	2011	Church essential part of society	Commemoration of national heroes defending ethic of nation and morality	Europe of nations, strong role of nation	Further stressing of national values

IDENTITY FORMATION

				Europe of nations	
PSL	2005	Church active part of society	-		-
	2007	Not specific mention	-	Europe of nations with shared interest	Weakening of national identity mentions
	2011	Not specific mention	Not specific mention	National interest in the EU	Further weakening
SLD	2005	Supporting secularism	-	Support of the EU integration	-
	2007	Secular society, decrease role of Church	-	Support of the EU integration	Weakening of national identity mentions
	2011	Secularization and equality of Churches	Change for improvement of RU-PL/EU relations	Support of integrated EU	Further weakening
LPR	2005	Society based Christian moral principles	-	Leaving the EU	-
	2007	National identity based on Catholic values	-	Against any deeper integration	Further weakening
SRP	2005	Church as a part of national identity	-	Country misused by EU, national interest	-
	2007	Not special mention	-	Europe of nations, national interest	Further stressing of national values
TR	2011	Against participation of Church on politics	Against glorification	Support of integrated EU	-

Source: Election manifestos

The issue of national identity has been a crucial element of rising political and social tensions during the period 2007–2015, when PO and PSL were in government. This resulted in rising tensions within both liberal and conservative camps (ceeidentity.eu 2016h). Interestingly, and reflecting the fact that national identity has been a highly relevant element of Polish politics, PiS started being attacked from far right formations for not being conservative enough (Vit 2014b). In addition to this, these tensions brought success to KNP in the 2014 EP election as well as a PiS majority victory, and the rise of the Kukiz15 movement in the 2015 general election.

The overview of the perception of issues in the election manifestos shows a penetration of issues related to the role of the Catholic Church and also European integration. It indicates the high relevancy of these issues through their translation into election manifestos; hand in hand also with the perception of other elements of national identity that profiles of individual parties display. In addition to this, the summary shows existing cleavages when it comes to national identity, as well as some very contradictory perceptions of individual parties. Deeper insights are brought to this topic in analysis published by EUROPEUM (2014), which explores the positions of individual parties towards several issues related to national identity. Following the overview above, it shows the significant extent of cleavages among Polish political parties when it comes to different policies but also offers an understanding of its relevancy. This is the case of the strong emphasis of PiS on individual questions, their evaluation, and further use in election manifestos.

122 Identity Formation

Table 19: Parties' positions on national identity relevant issues (2014)[77]

Party		Education towards patriotism	Church as an identity	Foreign policy towards RF	Banking union as threat	EU as federation	Reminding Smolensk crash
PiS		should be cornerstone of education	Church forms Polish national identity	Relations should never be based only on economic interests	limits national sovereignty	EU-superstate threats national sovereignty	state should develop the memory of plane crash
	relevancy	10	10	1	3	1	10
SLD		should be a side product of education about history	need to differentiate between state and church	relations should follow same principles as FR with other countries	not a threat	basic principle of social democracy	yes, they were state representatives of the state
	relevancy	5	1	10	1	10	10

77 Based on surveys sent to each parliament party.

Results

TR	relevancy	no, only in sense of education towards citizenship	Church as a negative impact on society	relations should follow civic and minorities situation in that country	not a threat	EU integration is the only way for PL to keep sovereignty	sufficient
		3	1		1	10	2
PSL		should be cornerstone of education	Church forms Polish national identity	relations should never be based only on economic interests	limits national sovereignty	not realistic, economic dimension should play crucial role	yes, they were state representatives of the state
	relevancy	10	10	10	6	2	3
PO		history education	not necessary; personal choice	relations should never be based only on economic interests	not a threat	not realistic, economic dimension should play crucial role	PO supports that
	relevancy	8	6	2	1	2	6

Source: Author

This detailed perspective shows some interesting patterns. Looking at SLD and TR, one can easily get confused about the differences between the two. Focusing on national identity, the main difference is the section of the electorate to whom parties try to appeal. SLD traditionally focuses on left conservative voters in contrast to TR who approached mainly young voters in the 2011 general election (Vit 2014c). Therefore, the framing of national identity played a significant role in the competition between them.[78] TR avoids any reference to myths of the Polish nation and calls for increasing ethnic diversity in society. In contrast to TW, SLD proved to have more conservative affiliations in the field of national identity, such as in its relations to the Catholic Church.

9.1.3.1. Civic Platform (Platforma Obywatelska, PO)

The Civic Platform is a liberal-conservative, Christian democratic political party. The beginning of the party goes back to the Solidarity Electoral Action (AWS) and aimed for cooperation of conservative right formations within Polish politics in the late 1990s. Its unification with other formations such as Freedom Union (UW) was short-lived and before the election in 2001 it formed a new political party, Civic Platform. PO was founded by a coalition of AWS members and those who had left UW. Both AWS and UW failed to enter parliament in the 2001 election (Černoch et al. 2011: 148). A clash over national identity within Polish politics emerged after the 2005 election, and out of an equivalent clash that occurred then between PiS leaders the Kaczynski brothers the leader of PO, Donald Tusk. Since the 2007 early election, PO has been the strongest political party in Poland.

---

78   The only significant difference is the emphasis on national mythology and attitude towards immigrants.

Table 20: Overview of development of policy of national identity of PO

2005	2007	2011
1. 1 Support of deeper integration	1. 3 Strong in the EU	1. 3 Strong in the EU
1. 3 Strong in the EU	2. 2 Individualism and freedom as a values	2. 4 Culture as a value
2. 2 Individualism and freedom as a values	2. 10 Christian values	4. 3 Western orientation
2. 10 Christian values		

Source: Election manifestos

The 2005 election manifesto attempts to shape the society in civic and significantly less ethnic terms. Despite this, it argues that Poland should be modernized in line with traditions, with a desire for freedom typical for Poland and in relation to a traditional system of values, based on the Ten Commandments of the Old Testament. Family, nation, community and state should cooperate together for the common good. The election manifesto shapes Poland in terms of a turning point for the self-identification of Poland in the West as well as within the eastern model of chaotic democracy. PO thus presents itself as offering "European normality".

The 2007 manifesto follows the core lines of the 2005 manifesto. Nevertheless, a shift towards a pragmatic perception of the EU is observable. Even if PO supports EU integration, emphasis on supranational integration has significantly weakened. Similarly, the 2011 election manifesto follows that of 2007. The European system represents a constant negotiation process in which the strength of arguments is most important. PO explains in the manifesto why Poland is so successful. It is not enough to be right; you still need to convince your partners. This applies both to the wider international environment, and in the European Union. The manifesto stresses the role of PO on the European level. The manifesto mentions that the party knows how to build effective coalitions, how to negotiate and how to convince partners. Even if the party supports closer political integration, the economic dimension should be, according the PO, the most important one. In this regard the manifesto calls for the strengthening of EU institutions as well as closer coordination of the economic policies of individual Member States as well as completion of the single market. In contrast to to the 2005 and 2007 manifestos, there are fewer references to Christianity and its need for social development has been significantly reduced.[79]

9.1.3.2. Law and Justice (Prawo i Sprawiedliwość, PiS)

This conservative party was founded in 2001 due to the fragmentation of AWS, the bearer of the revolution ethos. PiS started to unify the conservative branch of Polish politics. The key personalities were the twin brothers Jaroslaw and Lech Kaczyński, who were familiar to the public from the revolution and later from different political positions. Lech Kaczyński was Minister of Justice in the previous government (as a member of the AWS party). Most PiS issues were influenced by the activity of the Kaczyński twins. They were publicly known thanks to their very strong anti-communist opinions and their moral emphasis on social matters. As a result of his ministerial role, Lech Kaczyński attained an image of the hard and uncompromising fighter against violence and any kind of disorder in Poland.

During the period of left-liberal government, PiS boosted its popularity. Due to corruption and the ideological discrediting of the left, PiS gained a strong argument for justifying both its moral revolution and its call for a "new beginning". In the 2005 election PiS gained the best voting result ever (27 %) and formed a coalition with two controversial smaller parties SPR and LPR.

---

[79] According to former MEP Boguslav Sonik (2014), saying that the Catholic Church plays a significant role in shaping of European values and the legacy of the Church should be further developed because of Pope Jan Pavel II, but there is no need to artificially increase the role of the Church in Polish politics.

Table 21: Overview of development of policy of national identity of PiS

2005	2007	2011
1. 3 Strong in the EU	1. 4 Europe of nations	1. 4 Europe of nations
1. 5 Against the EU, leaving possible	2. 5 National culture as a part of identity	1. 5 Against the EU, leaving possible
2. 4 Culture as a value	2. 6 Traditional values	2. 5 National culture as a part of identity
2. 5 National culture as a part of identity	2. 10 Christian values	2. 5 National culture as a part of identity
2. 6 Traditional values	4. 8 perceived foreign economic threat	2. 10 Christian values
2. 7 Support of national culture	4. 3 Western orientation	4. 3 Western orientation
2. 8 support of national identity building		4. 6 negative perception of EU
2. 10 Christian values		4. 8 perceived foreign economic threat
4. 6 negative perception of EU		
4. 8 perceived foreign economic threat		

Source: Election manifestos[80]

The 2005 election manifesto defines the position of Poland in Europe as a strong state with deep roots in history. Very evident is the party's negative position towards Russia, as a result of historical experience – the three times division of Poland, the occupation during WW II and the subsequent communist era. Other foreign relations are also influenced by these experiences. This is the reason for a strong emphasis on national sovereignty and the desire for Poland to play a prominent role in Europe as a power. The definition can

---

80 Analysis based on the 2005, 2007, and 2011 election manifestos.

be found in Polish Christian heritage, the emphasis on national security and the responsibility for nation, the strong role of families, patriotism, and also the EU as a part of the national identity. Therefore the manifesto frames the role of a nation, its traditions and values, as well as morality as a core element of the manifesto; an emphasis on Christianity penetrates all these elements. The European integration is presented as a positive means through which nation states can cooperate ensure the strong role of the EU in world politics. The manifesto opposes accepting the Treaty on the European Union and also the Lisbon Treaty. Poland's entry into the monetary union should be made carefully and probably more in the long term, though timings are not specified.

The 2007 election manifesto sees the party soften slightly its negative perception of EU integration. The most significant feature of the manifesto is a detailed, elaborate European policy and the determination to strengthen transatlantic ties. Surprisingly, the manifesto is more forthright in its consideration of the question of the German minority in Poland and bilateral relations generally. At the same time, it calls for broader use of the subsidiarity principle, the modernizing of the functional structure of the EU, and a more positive attitude to the completion of the internal market. As with the 2005 election manifesto, it develops an understanding of the role of national culture and the need for a strong nation.

The 2011 manifesto develops key elements of the party's perception of national identity in a very similar way to in 2005 and 2007. However, it moves the role of the state towards responsibility for developing the nation even if this means increasing the role of the state in the economy. National pride is understood as an important element of Polish national identity. In addition to this, the party supports a strong nation-based sense of belonging that will contribute to the Polish economy. PiS stresses the role of a strong nation state in, among other things, its ability to defend civic rights, equality as well as the rights of national minorities. Contrary to previous election manifestos, the most recent one (2016) criticizes liberal and so-called western values to a greater extent. The manifesto emphasizes the spirit of Central Europe through common traditions and shared historical experience. Therefore for the future, the nation state should be the most important area of development.

9.1.3.3. Alliance of the Democratic Left (Sojusz Lewicy Demokratycznej, SLD)

Alliance of the Democratic Left was officially established in May 1999. However, the roots of this party lie in the fall of the communist regime in Poland and the transformation of the former communist party Polish United Worker's Party into the social democratic party, Social Democracy of the Polish Republic (Socjaldemokracja Rzeczypospolitej Polskiej, SdRP). From 1991 SdRP entered an electoral coalition with a number of left-wing parties and movements under the name SLD. The coalition won general elections in 1993 and formed a government with the agrarian PSL, which also obtained the right to nominate the prime minister. In the 1997 general election, SLD gained more than 27% of the vote, but for four years was the biggest opposition party. The general election of 2005 resulted in a major defeat for SLD, which received just a little bit more than 11% of the votes. The leadership of the party resigned in response to this fiasco and Wojciech Olejniczak replaced Józef Oleksy as the leader of the party (Černoch et al. 2011: 155). For the early general election of 2007, SLD joined forces with other left-wing parties, namely UP, SdPl and Democratic Party, coming together under the leadership of Poland's former president, Aleksander Kwaśniewski. After the 2007 elections the party did not manage to recover from its electoral defeat and, in the 2011 elections, registered its lowest number of votes.

Table 22: Overview of development of policy of national identity of SLD

2005	2007	2011
1. 1 Support of deeper integration	2. 1 Support of deeper integration	3. 1 Support of deeper integration
2. 7 Support of national culture	2. 1 Pluralism	2. 1 Support of new emancipation movements, open society
	2. 7 Support of national culture	2. 2 Individualism and freedom as a values
	3. 1 Inclusiveness	4. 5 positive connotation of Germany
	4. 2. 3 Pushing for human rights in foreign policy	

Source: Election manifestos[81]

The 2005 election coincided with a rising wave of nationalism in Poland and an increase in the politics of identity. SLD did not refer to the Polish nation in its manifesto but made reference to different social groups or citizens within Poland. In 2005 the Socialists considered it important to address the issue of the political exploitation of Polish history, and the artificial construction of myths and legends about Polish fate. The 2005 manifesto, therefore, condemned the falsification of history by some elements of Polish society and its political use. In this context, the manifesto perceives a danger arising from the influence of a nationalistic interpretation of history in the national education system. When it comes to European policy the manifesto is in favour of the European Constitutional Treaty and the common European security and defence policy. In this context Poland should become a modern European nation through contact and integration with the rest of the continent, and gain respect in this manner.

---

[81] Analysis based on the 2005, 2007, and 2011 election manifestos.

The 2007 election manifesto stresses observance of human rights within the state legislature and tolerance in society. In particular, it again stresses the importance of gender equality but also addresses issues associated with excluded communities and individuals, and supports policies against the segregation of the disadvantaged and handicapped. Interestingly, in comparison to the 2005 manifesto, the party sharpens its anti-nationalist language — the manifesto rejects the assumption that exclusively defined national interest and nation are of intrinsic moral value. At the same time it calls for an inclusive and open society based on social and ethnic equality.

The 2011 election manifesto follows a similar path to the 2007 and 2005 manifestos. In this context, the manifesto places a stronger emphasis on support for EU integration. The manifesto moves its support from the political to the social dimension. Therefore, the EU is presented as a community of European citizens instead of a combative arena for pushing national interests. In a similar context the manifesto understands Germany — not as a rival, but as the most important partner in the EU as well as in foreign policy. These elements, hand in hand with support for an inclusive society, make the SLD a liberal party ideologically comparable with its European partners.

9.1.3.4. *Polish People's Party (Polske Stronictwo Ludowe, PSL)*

PSL was renewed shortly after the fall of the communist regime in Poland in 1989. PSL played an important role in the Second Polish Republic after the First World War. However, under the regimes of Józef Piłsudski the party lost its influence in Polish politics. During the Second World War, PSL took part in the exiled government. After the war PSL was controlled by the communists and went under the name United People's Party (Zjednoczono Stronnictwo Ludowe, ZLN). In the general election in 1997, coalition parties suffered great losses. PSL managed to get just 7.3 % of the vote and lost more than one hundred seats in the Sejm. After the 2001 general election, it formed a left-wing government together with SLD. However it did not improve its gains as significantly as SLD, and received only 9% of the vote. In 2003, and due to growing disagreements with SLD, PSL left the government and went into opposition (Černoch et al. 2011: 159). In the general elections of 2005 and 2007, PSL gained respectively 7 % and 9 % of the vote. In 2005 the party remained in opposition but after the general elections of 2007 and 2011, it joined government as a junior partner of the centre-right Civic Platform. This meant a policy shift of the party especially when concerning the EU.

Table 23: Overview of development of policy of national identity of PSL

2005	2007	2011
1. 4 Europe of nations	1. 3 Strong in the EU	1. 3 Strong in the EU
2. 8 support of national identity building	2. 4 Culture as a value	2. 6 Traditional values
2. 7 Support of national culture	2. 6 Traditional values	4. 3 Western orientation
4. 8 perceived foreign economic threat	2. 10 Christian values	
	4. 3 Western orientation	

Source: Election manifestos[82]

The 2005 election manifesto emphasizes foreign capital and its negative influence in Poland. The manifesto criticizes the process of privatization after 1990, which it describes as the transfer of Poland's national wealth into the hands of foreign investors. The manifesto suggests that foreign investors and capital were exploiting Poland and the Polish population. Because of this any contracts made between the state and foreign investors should be re-opened and carefully audited. However, it was not just unprofitable contracts and disadvantageous conditions which the party stood against. Its 2005 manifesto criticizes the concept of foreign ownership of strategic businesses and sectors of the national economy. According to the manifesto, limitations to foreign ownership

---

82 Analysis based on the 2005, 2007, and 2011 election manifestos.

should apply to the energy sector, state forests, railway companies and even the media. The state should also support Polish enterprises and businesses. In order to develop and secure both Polish identity and culture, the EU is understood as an institution of sovereign nation states. In this context, Poland should be respected in Europe due to its historical achievements and its significant size and power.

However, the manifesto also emphasizes national identity as a key element through which citizens identify with the state. It stresses Polish identity and culture to be the object of the state's protection. When it comes to the EU, the manifesto weakens its anti-integration profile. The 2007 manifesto emphasized a European Poland because a strong Poland means Europe in Poland, and also that any improvement of Poland's international position is possible only through internal change.

The 2011 election manifesto shows a softening of support for nationality policies in regard to national culture. It also places much less emphasis on Christian values and the role of the Church in society. In addition to this, the party weakened its anti-globalization rhetoric. The manifesto exhorts the opposite: participating in the "Western club" of modern countries. This is understood mainly in terms of foreign policy and economics. In this context the manifesto also softens its negative perception of EU integration — the EU is presented as an element that contributes to the positive development of Polish agriculture.

9.1.3.5. *The League of Polish Families (Liga Polskich Rodzin, LPR)*

This party was founded shortly before the 2001 election and emerged as the sixth party in the Sejm, having gained 7.9 % of the vote. Although the grouping represented itself as a regular political party, the LPR was registered only four months prior to the election as a formation of various national, right-wing populist and ultra-Catholic groups: Catholic-National Movement, Polish Agreement and National Party. The formation was led by Maciej and Roman Gietrych. Thanks to cooperation with the very nationalistic broadcaster Radio Maryja, the LPR was able to successfully reach out and speak to a radical nationalist, religious right-wing electorate that it recruited from earlier right-national Solidarity formations (Černoch et al. 2011: 166). On foreign policy issues the party rejected Poland's membership of the EU. Due to this being a non-achievable goal, the party evolved its demand into the need for renegotiating the conditions of Polish membership of the EU. After participation in the government coalition between 2005 and 2007 the party lost relevancy after the 2007 general election.

Table 24: Overview of development of policy of national identity of LPR

2005	2007	2011
1. 5 Against the EU, leaving possible	1. 4 Europe of nations	
2. 10 Christian values	2. 10 Christian values	
2. 7 Support of national culture	2. 7 Support of national culture	
4. 8 perceived foreign economic threat		

Source: Election manifestos[83]

The 2005 election manifesto strongly emphasizes Polish national interests and the need to protect national identity and state sovereignty. The national identity is shaped by an emphasis on the Catholic Church and its role in society. The position of Poland in the globalized world is rather self-oriented; the main emphasis is self-sufficiency in agriculture, industrial and human sources, the natural conditions of the country and a politically self-sufficient and Europe-independent policy direction. The most important dimension of national identity is argued to be the morality of the society, with moral grounds based on Christian principles – the traditional value principle. It is claimed that this emphasis should bring about a strong and independent nation. Support for the national culture is thought to positively affect the moral and ethical development of

---

83 Analysis based on the 2005 and 2007 election manifestos.

Poland. In this context, the emphasis on Christian values is seen as a first step towards reclaiming the traditional morality and prosperity of the Polish nation.

The 2007 election manifesto is developed in a more pragmatic fashion in comparison to the 2005 manifesto. However, the fundamental elements of perception of national identity remained unchanged. The strong emphasis on nation and national identity is fulfilled by the stressing of family values, regional development and agriculture, and general dissatisfaction with the fragmentation of society. This party is the only party to promote a pure national policy with respect to the Catholic Church. As for European policy, the party has weakened its emphasis on rejecting the EU as such. Despite the negative attitude towards the Lisbon Treaty and the common currency, the manifesto softened its anti-EU policy in terms of not opposing Polish membership in the EU.

9.1.3.6. Self-defense of Polish Republic (Samoobrona Rzeczpospolitej Polskiej, SRP)

This party was founded in 1992 due to the fragmentation of the Labour Union of Farmers, "Self-defence". The party is evidently populist, with anarchical and agrarian influences. Its most important person during the researched period was its chairman, Andrej Leper. Leper's party role was very strong: he could decide on the exclusion of any member of the party and was the most important person when it came to policy-making. SRP's aversion to the free market and liberal economy is because the party views these as being antithetical to traditional values and especially harmful for rural areas. Those activities centred on the accumulation of profits and predatory competition, commercializing and 'perverted' consuming, are defined by the party as "evil activities". SRP opposes globalization, especially the influence of private capital and private banks. Most of the party's voters were located in rural areas that were strongly impacted by the post-communist transformation. After the 2005 general election the party formed a coalition with PiS and LPR. After electoral losses in the 2007 election, the party lost its parliamentary relevance.

Table 25: Overview of development of policy of national identity of SRP

2005	2007	2011
1. 4 Europe of nations	1. 4 Europe of nations	1. 4 Europe of nations
4. 8 perceived foreign economic threat	2. 7 Support of national culture	4. 6 negative perception of EU
2. 7 Support of national culture	4. 9 stressing sovereignty	4. 8 perceived foreign economic threat
	4. 8 perceived foreign economic threat	

Source: Election manifestos[84]

The 2005 election manifesto stresses defending the national interest, national culture, and national identity as the most relevant policies. This emphasis on the nation follows on from the anti-liberal emphasis and opposition to globalization. This opposition does not principally stem from regional or agricultural issues but from the perceived need to defend national identity. The party's strong anti-globalization agenda is directed to Washington as the "birthplace of globalization". It is also directed against key international organizations who it says do not consider the national sovereignty of their member states, and thereby cause harm to Poland. International capital flows harm the Polish people too. The manifesto emphasizes a stronger national economy and national ownership of Polish companies, and at the international level Poland should protect its economic interests.

The 2007 election manifesto focuses on the promotion of national identity, national culture, the strengthening of national sovereignty and the rejection of the contemporary economic system. In this sense, there is no significant development in the areas relating to national identity. The manifesto argues that the neoliberal economic system misuses Polish resources and does not bring any positive gains for Poland. It expresses its support for the EU in a more

---

84 Analysis based on the 2005, 2007, and 2011 election manifestos.

practical and technical way. Although SPR promotes an ambivalent attitude towards the EU, there are some issues where the party supports the EU line. Although the party rejects European integration in principle, the party is not against integration. SRP supports the integration of sovereign states but not the creation of a deeper, supranational institution. However, the manifesto opens the question of renegotiation of the entry conditions of Poland into the EU in order to strengthen national sovereignty and the national interest. Despite having a new leader of the party, Leszek Miller, the 2011 election manifesto did not change the key elements relating to the policy of national identity.

9.1.3.7. Your Movement (Twoj Ruch, TR)

The movement was founded in 2010 by the PO Member of Parliament Janusz Palikot as a new liberal political movement in Poland. In the 2011 election the movement gained 11 % of votes and became the third strongest political formation in Sejm. The party's main policy was to question the traditional understanding of Polish national identity and to embark on a quest for the "modernisation" of Poland in terms of being a truly European state. The party stresses its anti-clerical profile, its support of sexual minorities' rights as well as the legalisation of marihuana. Despite these liberal grounds, the party's success was rather an example of a protest party heavily operationalizing national identity. In the 2015 general election TR built up a coalition with SLD and other left formations but this did not help it to enter Parliament. Despite the emphasis of the party on the Europeanness of Poland and the acceptance of European social norms into a Polish context, the manifesto pays only limited attention to EU related policies. It stresses its support for the right of minority groups such as sexual minorities. At the same, its anti-clerical profile is not expressed as sharply as it was in public manifestations.

Table 26: Overview of development of policy of national identity of TR

2005	2007	2011
		2. 1 Support of new emancipation movements, open society
		4. 3 Western orientation

Source: Election manifestos[85]

9.1.4. Slovakia: Introduction into party system and national identity

Slovakia gained its independence in the 1993 and, together with other V4 countries, joined the EU in the 2004. Unlike the Czech Republic and Poland, Slovakia experienced a different path of transformation. Between 1993 and 1998 the country was governed by the sovereignist party LS-HZDS, under the leadership of Vladimír Mečiar. Together with LS-HZDS, nationalistic forces such as SNS played a significant role by not taking part in early post-transformation integration aims (Haughton, Rybář 2009: 138). This changed after the 1998 general election when a coalition opposing Vladimír Mečiar was formed under the leadership of Mikuláš Dzurinda and his SDKÚ party. This party shaped political and social consensus on Western integration aims, namely to the EU and NATO (Henderson 2002: 149). Despite the existence of nationalistic political forces in government between 2006 and 2006 such as SNS, Slovakia joined the eurozone in 2010 just when it was ruled a nationalistic coalition composed of Smer-SD, SNS, and LS-HZDS (Bilčík, Buzalka 2012: 60). The consensus led to a strong commitment by integration-supporting parties to be an effective and contributing member of the European political space (Haughton, Rybář 2009: 135). Therefore, from the EU perspective, the role of Slovakia on the European level remained mostly unchanged during the Dzurinda period between 2006 and 2010. There is also one significant aspect

---

[85] Analysis based on the 2011 election manifestos.

of Slovak political parties — similar to parties in Poland and the Czech Republic, they do not feel the need for participation in European politics and therefore they do not pay attention to aims in broader integration.

Table 27: Overview of political parties and their support

Party	profile	2006/seats	2010/seats	2012/seats	Government coalition
Smer-SD	Left	29.14/50	34.79/62	44.41/83	2006–2010; 2012–2016
SDKÚ-DS	Liberal-right	18.35/31	15.42/28	6.09/11	2010–2012
KDH	Conservative right	8.31/14	8.52/15	8.82/16	2010–2012
SNS	Nationalistic	11.73/20	5.07/9	4.55/0	2006–2010
SaS	Liberal right	-	12.15/22	5.88/11	2010–2012
Most-Híd	Centre-right	-	8.13/14	6.89/13	2010–2012
Ľ'S-HZDS	left	8.79/15	4.32/0	0.93/0	2006–2010
OL	Centre-right	-	-	8.55/16	-
SMK	Conservative right/minority	11.68/20	4.33/0	4.28/0	-

Source: Author, volby.statistics.sk

The most significant feature of the researched period is the rise in importance of ethnic cleavage after the 2006 general election as well as during the 2010 election campaign (Gyarfášová 2011). As various studies showed, the issue of national identity plays a significant role in constituting individual policies and cleavage order (see e.g. Deegan-Krause 2010; Učeň 2011). In the period 2006–2010, during the left coalition of Smer-SD, SNS, LS-HDZS, Slovakia was actively adopting nation-building policies hand in hand with continuing the construction of the state in ethnic terms (Černoch et al 2011: 183). This move was based on Smer-SD's adoption of nationalistic positions and its assimilation of these issues into mainstream politics (Gyarfášová 2011). Such policies are in line with the widely accepted foundational myth of a state of ethnic Slovaks who share a common culture, history, language, and future, and who were finally able to establish their own state after centuries of dominance by other nations, primarily Hungarians (Chudžíková 2014). Historical argumentation is used not only as a means to construct Slovak national identity but also has political meaning in building relations with Hungary and the Hungarian minority in Slovakia (Chudžíková 2014). Based on the 2012 election manifesto of Smer-SD, the party has softened from a conservative nationalistic rhetoric to approaching national identity from the perspective of a civic dimension. Despite this, the party is perceived as not stressing openness and liberal values (Haughton, Rybář 2009: 147). In contrast to Smer-SD, KDH incorporated a much more conservative and nationalistic rhetoric into its 2012 election manifesto in comparison to those of 2006 and 2010.[86]

---

86 In this respect, KDH proposed that the heritage of Cyril and Method missionaries, according to the manifesto, shape the groundings of Slovak historical heritage. In this context, the traditional role of Christian family should be secured by constitutional law (ceeidentity.eu 2016i).

Table 28: Overview of parties' positions on selected issues

Party	Election	National minorities	Shaping historical myth	The EU integration	Change
Smer-SD	2006	Inclusion of Roma	Historical values of nation in Christian tradition	Support of EU integration	-
	2010	Inclusion of Roma	Support for historical knowledge in schools about Slovak values and history	Support of EU integration, stability for Slovakia	Slightly stronger national identity emphasis
	2012	Respecting national minorities	Support for historical knowledge in schools	Support for integration, stability for Slovakia	Stressing openness
SDKÚ-DS	2006	Support for national minorities	No specific mention	Support for EU integration	-
	2010	Support of national minorities and language	Multicultural history	Support for EU integration with some exclusive competences on national level	Stronger emphasis on openness
	2012	Not specific mention	Slovak patriots in the EU	Support for EU integration with some exclusive competences on national level	Weaker emphasis on openness

142 IDENTITY FORMATION

SNS	2006	Against Hungarians and inclusion of minorities	Nation based on Christian tradition of Cyril and Method	Europe of nations	-
	2010	Against Hungarians and inclusion of minorities		Europe of nations, threatening sovereignty	Stronger nationalistic emphasis
	2012	Against inclusion of Roma	Slovak cultural values based on Cyril and Method legacy	Leaving EU	Stronger nationalistic emphasis
SaS	2010	Support of culture and language of minorities	Not specific mention	Support for the EU, but national states should have exclusive competences	-
	2012	Inclusiveness of all individuals	Not specific mention	Against deeper EU integration, threat for national state	Slightly stronger nationalistic emphasis
OL	2012	Inclusion of Roma	Low historical knowledge about nation	Limited EU integration support	-
ĽS-HZDS	2006	Respecting national minorities abroad and in Slovakia	Slovak cultural values based on Cyril and Method legacy	Not special emphasis	-
	2010	Slovak culture and language respected by minorities	No specific mention	No specific mention	Slightly stronger nationalistic emphasis
	2012	Limited rights for minorities	Cultural values based on Cyril and Method legacy	No specific mention	Slightly stronger nationalistic emphasis

RESULTS

KDH	2006	Inclusion of Roma	Culture and history as identification tool	Support of integration, but respecting national sovereignty	-
	2010	Inclusion of Roma	Values based on history and religion	Support for EU, but respecting national sovereignty	No change
	2012	Inclusion of minorities only if does not threat sovereignty	Cultural values based on Cyril and Method legacy	Support for EU, but national states should have exclusive competences	Slightly stronger nationalistic emphasis
Most-Híd	2010	Support of multicultural society	Not specific mention	Support of EU integration	-
Most-Híd	2012	Support of culture and language of minorities	Not specific mention	Support of EU integration	Weaker emphasis on openness
SMK	2006				
SMK	2010				

Source: Author, based on election manifestos

The overview shows similar positions of parties covered by analysis — with the exception of SNS. However, there are interesting developments when it comes to perception of deeper EU integration. It is evident that a strongly EU supportive environment has been shifted towards rather pragmatic positions when stressing certain limits of the integration process. At the same time, the role of history in political discourse is not a cleavage that would constitute party competition.

The government of Smer-SD between 2006–2010, from the perspective of nationalism and national identity, was very distinct. Insufficient electoral support meant it could not form a government on its own so Smer formed a coalition with the LS-HZDS, represented by Vladimír Mečiar, and the SNS, represented by Ján Slota. The controversial government coalition was characterized by producing explicitly nationalist policies against ethnic minorities living in Slovakia (Černoch et al. 2011: 181) such as stressing the Slovak language as the only lingua franca, and developing monuments connected to Slovak medieval history etc.[87] This period was a low point in Slovak-Hungarian relations as they became particularly strained due to disputes over double citizenship launched by the Hungarian government in the 2010.[88] In the 2012 preliminary parliamentary elections campaign, parliamentary parties largely shifted away from playing the nationalist card and focused on questions of social security. Since gaining a majority government in 2012, Fico, as Prime Minister, has also followed a more conciliatory line in the government's relations with Hungary. Nevertheless, Fico also declared a commitment to a pro-European orientation of his government.[89] This also shows that different language can be used in different arenas. On the national level, Smer-SD, and Robert Fico especially, used language stressing national identity when they discussed the role of Christianity, stressing Slovak national identity.

---

87 One example is the statue of Cyril and Method on the territory of the Hungarian minority.
88 During this period the Slovak Prime Minister, Robert Fico, labelled Hungary as a potential threat and appealed to Slovak youth to wear Slovak symbols and master the Slovak language, etc., see (ceeidentity.eu 2016k)
89 For more details about Fico's understanding of the party's European policy see (Gressel 2015).

Contrary to this, discussion on the European level is accommodated into the political mainstream and does not affect nationally coloured politics. However, the role of the EU has brought a new cleavage into Slovak politics, as showed by the fall of the centre-right government between 2010 and 2012 under the leadership of Iveta Radičová. Due to the different policies towards the EU of parties participating in the government, the government was not able to unify when faced with the issue of approval for the European Stability Mechanism (ESM) to secure Greece from bankrupty. The leader of the right-wing party SaS, Richard Sulík, claimed to keep the power of Brussels within national boundaries.[90] After the 1998-2006 consensus on the EU policy of Slovakia, this was the first time in the past decade that an EU issue caused a significant crisis.

9.1.4.1. Direction-Social democracy (Smer-Sociálna demokracia, Smer-SD)

The party was formed in 1999 by Robert Fico, a popular figure from the Party of the Democratic Left (SDĽ), which was, then in coalition. Fico left that party and also parliamentary coalition declaring that this was because of continuing corruption and unfulfilled government program and broken promises. Fico and his party, which defined itself as beyond a right-left dichotomy, quickly became very popular among voters partly due to its protest appeal and its refusal to join either Mečiar or the heterogeneous anti-Mečiar coalition. In the 2002 elections, Smer took over the whole electorate of the SD and despite gaining fewer votes than polls had predicted, it established itself as a relevant political force. Between the years 2002 and 2006, Smer moved from the centre to the ideological left (Černoch et al. 2011: 196). In 2004, Smer merged with most of the remaining left-wing parties in Slovakia and changed its name to Direction-Social Democracy (Smer-SD).

In the 2006 general elections, Smer won with almost 30 % of the votes and formed a coalition government with ĽS-HZDS and SNS. During the first premiership of Robert Fico, the Party of European Socialists for its decision to join a government with SNS, which was perceived as an extreme right-wing party, criticized

---

90 See more details about the approval of ESM by Slovak parliament here (ceskatelevize.cz 2011).

Smer-SD. Furthermore, relations with neighbouring Hungary deteriorated due to several incidents in both countries. After four years of being in government, Smer-SD managed to improve its electoral gains and again won in the 2010 general elections (Černoch et al. 2011: 196). In spite of this, Smer-SD did not manage to find enough partners to form a government and became the biggest opposition party.

Table 29: Overview of development of policy of national identity of Směr-SD

2006	2010	2012
2. 4 Culture as a value	1. 3 Strong in the EU	1. 3 Strong in the EU
4. 3 Western orientation	2. 1. 1 Nationalism negative	2. 4 Culture as a value
4. 9 stressing sovereignty	2. 4 Culture as a value	2. 5 National culture as a part of identity
	2. 5 National culture as a part of identity	3. 2 Protection of minorities
	2. 6 Traditional values	4. 3 Western orientation
	2. 7 Support of national culture	4. 4 Central European identity
	3. 2 Protection of minorities	4. 7 positive connotation of RU
	4. 3 Western orientation	
	4. 7 positive connotation of RU	
	4. 8 perceived foreign economic threat	
	4. 9 stressing sovereignty	

Source: Election manifestos[91]

---

[91] Analysis based on the 2006, 2010 and 2012 election manifestos.

The 2006 manifesto considers minority groups to be an integral part of Slovakia. In this respect, Slovak culture is deemed a sum of the cultures in the territory of Slovakia and also that of foreign Slovaks. We can see thus that to be a member of the Slovak nation even without Slovak citizenship constitutes a strong bond between the state and foreign, ethnic Slovaks. The Manifesto of Smer-SD in 2006 addressed one minority group in particular: issues concerning the Roma people were referred to as problems associated with their "status in society". Despite emphasising an anchoring of Slovakia within Western communities, the manifesto calls for a strong and confident foreign policy, based on sovereignty and independence from any foreign power. The manifesto also stresses the European identity of Slovakia, as being European was considered essential to being modern, prosperous and progressive. In order to pursue national and state interests, the manifesto proposed to enter into a strategic partnership with foreign countries, which would guarantee the sovereignty and integrity of Slovakia. Among these partnerships were some beyond the European Union, specifically the Russian Federation. A sense of potential danger was further heightened by the attitude towards the independence of Kosovo (ceeidentity.eu 2016).

In the 2010 election manifesto, the nation is understood to be a basic political entity centred on a culturally defined Slovak nation. Cultural and historical foundations of the nation should be protected and cultivated by the nation state's education system. However, this did not entail exclusion of minorities — on the contrary, while maintaining the foundations of the nation, minorities are to be respected and protected.

Although the 2012 manifesto politicizes some of the national coloured issues – e.g. the role of Cyril and Methodius in the historical shaping of Slovakia – it also displays a significant shift towards a liberal perception of national identity. The national culture is still understood as a basic identifying tool of the society; the traditional role of family should be strengthened. On the other side, the manifesto emphasizes support for and inclusion of national minorities and marginalized communities, especially the Roma minority, who should be encouraged in education and employment. The national sovereignty and national interests should act as a guide for decision-making in European politics. On the other side, the role of national sovereignty helps to identify citizens and the state. In a similar context, globalization is perceived only positively; it brings pressure on the national and social stability of Slovakia.

9.1.4.2. Christian-Democratic Movement (Krestansko-demokraticke hnuti, KDH)

The party was formed in the wake of the Velvet Revolution – by dissidents and other elements of the Catholic anti-communist opposition in Slovakia. In the first free elections in Czechoslovakia in 1990, KDH received almost one fifth of the votes in the Slovak part of the Federation. KDH joined the coalition governments both on the level of the Republic and at the federal level. In 1991, an internal struggle in the senior coalition partner Society Against Violence (VPN) led to the division of that party, and in order to secure the continuation of the coalition, VPN offered the post of prime minister to KDH's chairman, Ján Čarnogurský. After the period of Mečiar dominance and before the election of 1998, KDH joined forces with other opposition parties from both the right and the left of the political spectrum and formed the political party Slovak Democratic Coalition (SDK). The leader of SDK was the prominent KDH figure Mikuláš Dzurinda. In the 1998 election, parties of the anti-Mečiar opposition succeeded in keeping HZDS and SNS from power (Černoch et al. 2011: 214). However, shortly after the formation of the government, disagreement arose in SDK between those who preferred to fully integrate the original parties into SDK and those who insisted on the autonomy of the original parties of the Coalition. This conflict was resolved when Dzurinda and his followers left KDH and formed the new party SDKÚ. In the 2002 general election, KDH did not reach the position of being the strongest right-wing movement and lost mainly against SDKÚ. Nevertheless, KDH participated in the centre-right coalition led by SDKÚ between 2002 and 2006. Government cooperation also continued between 2010 and 2012 under the leadership of SDKÚ.

Table 30: Overview of development of policy of national identity of KDH

2006	2010	2012
2. 4 Culture as a value	1. 3 Strong in the EU	1. 2 Support of the EU but not deeper integration
2. 6 Traditional values	3. 6 Traditional values	2. 4 Culture as a value
2. 10 Christian values	2. 7 Support of national culture	3. 6 Traditional values
3. 6 Against immigration	2. 10 Christian values	2. 7 Support of national culture
4. 3 Western orientation	4. 1 Support of the EU	2. 10 Christian values
	4. 8 perceived foreign economic threat	3. 3 Dialogue with minority
	4. 9 stressing sovereignty	4. 3 Western orientation
		4. 9 stressing sovereignty
		4. 12 negative towards neighbouring country

Source: Election manifestos[92]

In the 2006 election manifesto for KDH, the Slovak nation is understood to be a community with a common Christian culture and shared life experiences. The manifesto stresses the civic approach when shaping a sense of belonging. Nevertheless, it argues that a shared cultural heritage of Christian civilization is important. Based on this attitude towards cultural difference, policies were derived that were advocated in the manifesto. The manifesto calls for cautious asylum procedure in order to prevent the misuse of asylum. It praises Andrej Hlinka, the Christian autonomist politician from the interwar period. However, while expressing a preference for a similar cultural background and Christian values, KDH stresses the need for equality, freedom and autonomy for all citizens. So, one

---

92 Analysis based on the 2006, 2010 and 2012 election manifestos.

can conclude that their manifesto did not try to impose Christian values on society as a whole but rather emphasized their importance and relevance even in the modern era.

Despite a positive attitude towards the EU in the 2010 manifesto, it also stresses that the EU should be approached cautiously and the state should have control over its future perspectives. In this respect, the manifesto emphasizes the principle of subsidiary and unanimity in key issues such as the foreign policy of the Union. In its 2010 manifesto, KDH emphasized that Slovak society should be built on the principles of tolerance, equality and respect for the individual, with special regard to the Roma population. The manifesto calls for such measures that would prevent discrimination against the Roma but at the same time stimulate their self-responsibility. Integration of the Roma population into society was seen as a very important goal. The cultural tolerance of KDH, however, had its limits. The party approached people of completely different cultures with suspicion, especially those who did not come from a Christian tradition.

The 2012 election manifesto consists of two contradictory parts: in the first one, the manifesto pushes Slovak culture, and in the second part, it emphasizes support for European integration and belonging to the "EU club"; as well as support for national minorities and their inclusion. Culture and national heritage play a crucial role in the manifesto. Even if the party shows its openness in terms of European integration, national history is perceived as a source of national legitimacy. However, this claim does not exclude national minorities. Therefore, Roma culture and identity should also be strengthened. Christianity plays a significant role in the manifesto, namely with references to the heritage of Saint Cyril and Method. These two missionaries, according to the manifesto, shaped the groundings of Slovak historical heritage. In this context, constitutional law should secure the traditional role of the Christian family. The party's European policy seeks to accommodate the national interest; the EU should respect national sovereignty and identity according to the necessary adaptation to globalization. Slovakia profits from membership of both the EU and the eurozone. However, the EU should respect the individual national constitutional traditions, which makes the manifesto one of the most pragmatic among centre-right formations. In this respect, the EU should be developed as a cultural and identity-based entity (ceeidentity.eu 2016l). Despite this generally positive attitude towards the EU, there are a few elements in the manifesto aimed at strengthening the notion of national identity, such as stressing sovereignty and the role of nation states over selected policy areas.

9.1.4.3. Slovak Democratic and Christian Union-Democratic Party (Slovenská demokratická a kresťanská únia-Demokratická strana, SDKÚ-DS)

The Democratic Party of Slovakia and the Green Party in Slovakia formed a coalition before the general election of 1998, due to a new amendment to the electoral law that they would need to get 25 % of the votes to enter the National Council. That was the reason why they took part in the establishment of the new party Slovak Democratic Coalition (SDK). SDK competed in elections instead of the five parties and all membership of the new party comprised of the leaders and politicians of the five coalition parties. SDK succeeded and after the elections led as a senior partner wide so called anti-Mečiar coalition. During 1999 and 2000, the leadership of the SDK, namely Mikuláš Dzurinda and Ivan Šimko (originally from KDH), pushed for further integration of the right-wing parties in SDKÚ. However, this internal struggle in the main government party SDKÚ did not lead to a serious weakening of the coalition and it survived for a full term until the elections of 2002. SDKÚ then joined a coalition with other centre-right parties and Dzurinda formed his second government. Alongside this development, the party also witnessed a rise in popularity of the former Minister of Social Affairs Iveta Radičová who joined SDKÚ-DS in 2006. She became electoral leader of the SDKÚ-DS in the general elections of 2010, in which SDKÚ-DS proved to be the strongest right-wing party with 15.42 % of the vote. After the elections, Radičová became the first female prime minister of Slovakia leading the centre-right coalition of SDKÚ-DS, SaS, KDH and Most.

Table 31: Overview of development of policy of national identity SDKÚ-DS

2006	2010	2012
1. 1 Support of deeper integration	1. 2 Support of the EU but not deeper integration	1. 3 Strong in the EU
2. 2 Individualism and freedom as a values	2. 1 Support of new emancipation movements, open society	2. 2 Individualism and freedom as a values
2. 4 Culture as a value	2. 3 Human rights as a value	2. 3 Human rights as a value
2. 6 Traditional values	2. 5 National culture as a part of identity	2. 4 Culture as a value
4. 1 Support of the EU	2. 6 Traditional values	2. 5 National culture as a part of identity
4. 2. 2 International solidarity	3. 2 Protection of minorities	4. 1 Support of the EU
4. 2. 3 Pushing for human rights in foreign policy		4. 4 Central European identity

Source: Election manifestos[93]

The 2006 manifesto emphasizes respect for human rights and values tolerance and individualism. These principles are mirrored in a call for equality for all citizens and in condemnation of the social exclusion and segregation of the Roma population. The manifesto places high value on a civil society based upon individualistic and active citizens. According to the manifesto, Slovak foreign policy should push human rights in the developing world and should not neglect them. The manifesto stresses the importance of equality, individualism and the development of civil society. As with other liberal-wing parties, SDKÚ-DS tends to be open to external influences.

---

[93] Analysis based on the 2006, 2010, and 2012 election manifestos.

This also means vertical support for EU integration in its supranational substance.

The 2010 election manifesto addresses the issue of national culture in greater detail than in 2006. Slovak cultural heritage, which is connected with national pride and patriotism, should be supported. However, this emphasis on the cultivation of Slovak culture is framed as Slovakia being a community of all its citizens. A significant part of the manifesto is dedicated to cultural policies, with policies related to minorities and their relation to the majority population. The manifesto stresses the importance of equality, individualism and the development of civil society. However, the party shifts from strong support of deeper integration towards a slight reluctance to support integration, where that integration shifts towards a supranational union such as a harmonised EU tax.

The 2012 manifesto stresses individual responsibility in terms of an open and modern society. However, one has to consider the country-specific context; the role of family and Christianity is significant in this manifesto as well. The liberal emphasis on the freedom of all individuals in the manifesto is, thus, accompanied by requests for the observance of rules. The manifesto continues to stress support for European integration, but it rejects harmonisation in tax and social policy. EU support is connected to individual responsibility, for instance in perceiving Slovakia as a strong country defending its national interest. The manifesto tries to find a modus operandi between the defence of national interests and its liberal commitment to, for example, constituting an open country (ceeidentity.eu 2016l). In the field of foreign policy, the party supports EU enlargement as well as values promoting human rights abroad. Slovakia, the party believes, should be able to effectively cooperate with its neighbours, especially on the V4 platform.

9.1.4.4. Freedom and Solidarity (Sloboda a Spravodlist, SaS)

The economist Richard Sulík and some other entrepreneurs and economists founded this party. Sulík served as an advisor under two ministers of finances from both the right-wing governments of Mikuláš Dzurinda and the centre-left government of Robert Fico. Sulík was the main designer of the pension system reform. The new party was established in 2009 in time to take part in the European Elections of that same year. SaS gained almost five percent of the votes. Before the general election of 2010, SaS persistently criticized Fico's government and refused to enter any potential coalition with Smer (Černoch 2011 et al. 2011: 200). In the elections, SaS managed to enter parliament and even became the third largest party with more that twelve percent of the popular vote. SaS also entered the newly formed government led by Iveta Radičová from SDKÚ-DS.

Table 32: Overview of development of policy of national identity of SaS

2006	2010	2012
	1. 3 Strong in the EU	2. 2 Individualism and freedom as a values
	1. 4 Europe of nations	2. 4 Culture as a value
	2. 1 Support of new emancipation movements, open society	3. 1 Inclusiveness
	2. 2 Individualism and freedom as a values	3. 2 Protection of minorities
	2. 4 Culture as a value	3. 3 Dialogue with minority
	3. 1 Inclusiveness	4. 4 Central European identity
	3. 2 Protection of minorities	4. 6 negative perception of EU
		4. 9 stressing sovereignty

Source: Election manifestos[94]

The 2010 manifesto emphasizes a strong commitment to the principles of equality, tolerance, human rights, freedom and secularism. These principles are almost omnipresent in the manifesto—the party supports the legalization of gay marriage and some classes of soft drugs. It strongly opposes any church involvement in public affairs and proposes the fiscal separation of church and state. In the manifesto, there are no references to the Slovak nation. Clearly, the

---

94 Analysis based on the 2006, 2010 and 2012 election manifestos.

target audience of the manifesto is intended to be citizens of the Slovak Republic rather than members of the Slovak nation. On this issue SaS strongly opposes Roma segregation and suggests policies, which aim at non-discriminatory practices in the classification of pupils' mental capacities. While supporting Slovak membership in the European Union, SaS also cautiously approaches any further integration into the Union. Each step towards further transfer of competencies from the states to the Union is to be subject to approval by the National Council. Furthermore, not everything derived from the European Union is considered to have a positive effect on Slovak society. In this respect, we should also interpret the party's cautious approach towards Turkey and its membership in the European Union. SaS refused full membership and instead advocated a privileged partnership for the Islamic country.

In regard to national identity, the 2012 election manifesto focuses on European integration issues. Although SaS proved committed to EU integration, the 2013 manifesto set certain limits in this area. The party rejects any deeper supranational integration that can affect national sovereignty. Therefore, the party does not accept any European fiscal packet and argues that the role of the ECB must be purely independent. Nonetheless, the manifesto perceives the EU and NATO as guarantors of stability and security. The party supports the enlargement of both the EU and NATO. In this respect, the democratization of Ukraine should continue with EU assistance. The manifesto stresses individual freedom and responsibility as one of the core elements of the party's ideological grounds. However, the manifesto emphasizes collective feelings in that it uses culture and national pride—a significant change in comparison to its previous manifesto (ceeidentity.eu 2016o). The Roma issues should be perceived as a social problem without any ethnic dimension. In a similar sense, Slovak-Hungarian relations should be strengthened by civic society activities. Still, a sceptical view towards the EU and supranational integration remains a significant aspect of the party's ideological orientation.

9.1.4.5. Most-Híd (Bridge, Most-Híd)

The official name of the party Most-Híd consists of the Slovak and Hungarian words for bridge. It was formed in 2009 by Béla Bugár and other politicians defecting from the Party of the Hungarian Coalition. Bugár served as a chairman of SMK-MKP for almost ten years from 1998 to 2007. In 2007, Bugár lost intra-party elections to Pál Csáky who represented the more radical platform of the party. After several conflicts with its new leadership, Bugár left SMK-MKP and, together with his followers and some intellectuals of Slovak nationality, founded Most-Híd. In contrast to SMK-MKP, this new party was supposed to be a platform of cooperation for all citizens of the Slovak Republic regardless of their nationality (Černoch et al. 2011: 205). The party succeeded in replacing SMK as the main representative of the Hungarian minority.

Table 33: Overview of development of policy of national identity of Most-Híd

2006	2010	2012
	1. 3 Strong in the EU	1. 2 Support of the EU but not deeper integration
	2. 1 Pluralism	1. 3 Strong in the EU
	2. 2 Individualism and freedom as a values	2. 3 Human rights as a value
	2. 3 Human rights as a value	3. 1 Inclusiveness
	3. 1 Inclusiveness	3. 2 Protection of minorities
	3. 2 Protection of minorities	4. 8 perceived foreign economic threat
	3. 3 Dialogue with minority	
	4. 3 Western orientation	
	4. 8 perceived foreign economic threat	

Source: Election manifestos[95]

---

95 Analysis based on the 2006, 2010, and 2012 election manifestos.

The party manifesto for the general election of 2010 was carefully written in order to present a program of cooperation and tolerance among Slovakia's citizens, including minority groups. In the manifesto of 2010, tolerance and minority rights enjoyed a special importance and relevance. It was also stressed in the document that there is not just one minority in Slovakia, but rather many, and that attention should be paid to each and every one. Instead of reciprocal attacks and tensions, it proposed true cooperation between the two countries in order to solve their disputes. Both should focus on the well-being of Hungarian and Slovak minorities in their respective countries. In this respect we should also understand the support by Most-Híd for decentralization and regionalization (ceeidentity.eu 2016p).

In the 2012 manifesto, national minorities do not threaten national sovereignty or the national majority. The manifesto supports a wide discussion of demands by national minorities in order to involve them in a multicultural society. In this respect, the party emphasizes socialization of excluded people. The manifesto favours education about human rights in schools instead of education that aims at inculcating historical pride. Therefore, education on the issue of national minorities should be strengthened. National minorities should have the right to be educated in their mother tongue. Although the manifesto speaks for strengthening national minorities' rights, it also suggests that all nations and cultures in Slovakia should converge, including the Roma minority. In a similar vein, it pushes for the acceptance of minority culture to be strengthened.

9.1.4.6. *Ordinary People (Obyčajní ľudia, OĽaNO)*

The success of the centre-right political movement stems from a deep fragmentation of the Slovak centre-right ideological camp. The representatives of this movement came from very different fields and were perceived rather as a non-formal group with political interests. Some of them were MPs elected for the liberal-oriented party, SaS. Due to fragmentation of the centre-right government and a general feeling of disappointment in the centre-right electorate, the movement joined the Parliament in the 2012 as an independent party. However, the manifesto consists of a mixture of liberally open statements as well as claims coloured by national culture (ceeidentity.eu 2016q).

Table 34: Overview of development of policy of national identity OĽ

2006	2010	2012
		1. 3 Strong in the EU
		2. 4 Culture as a value
		2. 5 National culture as a part of identity
		2. 6 Traditional values
		4. 4 Central European identity
		4. 12 negative towards neighbouring country

Source: Election manifestos[96]

The perception of national Slovak culture is a very significant feature in the 2012 manifesto. Slovakia is perceived as a predestined place for good living. Traditional cultural, natural, and historical values should be defended and, at the same time, cultivated for future generations. The current under-financed cultural institutions are not able to secure sufficient development of national history and patriotism in the society. As with other parliamentary parties, OĽaNO describes the Roma issue as a social problem that must be solved to help Roma people to integrate into society. In this sense, Roma children should be educated in a more effective way. Although the movement stresses the country's openness and supports membership in the EU, it perceives Brussels as the domain of non-elected bureaucrats delivering more and more regulations. Nevertheless, it claims that Slovakia should be a proud member of the EU.

---

96   Analysis based on the 2012 election manifesto.

9.1.4.7. Slovak National Party (Slovenská národná strana-SNS)

The party claims to be the oldest Slovak political party, tracing its roots to the 19th century Slovak National Party. With the exception of the periods from 2002 to 2006 and from 2010 to 2012, SNS was a permanent parliamentary party. Since March 1990 when it was established, SNS has experienced several internal conflicts and secessions. After the first general election in 1990, Stanislav Pánis, a proponent of the ultra-nationalistic faction of SNS, left the party and formed the party Slovak National Unity (Slovenská národná jednota, SNJ).

After elections in 1998, SNS found itself in opposition and many started to question the leadership of Ján Slota, who was repeatedly seen drunk in public. In 1999, Anna Malíková replaced Slota as chairwoman of the party and internal tensions resulted in a split of the party and the creation of the Real Slovak National Party by Slota and his followers. Both parties shared a principle ideology and policies and so they competed against each other for the same electorate, which resulted in almost an equal division of their votes in the general elections of 2002 and the first absence of the SNS from the National Council since 1990. After this electoral defeat of both SNS and the Real Slovak National Party, the parties again merged in 2003 with Slota as chairman and in 2006 SNS gained 11% of the votes and became the third biggest parliamentary faction. Between 2006 and 2010 the party was also part of the ruling coalition with Smer as its junior partner (Černoch et al. 2011: 184). In the general elections of 2010 SNS lost more than half of the votes and, with 5 %, barely entered the National Council.

Table 35: Overview of development of policy of national identity of SNS

2006	2010	2012
1. 4 Europe of nations	1. 3 Strong in the EU	1. 5 Against the EU, leaving possible
2. 4 Culture as a value	2. 6 Traditional values	2. 5 National culture as a part of identity
2. 8 support of national identity building	2. 7 Support of national culture	2. 7 Support of national culture
2. 9 Soil as proof of nation	2. 10 Christian values	2. 8 support of national identity building
2. 10 Christian values	4. 8 perceived foreign economic threat	2. 10 Christian values
3. 5 Limited rights for minorities		2. 11 Nation is threatened
3. 7 Against minority rights		4. 6 negative perception of EU
4. 7 positive connotation of RU		4. 8 perceived foreign economic threat
		4. 9 stressing sovereignty
		4. 11 Slavs positive
		4. 12 negative towards neighbouring country
		4. 14 otherness as a threat
		4. 15 militarization

Source: Election manifesto[97]

The Slovak National Party's campaign and manifesto for the election of 2006 were conducted under the slogan "We are Slovaks. A Slovak Government for Slovaks". This slogan in and of itself captures the key message and goal of SNS in 2006. As the manifesto stresses, the aim is to shape a government composed only of Slovak

---

97 Analysis based on the 2006, 2010, and 2012 election manifestos.

political parties – meaning a government without any party representing the interests of the 10% of the country who are Hungarian. The creation of this so-called "Slovak government" was necessary, according to SNS, because Slovak national interests were in grave danger. Two principal sources of danger were identified by SNS in their 2006 manifesto. The first was the threat of so-called Hungarian chauvinism and revisionism. In the view of SNS, Hungarian political representation, either in Hungary or in neighbouring countries where there is a significant Hungarian minority, is trying to change the borders established after the First World War. However the nation is not defined by race or blood but rather by culture, a shared history and – most importantly – by language and values. In the view of the SNS manifesto of 2006, nation states are the most natural organizational entities for people to live in. The main purpose of the nation state is to defend its national identity from alien influences. SNS does not distinguish between the Hungarian minority in Slovakia and the Hungarian government in Budapest. In their view, Hungarian political representation as a whole is working against Slovak national interests, with one goal: to reunite all the Hungarian population in central Europe into one country by annexation of at least some parts of Slovakia and other neighbouring countries. Slovakia is understood primarily as the nation state of the Slovak nation. Therefore, while not denying the concept of minority rights, SNS was very cautious in applying them. It considered minority rights as something to be granted by the state rather than defined by some higher principle.

In their 2010 manifesto, SNS also emphasizes the need for economic sovereignty and autarky, especially in the sectors of food production and the energy industry. SNS does not trust foreign capital or big corporations, preferring Slovak companies instead. Concerning the EU, the manifesto calls for a Europe of sovereign nation states and rejects the bureaucracy of EU institutions. In this sense, the manifesto stresses deeper cooperation among Slavic countries. The manifesto defines the nation in terms of values and culture. It includes ethnic minorities into the definition of national culture but claims the state's purpose is to serve Slovaks without mentioning other minorities. This approach can be discerned by the suggested treatment of the Roma minority in the manifesto. Rather than speaking about helping this community, the manifesto calls for control of this ethnic group. Also very apparent is the polarized understanding of Slovak-Hungarian relations. SNS considers almost the entire community of the Hungarian minority in Slovakia to be disloyal to the country of their citizenship, and considers them to be a 'fifth column' of Hungarian revisionism. Roma people are not accused of being a fifth column, but 'merely' of misusing the social security syste. For SNS, the society must act collectively. Children should be educated to foster patriotism and national pride. Christianity plays very important role: 2013 should be a "Year of Saint Cyril and Method". The EU is defined as an institution importing liberal policies such as multiculturalism; while it misuses Slovakia by ignoring its national sovereignty and acts to serve global capitalism.

Despite softening these nationalizing policies from the 2010 election manifesto, the 2012 one continues to emphasize its nationalizing profile. This is most evident in the case of the Roma issue, perception of culture, and the EU. The Roma issue is framed as an ethnic issue and around the labelling of Roma as extremists who misuse the hospitality of the Slovak nation. When speaking about the role of culture and values, the language of mythology of an independent Slavic nation is invoked, and the possibility of using military response to defend the nation is not excluded. At the same time, it is penetrated by an emphasis on Christian values and the need to practice them within society. It is presented as a necessary tool against any possible rise of Islamic religion in Europe and particular in Slovakia. When it comes to the EU, the manifesto mentions the possibility of leaving the EU due to its undemocratic structure and its damage to the unique culture of Slovakia. This is the first time that a parliamentary party calls for leaving the EU.

9.1.4.8. People's Party – Movement for a Democratic Slovakia (Ľudová strana – Hnutie za demokratické Slovensko ĽS-HZDS)

ĽS-HZDS was formed in April 1991 after internal conflict in the senior coalition party VPN. As a consequence, Mečiar and his followers left VPN and formed the new party ĽS-HZDS. Mečiar has been the one and only chairman of the party since then. In the subsequent general election, ĽS-HZDS won with a landslide support of 37 % of voters. Due to the electoral system, it took almost half of the seats in the National Council. Between 1992 and 1994, many prominent figures left ĽS-HZDS, mostly because of the political style of its chairman Mečiar. However, none of these defections harmed ĽS-HZDS considerably and it managed to win the next elections. In 1994 ĽS-HZDS formed its second government—the third for Vladimír Mečiar. In the following years, the coalition of ĽS-HZDS, SNS and the small Union of the Workers of Slovakia ruled Slovakia in a way which was considered by many to be authoritative and Mečiar was accused of misuse of state power to curb the democratic process and of attempting to influence election. In 1998 the movement was defeated by a coalition of centre-right parties under the leadership of Mikuláš Dzurinda.

Table 36: Overview of development of policy of national identity of HZDS

2006	2010	2012
2. 5 National culture as a part of identity	2. 5 National culture as a part of identity	2. 5 National culture as a part of identity
2. 10 Christian values	2. 10 Christian values	

The national principle in the 2006 manifesto was clearly understood as important to Slovak national interest, which should be followed in a manner in accordance with European standards for the protection of ethnic minorities. In this regard, it is very interesting to note the connection made by the manifesto between support for minority cultures in Slovakia and support provided for Slovak communities in foreign countries. In the words used in its manifesto of 2006, ĽS-HZDS would propose the monitoring and solidarity of the symmetric development of both minorities in Slovakia and Slovak minorities abroad.

In the 2010 election manifesto, ĽS-HZDS stressed the need for the defence of Slovakia, but in principle it stuck to its understanding of the Slovak nation and its relation to the state and minorities from its 2006 election manifesto. Analyzing the 2010 election manifesto, it is evident that the party aims to sever the political connection between the Hungarian minority in Slovakia and Hungary because this connection is perceived as a threat to the integrity of Slovakia. In regard to shaping national unity, the manifesto stresses integration of the Slovak nation in order to secure the Slovak character of Slovakia in terms of ethnicity.

The 2013 manifesto stresses the importance of national culture and historical heritage. According to the manifesto, the Slovak language should be the main language of communication in Slovakia regardless of any ethnic minorities living in the country. Christianity plays an important role in the party manifesto: the legacy of Saint Cyril and Methodius should have a greater impact on the society. Culture serves as an identification element with Slovak history and keeps folk traditions alive among the people.

10. Conclusions

This chapter is devoted to evaluating the results of the individual countries introduced above in the subject context of policies related to national identity. This context serves as a basic information kit for a better understanding of developments relevant to national identity. It also puts the data that emerged from the election manifestos into a broader as well as more accurate framework. Based on this context, the analysis is evaluated by focusing on individual countries as well as political parties.

Each country is analyzed in greater detail with a focus on the most relevant findings, followed by a final comparison of individual case studies. Importantly, this section is not intended to be an exhaustive analysis of all political parties included in the study. Its aim is rather to highlight the principal elements related to the development of how political parties perceive national identity by. This evaluation of results is also not intended to be a complete description of all social developments related to national identity. The analysis provides an insight into the transformation of the perception of national identity, quantified as the number of changes in election programmes, but also into shifts in nationalistic rhetoric related to the parties' participation below offers a general key to analyzing the ideological transformations of individual political parties in this regard. The assessment of the transformation of the perception of national identity by political parties would, however, be incomplete without considering one essential factor — the influence of the European political environment on the individual political parties in matters related to national identity. Individual sections of the following chapter thus always reflect both the changes in the perception of national identity in the respective manifestos (expressed by the number of changes in the number of nationalism positive or nationalism negative codes) and the fragmentation of the party system (the number of parliamentary political parties). The table below shows the rising fragmentation of party systems in the Czech Republic and Slovakia as well as stabilization when it comes to the number of parties in Poland. This serves to get a better overview when analyzing individual countries in terms of the rise of movements operationalizing national identity.in the context of European politics.

The influence of the European political space on the political parties' perception of national identity is evaluated for those parties that were represented in European institutions and, at the same time, in the national Parliament during the time period of the study. As such, it does not include parties that were represented in Parliament for the duration of one election period but did not participate in the shaping of the European political space. Focusing on the evaluation of election manifestos, these parties are included in the evaluation of individual countries in order to provide for a complete country context and allow for a meaningful comparison between the three countries. Although it is beyond the scope of this work to elaborate in detail on the relationship between the relevance of issues regarding nationality for voters and the political parties' subsequent reflection of this demand, the evaluation of results outlined

Table 37: Overview of parties covered by research and number of parties reaching over 3 % public support

	Parliamentary parties	Parties over 3 %
CZ		
2006	5	5
2010	5	8
2013	7	8
SK		
2006	5	7
2010	6	8
2012	6	8
PL		
2005	5	6
2007	4	4
2011	5	5

Source: Author

10.1. Czech Republic

A closer look at the Czech parliamentary parties offers two main insights. First, only three codes denoting a nationalistically coloured program are relevant for the parliamentary parties studied. Movements that have been voted into the Czech Parliament for the first time join the ranks of parties examined for their nationalistically coloured program. Interestingly, ODS, the main liberalising political formation in the post-1989 period, displays characteristics for three of these codes. As a result, it is necessary to explore the development the party has undergone after 2004, when its integration efforts (in the sense of supranational integration in the EU) slowed down and, as is apparent from its 2013 election program, it shifted to a position characterized by nationally coloured codes. Second, KDU-ČSL, a party symbolizing the ideological centre of the party system's political spectrum, also underwent such a transformation related to national identity in its party programs.

Table 38: Results of analysis

Party	Year	NAT_positive	No. of changes	NAT_negative	No. of changes	Changes	CMP_pos	CMP_neg	% of votes
ANO	2013	2	-	1	-	-	1.013	0.000	18.65
ČSSD	2006	1	-	1	-	-	1.703	0.000	32.32
ČSSD	2010	4	3	1	0	3	1.169	0.000	22.08
ČSSD	2013	3	1	0	1	2	1.240	0.000	20.45
KDU	2006	2	-	0	-	-	0.856	0.050	7.22
KDU	2010	7	5	2	2	7	1.081	0.085	4.39
KDU	2013	3	4	1	1	5	1.098	0.000	6.78

KSČM	2006	0	-	0	-	-	1.083	0.000	12.81
KSČM	2010	1	1	1	1	2	0.364	0.242	11.27
KSČM	2013	1	0	2	1	1	1.003	0.000	14.91
ODS	2006	2	-	0	-	-	0.683	0.049	35.38
ODS	2010	5	3	3	3	6	1.693	0.556	20.22
ODS	2013	2	3	3	0	3	0.895	0.447	7.72
TOP09	2010	2	-	0	-	-	1.116	0.000	16.70
TOP09	2013	3	1	0	0	1	1.282	0.000	11.99
Úsvit	2013	0	-	2	-	-	0.115	0.573	6.88
VV	2010	0	-	1	-	-	1.226	0.079	10.88

Source: Vít, Němčok 2016

On the basis of these two examples, it is possible to identify certain general trends in the perception of national identity and related issues. The first observation is that parties which most reflect new developments in the social context—and contribute towards its transformation – are drafted from the political centre. As a result, and judging by the content of the election programs, one can observe less significant shifts within manifestos for general elections, but rather the parties' search for a convenient handling or framing of issues related to national identity. With ODS and KDU-ČSL being parties in the centre-right of the political spectrum, it may be the case that it was precisely these parties that were most exposed to the changing perceptions of national identity during the captured time period—and as a result had to look for responses to this development. In that time period, both parties also underwent significant shifts in electoral support. From its position as a party with the greatest electoral support (the victorious party with more than 30 % of votes in 2009s), to receiving only 7.6 % of votes in 2013, ODS evolved into a party whose main mission was to survive. Even though this development cannot be ascribed solely to a changing understanding of national identity and its manifestation in election programs, it is clear that the party crisis, which peaked in 2013, followed a shift in its understanding of national identity. The manifestos similarly suggest a shifting of the party's priorities.

In the same time period, at the European level, ODS decided to cease its membership in EPP and establish a new political group in the European Parliament whose stance towards deeper integration is decidedly negative. Although ODS has, for a long time, been represented in various institutional structures, its adjustment to European norms (as being integration supporting) arising from the party's socialization in the European environment has not been taking place. In other words, the Lisbon treaty was a step too far for ODS. It may thus be concluded that the party's perception of national identity was transformed due to tensions within the party in response to the deepening integration of Europe, particularly the Lisbon Treaty. Nevertheless, this transformation may be thought of as belonging to a wider topic—the extent to which this transformation is related to the party's constitution of the liberal-conservative politics from the transformation period and an objective crisis of human resources of the party as such. Moreover, the party's membership in a European political group with whom it does not completely share a mission constitutes another factor in this regard. This is due to the fact that under such circumstances, the European group does not serve as an ancillary anchor, which could contribute towards upholding the ideological framework in relative concordance with that of the European political group. Consquently, it may be concluded that the party's mission and ideology play a greater role than a sort of ad hoc identification of individual and rather haphazard political topics and their prioritisation.

A glance at parties in the centre of the political spectrum offers an insight into how parties deal with a changing environment, which in turn shapes their priorities. Another party that has undergone a significant transformation in the formulation of its policy of national identity is KDU-ČSL. Although this transformation has not been one that would accentuate topics strongly coloured with national identity, a tendency to take advantage of nationalism negative references was so distinct that it deserves attention. The party's election programme underwent the greatest transformation in 2010, when KDU-ČSL did not overcome the electoral threshold of 5 % necessary to enter the Parliament. In the following election in 2013, the party successfully re-entered the Parliament with an electoral programme that placed much less emphasis on national identity and related issues. Importantly, during the time period studied KDU-ČSL was anchored in the EPP group without considering leaving the group. In this regard, it would be worthwhile to devote further research activity to the question of whether reduced emphasis on national identity and related issues is caused by a party's being anchored in the European political arena, or is the result of intra-party dynamics such as staffing considerations (especially with regard to the party chairman position).

In the studied period, the number of parliamentary political parties has remained constant, with the exception of the year 2013 when it increased by two. Our investigation of issues related to national identity through electoral programmes shows that new political parties have generally not reflected an escalation of such issues.[98] The rise of the ANO and the Dawn of Direct Democracy political movements did not represent a fundamental shift in the handling of issues of national identity, even though the parties subsequently thematized these issues intensely (especially the Dawn movement). As a result, it cannot be said that an increased number of parliamentary parties would have an effect on the intensity of the use of national identity and related issues. From the perspective of strategic, purposive and instrumental use of national identity, it is expedient to focus on the ideological centre of the party system. These are parties that are anchored in the European political space, but at the same time are faced with a constant transformation of the ideological centre — more so than other parties; as a result, their perception of this issue is subject to various influences that are oftentimes contradictory. The cases of ODS and KDU-ČSL demonstrate the varied reactions to this phenomenon by parties that are institutionally anchored in the European political space, as well as the effect it has on their perception of national identity.

In both cases, the analysis does not focus on specific policy areas, but on the impact of external influences shaped by the parties. In the case of Czech political parties, interestingly, it is parties other than those on the ideological fringes that display the greatest changes in their electoral programmes. In the case of the Czech political parties, it is possible to observe the following tendency: with their increased involvement in the structures of the European political space, their emphasis on nationalism-coloured politics decreases. As a result, it would be fruitful to focus further research on the ideological centre, the main ideological force during the transformation period, and the ways in which it is influenced by developments relevant in this regard (such as the challenge presented by the immigration wave of 2015).

---

98 Due to its research design, this work and its conclusions are necessarily limited by the time frame captured. In particular, the 2013 post-election rhetoric is not included in the analysis. The political movement the Dawn of Direct Democracy of Tomio Okamura would, for example, be evaluated much more nationalistically than is the case based merely on its 2013 election programme.

10.2. Slovakia

Slovak parliamentary political parties and their electoral programmes offer another perspective on the transformation of political parties' perception of national identity. The increased fragmentation of the party system has, particularly since 2010, brought an increased number of actors, and thus, also a broader spectrum of national identity perceptions to the study. The three main characteristics that may be identified based on the study of the given cases in the specified time period are the following. First, there is a wide spectrum of parties that either emphasize or refuse the stressing of national identity. Second, there is an influence of national identity and related issues on the division of political parties in the centre and right-wing of the political spectrum. We may speak of a gradual centralization of parties of the political right and their shift towards a similar position with regard to national identity and, at the same time, of a significant strengthening of those tendencies that stress national identity within the SNS political party. Third, in contrast to the image of the party in the media, in the Smer-SD manifesto, there is a discernible tendency towards a civic conception of nationalism.

Table 39: Results of analysis

Party	Year	NAT_positive	No. of changes	NATnegative	No. changes	Changes	CMP_pos	CMP_neg	% of votes
SMK	2006								13.33
SMK	2010								3.28
HZDS	2006								10.00
HZDS	2010								
KDH	2006	1	-	1	-	-	1.083	0.950	9.33
KDH	2010	1	0	3	2	2	4.485	0.000	10.00
KDH	2012	3	2	4	1	3	2.904	0.116	8.82
MOST	2010	7	-	1	-	-	1.609	0.041	9.33
MOST	2012	4	3	1	0	3	1.342	0.000	6.89

Conclusions

OL	2012	0	-	1	-	-	0.617	1.157	8.55
SaS	2010	5	-	1	-	-	0.635	0.544	14.67
SaS	2012	4	1	2	1	2	0.424	1.086	5.88
SDKU	2006	6	-	0	-	-	2.093	0.000	20.67
SDKU	2010	4	2	0	0	2	0.786	0.098	18.67
SDKU	2012	4	0	0	0	0	1.109	0.139	6.09
SMER	2006	1	-	1	-	-	1.247	0.000	33.33
SMER	2010	3	2	3	2	4	4.016	0.045	41.33
SMER	2012	2	1	0	3	4	3.158	0.043	44.41
SNS	2006	0	-	5	-	-	1.717	0.693	13.33
SNS	2010	0	0	3	2	2	1.625	0.952	6.00
SNS	2012	0	0	10	7	7	0.779	6.075	4.55

Source: Vít, Němčok 2016

The wide diversity in political parties' perception of national identity and related issues demonstrates that, in Slovak politics, this is indeed a relevant topic. The differentiated thematisation of national identity and related issues indicates the extent to which identity topics constitute substantial and relevant content in Slovak politics. It is worth noticing that most of the Slovak political parties do in fact deal with the question of Slovak modern historical heritage and the issue of Slovak national independence during World War II. The electoral programmes of most political parties could be accused of inadequately addressing history. Interestingly, however, no parliamentary formation tends to present itself as a civic liberal party, strictly opposed to SNS with regards to history. From perspective of temporal development of the issue of national identity, it is surprising that differences among political parties, with the exception of SNS, generally do not increase. In fact, political parties' attitudes towards this topic gradually converge, a phenomenon that is particularly apparent in manifestos from 2012. It may be concluded that the topic of national identity is not crucial in the polarization of voters, despite the fact that related themes are used intensely and form a permanent feature of the political discourse.

The relationship of the right-wing SDKÚ-DS, MOST, KDH, SaS and OL to issues related to national identity demonstrates that, despite these parties' attempts to set themselves apart from the other parties to whom they are ideologically close, their attitudes in this regard nevertheless do converge. This trend is particularly noticeable in the case of the SaS and MOST parties, which in the second election of 2012 brought their perception of national identity closer to that of SDKÚ-DS and KDH. Although it is impossible to track down the specific reasons for the shift in individual political parties' priorities, it is conceivable that the liberal conception of topics related to national identity does not resonate with voters. As a result, parties differentiate themselves from others at the level of personal relationships and political issues chosen at random. This phenomenon also illustrates that an increased number of participants in the party system does not necessarily lead to a polarization of the party system. In other words, the issue of national identity pervades several policy areas and is not the main dividing line. This argument may be supported by the fact that parties that have recorded a significant drop in electoral support have not subsequently resorted to a sudden and purposeful use of national identity in their political programs. This is the case for SDKÚ-DS and, to a lesser extent, SaS, which did not resort to the excessive use of issues related to national identity after their electoral down swings in 2010 and 2012.

The case of SDKÚ is particularly interesting; it is a party that has, since circa 2009, been experiencing a crisis related to human resources, coupled by a substantial drop in voter support. The party has long been present in the European political space, which may be one of the significant reasons why the party has not opted for nationalistically coloured politics. The European political space may have played a fundamental role in anchoring a party that generally accentuates nationalistically coloured politics. As can be illustrated from the election programme of SNS in 2012, the absence of a wider ideological framework supported by the party's allegiance to an influential political grouping at the European level undermined the party's successful response to its 2010–2012 intra-party crisis. In an attempt to address its decline in voter support, in its 2012 manifesto, SNS resorted to making the most changes between two consecutive election programmes compared to any other Slovak political party in the course of the studied period.

However, this strategy was unsuccessful and the party did not overcome the 5% threshold necessary to enter the Parliament. It is difficult to estimate the likelihood of SNS overcoming its inner crisis had it been more anchored in European politics. Nevertheless, the membership of SDKÚ in EPP, a group supporting deeper European integration, serves as a safeguard against the party's stepping out of line from the general ideological direction of EPP.

The third point that deserves attention is the position of Smer-SD towards the subject of national identity, particularly the difference between the party's image in the media, in this regard, and the actual content of the party's election programme. In its 2012 manifesto, the party significantly attenuated nationalistic references used to purposively contribute towards the building of national identity compared to its previous programme. This is all the more surprising considering the fact that Smer is dominant on the left side of the political spectrum and represents a substantial part of the Slovak public that does not show affinity towards the liberal conception of a nation. It is, however, possible to look for a link between the party's anchoring in European politics and its subsequent manifestation of a positive stance towards European integration.

At the same time, it is impossible to conclude that Smer's attempt to broaden its influence in European politics will lead to a relatively smaller emphasis on national identity in the election programme. Nevertheless, the fact that it identifies an interest in the exercise of its influence at the European level may contribute to the broadening of the ideological basis for its politics at a national one.

10.3. Poland

Closer scrutiny of Polish election manifestos largely challenges the perception of the Polish party system's fragmentation as experienced in the early post transformation period. Two main features emerge as noteworthy for the studied period. First is the emergence of political movements that intensely thematize issues related to national identity – both emphasizing and refusing this concept as a whole. Second is the transformation in the perception of national identity in the case of the centre party PSL, which in the studied period underwent the most significant shift in political priorities. A general characteristic that may be identified in the election programmes is the following: the two largest political parties, PO and PiS, express conceptions of national identity that are very different.

The parties that used the issue of national identity as their main differentiating feature – particularly LPR, SPR (in years 2005 – 2007) and TR (2011 – 2015) – lacked, during their short activity span, any anchoring in European politics. As a result, it is rather complicated to evaluate in this regard. These parties' purposive use of national identity turned out to be, in both time periods, rather easy to thematize as an issue, yet difficult to sustain in the long term. This can be demonstrated by the example of the above-mentioned parties that could not retain their electoral success in the next election. In particular, the manner in which TR uses issues related to national identity amounts to, according to TR itself, a liberal questioning of the conservative conception of Polish national identity for which TR found allies in European politic.

Nevertheless, in the Polish context this relatively radical step was not matched by a gain in the 2015 election. In the case of Polish politics, we may speak of a significant demand for a conception of national identity that is not systemic; this demand regularly manifests itself in the emergence of new political groupings.

Table 40: Results of analysis

Party	Year	NAT_positive	No. of changes	NAT_negative	No. of changes	Changes	CMP_pos	CMP_neg	% of votes
LPR	2005	0		3					8.00
SRP	2005	0		5					11.40
SLD	2005	0	-	1	-	-	2.549	0.000	11.30
SLD	2007	4	4	1	0	4	4.137	0.000	13.15
SLD	2011	4	0	0	1	1	1.583	0.000	8.24
PSL	2005	0	-	0	-	-	0.329	0.000	7.00
PSL	2007	1	1	4	4	5	1.337	0.000	8.91
PSL	2011	2	1	0	4	5	0.142	0.000	8.36
PO	2005	2	-	0	-	-	0.000	0.000	24.10
PO	2007	2	0	0	0	0			41.51
PO	2011	2	0	0	0	0	2.664	0.000	39.18
PiS	2005	0	-	5	-	-	0.745	0.852	27.00
PiS	2007	0	0	1	4	4	0.423	0.690	32.11
PiS	2011	0	0	3	2	2			29.89
Palikot	2011	2	-	0	-	-	0.000	0.000	10.02

Source: Vít, Němčok (2016)

The second feature relates to a party that belongs to the ideological centre of Polish politics, the PSL. In the studied period, this party underwent a significant transformation in its perception of national identity. As may be concluded from its 2007 election programme, at a time when it entered into a coalition with PO, its approach to national identity was much less nationalistic compared to 2005. Above all, this transformation has been influenced by a shift in the party's approach to European integration – specifically, a shift from the framining of European integration as a threat to Poland, to its presentation as an opportunity. Considering the party's focus on rural areas, it is worth noticing that European integration was, in this regard, presented as a modernising factor. The party confirmed this transformation in its 2011 election programme. That said, it is important to consider the influence of PSL's membership of EPP, a group which is characterized by a much more positive attitude towards European integration than that captured in PSL's 2005 manifesto.

Understandably, the change in the party's perception of national identity cannot be interpreted as a result of its membership in EPP or its participation in European politics. Particularly so, as PSL presents itself as a party that pays close attention to identity and Christianity, representing mainly rural, conservative voters.[99] It is also interesting that, despite the significant transformation in the perception of national identity, in the case of PSL, this development was not matched by significant changes in voter support (signified by its failure to get beyond the 5 % electoral threshold, for example). The case of PSL demonstrates that, also in Polish politics, parties of the ideological centre need to react to changing societal demands and, at the same time, be attentive to external impulses. This is especially the case when a party belongs to one of the most influential political groups on the European level. The speed with which this transformation occurred, under circumstances that did

---

99 Interview with Jerzy Stefaniuk. It is worth mentioning that, for more than 20 years, Waldemar Pawlak was the chair of PSL, which certainly does not attest the party's tendency to alter ad hoc its ideological profile to suit societal demand.

not present PSL with a relevant political challenger of the same ideological background or with an existential crisis, nevertheless remains noteworthy. Last, but not least, it is also remarkable that, in the studied time period, an increase in the number of parliamentary parties leading to the fragmentation of the party system was not recorded.

The varied degree to which national identity and related issues are used by parties is a distinctive feature of the Polish party system. On one hand, there is the liberal conception of national identity on the part of SLD and partially TR that had, in the studied period, rather centrifugal tendencies, particularly in the 2007 election. At the same time, in the 2011 election, we may speak of a sort of stabilization in the perception of national identity in all parties except for TR. This trend is also interesting from the perspective of SLD, which had been losing electoral support in the course of the studied time period despite the fact that its perception of national identity had been shifting towards a more liberal position. Although the party has long been anchored in European politics, it was unable to explain its shift towards a more liberal position to its voters.

It is also interesting to note that the two largest Polish political parties have perceptions of national identity that are divergent. This fundamental difference illustrates the relevance of the topic of national identity in the Polish political space. This argument is supported also by the fact that PiS is becoming de facto immune to the influence of the European political space. Despite its active participation in European politics and representation in EU elected offices, PiS declares that it does not recognize the current shape of the European political environment and merely focuses on defending its own interests and priorities arising from national politics. It follows that even a dominant actor of a party system participating at the European level may be resistant to external influences and grounded in self-determination.. The party's ability to provide a credible, alternative ideological framework is a necessary condition in this regard.

10.4. Comparison

When it comes to the development of the perception of national identity in political parties and the influence of the European political environment on the process of (their) formation, a comparison of the three country cases offers several parallels. The main observations may be summarised as follows:

Political parties of the ideological centre are subject to intensive influence by the European environment through existing institutional links. This is particularly the case with political parties that are members of the EPP. This influence could be a supporting factor in overcoming an inner crisis in the party, as was the case with KDU-ČSL. Nevertheless, what remains a challenge for the parties is how to handle this influence in their relations with voters. The symptoms of such a complicated task are especially evident in the case of SLD.

The degree to which issues related to national identity are used cannot be treated equally in all three countries. Despite the fact that national identity tends to manifest itself in a similar manner, the extent of its relevance remains different in each context, because of the particularities of the individual party systems.

At the same time, national identity cannot be perceived as a manifestation of the fragmentation of party systems, despite the fact that in the Czech Republic or Poland we witness the rise of parties that use these issues in a nationalistic or a liberal manner to either emphasize or downplay national identity.

Where party systems display an increased presence of issues related to national identity, there are political parties that thematize national identity in a manner that solidifies it without regard for the development of the European political space. This is particularly so in the case of PiS. On the one hand, the party does participate in the European political space, but on the other, it refuses to participate in its integration project. SNS participates much less in the European political space, and its activities are aimed at maintaining its position in domestic politics. SNS also emphasizes the building of national identity much more vehemently – an observation that is also confirmed by the high number of nationalistic codes in its manifestos. In this case, the European space may be understood as helping the political party to create an opposition against undesirable external influences—provided the party participates actively in the European political environment. However, this argument needs to be expanded further; the party needs to struggle to achieve the creation of an alternative European political space. This is particularly the case for PiS, rather than other nationalistic parties in the Czech Republic and Slovakia.

10.5. Effects of participation of political parties in the European political space

Social science allows for multiple analyses of political parties' behaviour in the European arena or nation states but the question of whether their politics is consistent on both levels stands somewhat outside the researchers' interests. The aim of this research was to compare the development of perception of national identity and how it is influenced thorough transnational cooperation outside the nation state with their integration into the structures of the European Union.

At first glance, the introduced findings are not surprising. The representatives of those parties that promote international cooperation, further European integration and who avoid using nationalistic rhetoric also occupy more positions within the European political spaces. This relationship also works the opposite way, with those parties who promote the importance of preserving national sovereignty and refusing any form of transnational cooperation showing a reluctance to integrate into the structures of the European political space. What needs to be said—in context of the CEE region—is that the outputs of the analysis revealed either the tendencies outlined above or no relationship at all. That basically means that parties such as PiS and ODS, who emphasize nationalism, tended to penetrate EU structures in order to support their attitudes on the European level.

Based on the above, the research questions can be answered as follows:

1. How does the perception of the national identity of political parties change while they are participants in the European political space?

Looking back on the decade between 2004 and 2013, one can conclude that most of the changes in attitude occurred in parties belonging to the centre of the political spectrum, with special emphasis on PSL (Poland), KDU-ČSL (the Czech Republic) and SDKÚ-DS (Slovakia). Among these parties there was a visible shift towards more nationalism negative perceptions of national identity. This trend can be explained by their long-term commitment to European integration as well as their will to be integrated in the European political space. From the long-term perspective, the issue of the constitution of the European political space should be observed carefully. If the European space will be reshaped in terms of softening EU integration, centre-right parties will be faced with the need to redefine their "belonging" to the higher political body/space.

Those parties that did not prove to be influenced by participation in the European political space do not consider that space as something they should pay attention to and therefore do not even have the intention to spread their influence beyond the national arena in the context of the CEE region. This is the case with PiS, which remains consistent in its nationally focused policies. In contrast to PiS, ODS aimed to develop new European partnerships in the European Reformist Group and to move from a position supporting integration to one of stressing its negative effects of integration. This goes against the core idea of the socialization process within the EU. Nevertheless, it also shows that individual parties have to identify with either the ideological reasons to support European integration, or the clear and pragmatic gains and opportunities the European political space can bring. From this perspective, one can see ODS as a party who have spied an opportunity rather than an answer to their long term political goals since they left the mainstream European parliament fraction EPP and participated in the founding of the ERG faction.

2. How is the length of membership in the EU translated into a party's perception of national identity and how does this affect the constituting of policies relevant to national identity?

Based on the data explained in the previous section, one can observe a positive correlation between an increase in a nationalism-negative perception of national identity and length of participation in the European political space. From this wider perspective, one can agree that a key characteristic of the European political space is its ability to socialize new participants into European politics towards softening nationalistic views and increasing European shared understanding. This characteristic can be seen especially in the case of social democratic parties in each of the three countries. These parties have a long tradition of internationalism and therefore one can expect them to be rather open to incorporating such inputs in their manifestos. One cannot omit the fact that in the past 25 years they have undergone significant developments from nationallyfocused parties – in SLD's case, even from an ex-communist party – towards international openness. In addition to this, those who vote for social democrats in the CEE region tend to be rather conservative in terms of social values.

Based on the qualitative and quantitative analysis mentioned above, Christian and social democratic parties prove to have the highest ability to incorporate inputs from the European political space. It shows the importance of the existence of a Europe-wide structure of political parties. In addition to this, the research showed that those parties that are able to anchor their ideology to a higher structure, such as a functioning platform of Christian or Social democratic parties demonstrate a willingness to incorporate inputs from the European political space. Results of quantitative analysis do not cover the tendencies of individual parties. In addition to this, a pattern of parties belonging to similar ideological camp was observed, such as ČSSD, SLD, SMER-SD, OR KDU-ČSL. However, a deeper analysis of individual parties is need.

3. Why do some parties change their understanding of national identity whereas other parties resist any significant influence?

In regard to the research question answered above, focusing on Christian and social democratic parties, these are the parties who are the subject of influence and therefore change their perception of national identity. It was found that Christian democratic parties in all three countries occupy the ideological centre and change the most. Besides those parties belonging to the ideological centre, nationalistic parties have also significantly changed their perception of national identity in the researched period. Since only one Slovak party, SNS, has been part of parliament, broader conclusions cannot be made. Nevertheless, the rise of parties using nationally coloured policies has appeared in the Czech Republic and Poland as well. In contrast to Slovakia, they never become a significant and long-term formation of the Czech and Polish party system. Therefore, similar patterns can be observed, meaning different variations of the use of policies based on national identity. Given that only SNS proved to be a relevant party during the researched period, one should pay attention to nationalistic parties in general. In the argumentation developed above, parties participating in European politics as well as cultivating contacts with other parties of similar ideological background are most open to policy change. Contrary to this, nationalistic parties such as SNS or, to some extent, PiS do not consider the cultivation of international contacts to be significant As a result, even if they participate in European politics, they are remain unsusceptible to influence.

From a methodological perspective, the research aims to apply a research framework when analyzing the perception of national identity by political parties. Since the attitudes towards various policy issues are hidden in the abstract space, political science has no method capable of mapping the policy preferences objectively. For this purpose, this analytical framework was implemented and compared with a prior framework for analyzing political texts. The Deductive Manifesto Project methodology and the inductive Grounded Theory each bring arguments to support this selected analytical approach, and to increase the reliability of results. At this point, reference to the methodology used has to be made—this work tried to carefully set the framework for analyzing the perception and framing strategies of political parties as well as elements influencing the main data source, i.e. election manifestos. Despite this, the researcher cannot escape from normative judgements and perceptions of the analyzed topics.

Since the presence of nationalism or support for transnational cooperation is more or less a dichotomous question, it must be said that the methodological imperfection can be reflected only in the robustness of presented tendencies that were omitted from the interpretations while their direction should still be correct. The research opens a new field of research, namely the consistency of political parties' politics in the nation state and in the European arena, with a focus on the perception of national identity from two inquiring perspectives. First, from the perspective of accommodating the framework used in order to provide a context for any liberal democracy, where political parties aggregate the interests of the public and vice versa. Secondly, and more specifically, in the context of the EU, from the perspective of whether the European political space affects the perception of national identity in the same way; or if there are any differences that require our further analysis and explanation.

At the same time, this thesis contributes to research focusing on the rise of nationalistic tendencies in the EU and their reflections in party policies and in election manifestos. It shows how parties react to developments in the European political space. This means that the research contributes to a deeper understanding of "identity cleavage" in party systems—focused here on election manifestos. Therefore, the research helps to achieve a deeper understanding of political parties' aims in terms of shaping their societies. It focuses on the various aims and shaping tools of liberal or nationalistic parties in a changing European context. The research also contributes to a better understanding of the CEE region (here as the Czech Republic, Poland, and Slovakia) in the first period after joining the EU. Although a body of literature focusing on changes in political parties of the CEE region after 2004 already exists, this work develops the scope of this literature further, in terms of an evaluation of their policy transformations while being part of the European political space. It also shows how inputs of the environment are transformed into parties' understanding of national identity.

11. Appendix A:

Monitored positions in the EU structures

European Parliament:	Conference of Presidents
	President of delegation
	Vice-President of delegation
	President of committee
	Vice-President of committee
	President of intergroup
	Vice-President of intergroup
	President of political group
	Vice-President of political group
European Commission:	Membership
	Member of Conference of Presidents
Council of Regions:	Membership in Commission
	President of Section
	Vice-President of Section
ECOSOC:	Membership
	Member of Conference of Presidents
European political parties:	Membership
	Member of Conference of Presidents

12. Appendix B: The Grounded Theory Codebook

I) European Union

This area covers issues relating to how the EU is perceived within manifestos. The purpose is to enhance the party's attitude towards issues related to the EU. The most crucial point is the party's position towards deeper integration of the EU. In other words, the party's commitment to the European idea. This example shows the complexity of the whole issue. Usually, the manifesto does not contain a statement supporting or rejecting deeper integration. It might be collected from various mentions such as support of joining the monetary union or explicit mention of nationally sensitive policy such as integration of tax policy. The domain of the EU consists of declaratory statements as well as its mention in various policy fields. It also shows how EU affairs penetrate each national context; and the extent to which issues relating to the EU are politicized.

The area of the EU contains the following codes:

1.1 Support of deeper integration

> The manifesto mentions the support of deeper integration that will lead to a federalized EU. The manifesto explicitly mentions the federalization of the EU or, for instance, perceiving the common currency as a value instead of only a source of economic gains. The manifesto proves support of the EU institutions' activities in the way of competence transfer to the EU level. In regard to the last period of the integration shifts, the manifesto refers to support of the Lisbon Treaty. The code does not cover the general meaning of support of the EU.

Examples:

Entering the eurozone, once our economy is ready for it; EU policy of education and research.

TOP 09 also makes maximum effort to ensure that the Czech Republic accedes to the European financial agreement ("Fiscal Compact") and adopts the financial constitution. We want to achieve savings in expenditures of the state primarily through the increase of their effectiveness and a consistent system of checks.

We will prepare CZ for its entrance into the eurozone. We want to enter when it becomes economically and socially beneficial for us.

Parties: KDU 2013, KDU 2010, PO 2011, PO 2005, TOP 09 2010, TOP 09 2013, ČSSD 2010, ČSSD 2013, SDKU 2006

1.2 Support of the EU but not deeper integration

This code covers mentions of general support of European integration, but without the party's commitment for supporting further deeper integration. Simultaneously, the manifesto does not contain any signs of rejection of certain policy integration. In other words, the code reflects the party's general position.

Examples:

The fact that we have become a full-fledged member of the European Union and the eurozone is the most positive fact in the modern history of Slovakia. This fact includes successful times and must also count in times of difficulty.

Constructing Europe as a community of values. We want Slovakia to be an initiative-taking, active, reliable and proud member of the European Union and especially the European Monetary Union.

ODS seeks further enlargement of the EU as an area of stability and economic prosperity based on democratic principles, respect toward human rights, and free competition.

> *We are in favor of preserving the sovereignty of member countries in the area of economic and social politics wherever it clearly and unambiguously does not conflict with the needs of the Common European Market. Nevertheless, we will fully support the policies and instruments of the EU and EC, through which these institutions contribute to the long-term preservation of public finance and responsible economic policy.*

Parties: Most 2012, SDKU 2012, KDH 2012, SDKU 2010, ODS 2010

1.3 Strong in the EU

> The European arena is not perceived as a shared political space but as an environment of different national interests that must be defended by each party. The party stresses the EU's unilateral (concrete) benefits. The party openly aims to push through national interest; also in terms of a higher role of national representatives within the EU. EU funds, as well as Common Agriculture Policy (CAP) without connection to the "European idea" also belong to this code.

Examples:

> *We want to preserve the permanent sovereignty of Slovakia in the areas of taxation and social policy. The politics of Slovakia in the EU should be confident, forward-looking, and balanced. Slovakia cannot surrender the strategic benefits of membership in the EU and its participation at the main negotiating table.*
> *Therefore, it is of strategic interest for Slovakia to participate in the protection of our common European currency, both in the processes and the economic strengthening of the eurozone.*
> *Slovakia belongs in the EU and must be a proud and stable member. This of course cannot mean that we will obey silently. We also have the right to our own view on solutions.*

> *The developments in Europe in recent years, and particularly the euro crisis, made it clear that our realistic approach toward European integration is correct. We are aware that European integration brings the Czech Republic a number of advantages, but we need to approach it in such a manner that it doesn't proceed at the expense of some of its members. We do not wish to act irresponsibly by leaving the EU, but this isn't to say that we will blindly accept everything that comes from Brussels. We will measure every element of the European integration with Czech eyes and from the angle of Czech national interests. We want the EU as a space for economic freedom and not as a space for European bureaucracy. We want the Czech Republic to act as a proud and confident country in Europe. We will ensure that Czech representatives represent the Czech Republic in Brussels and not Brussels in the Czech Republic.*

Parties: SDKU 2012, OL 2012, TOP 09 2013, KSČM 2013, ČSSD 2006, ČSSD 2013, ODS 2006, ODS 2010, ODS 2013, PSL 2005, PSL 2007, PO 2011, PO 2005, KDU 2006, SNS 2010, Smer 2010, Smer 2012, Most 2012, OL 2012, Most 2010, SaS 2010, PSL 2011, PiS 2005

1.4 Europe of nations

> The party categorically opposes the idea of deeper integration and supports the return of some competences back to the national level. Negative statements about the EU are evident as are depictions of the EU as a threat to national sovereignty. In addition to this, the party stresses national uniqueness and criticizes the EU as a "melting pot" at the same time. The role of the EU should be limited to grounds of economic cooperation.

Examples:

> *We will prevent the take-over of the competency of the European Union, for example in the area of taxation or criminal law, where it lacks the proper approval of elected representatives of Slovak citizens.*
> *SNS will therefore promote that in the future, a community of individual sovereign states form out of the EU.*

Utilization of the skill and knowledge capital for the economic and social development of Poland and assertion of a better future of the nation as well as multiplication of this capital in the course of advanced education that leads to the creation of an information society.

Parties: PSL 2007, PiS 2007, SaS 2010, SNS 2006, ODS 2010

1.5 Against the EU, leaving possible

The party openly criticizes the current state of the architecture of the EU, and explicitly mentions the possibility of leaving the EU. This critique focuses on a so-called democratic deficit, doubtful legitimacy and the EU's threat to national sovereignty.

Examples:

Equally dangerous in this area are strong centralizing trends occurring in the European Union, binding hopes for the future of our continent with building a superstate and forming a new "pan-European" identity at the expense of nation states and the identity of European nations. In social practice, the project of the construction of a new "European" consciousness must lead to identities of stronger nations being foisted on the weaker nations.

In cases of extreme necessity to protect the property and values of citizens and state sovereignty, there should be the option of withdrawal from the EU and the termination of the current common currency – the euro.

Parties: PiS 2005, SNS 2012

II) Values

This area covers party statements that imply fluidly defined notions of the values of the society. In addition to this, it is important to pay attention to how the party understands its role in shaping and communicating those values. In other words, to what extent the party understands its role as a generator or cultivator of particular values. Although this area might be perceived as unclear, the emphasis on the party's role in the system that shapes values brings new perspectives into the analysis. In addition to this, the context of an individual country plays a crucial role; e.g. whether there are any national minorities in the country and how they are asked to participate in the society values' system.

Attention is also given to the party's perception of culture and cultural heritage and the role it assigns to culture; whether it perceives culture as playing any role in national identity consciousness or perceives it as a civic service. The role that parties believe culture should hold must be distinguished. Do they emphasize the active development of national culture and national feelings; or the cultivation of certain traditions and cultural heritage? One of the most important aspects is the role of language; if the party considers this as an entity to be protected in its fine form or left to natural development. In addition to the examples mentioned above, attention should be paid to parties' attitudes towards the culture of national minorities.

This area is covered by the following codes:

2.1 Support of new emancipation movements, open society

> The party's call for a redefinition of entire values of the society, which means rejection of the current system. Redefinition, in the context of this research, means redefinition from a liberal perspective and in opposition to the Catholic Church. This concerns the matters of homosexual partnership or acknowledging minorities' rights to a maximal extent, or rejecting the use of the term nation/national state. The party supports openness towards immigrants and general openness of the society.

Examples:

> *The legalization of civil partnerships without the right to adopt. Both heterosexual and homosexual individuals, who live together for at least five years, should be given the same rights and freedoms. The law will be transparent and understandable for people.*

Slovak citizens of the same sex, living together as life partners, do not have the option to relieve society through the acceptance of mutual maintenance obligations for one another. Their daily partner co-existence is uncertain, legal certainty is reduced, and conditions for security in old age are not being created. Even their parents are left uncertain.

Parties: KDU 2006, KDU 2010, SLD 2011, SDKU 2010, SaS 2010, Palikot 2011, SLD 2011

2.1.1 Nationalism negative

> The party rejects any use of nationalistic feeling in regard to the majority population. The party openly refuses the term nationalism as a mobilizing tool as well as a general concept of shaping of society.

Examples:

The Czech Republic should actively support the respect of basic human and civil rights, as well as freedoms everywhere in the world, including national, religious, and ethnic minority rights; in this regard, the Czech Republic should reject any kind of double standard. At the same time it should also oppose all forms of suppression of fundamental freedoms of citizens, genocide, racism, extreme nationalism, xenophobia, intolerance, anti-Semitism, and especially all forms of terrorism, individual or state-run.

Parties: ČSSD 2010, SLD 2011, Smer 2010

2.2 Pluralism

> This code covers the party's emphasis on equality of all individuals, religions and nationalities, and respect in the matters of individual freedom. This also relates to the party's commitment to participation in the Western values' system.

Examples:

Political party MOST-HID is aiming for reconciliation between the Hungarians and Slovaks, between the Hungarians themselves, and even among other national minorities and ethnic groups.
We support a politically and economically pluralist society.

Parties: KSČM 2010, KSČM 2013, ODS 2013, KDU 2010, Most 2010, ČSSD 2010, SLD 2007

2.3. Individualism and freedom as values

> The party treats the role of the individual as one of the most important achievements of Western societies. For its further development, it is important to be conscious that individuality is the basic unit of society. The parties stress the cultivation of freedom within society, often in response to the legacy of communism.

Examples:

SDKÚ-DS will therefore in the following period of time also be the party that its citizens knew during its better days. Our main principle will be the promotion of individual freedom, responsibility, and justice instead of populism.

Parties: PSL 2011, SDKU 2006, SDKU 2012, Most 2010, SaS 2012, PO 2005, SaS 2010, SaS 2012, ODS 2010, SLD 2011, PO 2005

2.4. Human rights as a value

> Human rights are perceived as an integral part of liberal western societies and should be further cultivated as its part. It means that human rights are perceived through a wide range of policy fields.

Examples:

Human rights are not an empty concept to us, but rather a value upon which our society stands, and which should always be respected and fulfilled.
Slovak foreign policy must promote values upon which the country is built — freedom, responsibility, protection of human rights, pluralist democracy, and a functioning market. We want these principles and values reflected in the external policies of the EU, in the policies of our neighbors, allies in international organizations, and alliances such as NATO.
CZ cannot and must not let up in its foreign policy in the field of human rights; this concerns the basic component and the very essence of a "ZP" democratic country; simultaneously, it must carefully balance this policy with the implementation of our economic interests.

Parties: SKDU 2010, SKDU 2012, Most 2010, Most 2012, SaS 2010, TOP 09 2013, ANO 2013, ČSSD 2013, ČSSD 2010, ODS 2010, KDU 2010

2.5 Culture as a value

Culture is perceived as a source of knowledge that serves the cultivation of a society. This level proves a disconnection with any emotional feelings.

Examples

An educated nation, conscious of its own history and valuing its own culture, has the potential for its own successful development.
The promotion of free access to the National Museum, National Gallery and other similar cultural institutions is an element of educating the entire nation.
The government perceives culture not only as the basis for identity and spiritual life in Slovak society. According to the political principles of SNS, the state has to support national culture. Artists can create cultural values, which assist in cultivating Slovak society, and so that they also challenge the culture of death, trash, and kitsch, with the state, regional governments, cities, and municipalities having to equally support traditional culture and contemporary culture an –d according to needs – help with the culture of all nationalities and ethnic groups.
We take responsibility for the cultural heritage of our country, as well as allowing for culture to have a vital space at the present time and be a support for upcoming generations, so that it can play an important role in their lives, i.e. the future. The relationship towards culture is provided by upbringing and education, through the action of cultural associations or institutions, as well as through the media. It turns out that an entirely different civil comfort is provided by places where people actively dedicate their time to culture with either the help of philanthropists, municipalities, or cities.

Parties: SNS 2006, SDKU 2006, SDKU 2012, Smer 2012, KDH 2006, KDH 2012, SaS 2010, SaS 2012, OL 2012, Úsvit 2013, TOP 09 2013, KSČM 2010, KSČM 2006, KSČM 2013, ODS 2010, ODS 2006, ČSSD 2013, PSL 2007, PiS 2005, PO 2011, Smer 2006, Smer 2010, TOP 09 2013, KDU 2013

2.6 National culture as a part of identity

The party understands the national culture as given. Therefore, national identity cannot be separated from culture that shapes the social and political context.

Examples

We will protect and enhance the Slovak culture and spiritual heritage. The nation understands SNS as a collective individuality, with which every Slovak shares a common historical memory, fate, and future. Culture is essentially always national, and therefore SNS puts an emphasis not only on its protection, but also for new Slovak creations.
In terms of streamlining the central government, we want to merge the ministries of education and culture into one. We want the Ministry of Culture to lead a continuous dialogue with the cultural community so that an independent section of national culture and protection of the state language is established.
Culture should be accessible to the general public, including children, youth, and retired.
Culture is perceived by the government not only as the basis of identity and spiritual life in Slovak society.

Parties: OL 2012, SDKU 2010, Smer 2010, Smer 2012, PiS 2005, SNS 2012, HZDS 2012

2.7 Traditional values

The party emphasises national and/or regional traditions in order to naturally cultivate values that are in the party's perception of tradition. This can be, for instance, landscape, folk traditions, or the cultivation of historical monuments. It is important to stress that the party does not discuss these values in an emotional way.

Examples

> *In every gmina, in every city, powiat and voivodeship, in which it participates in the local government – a good government – PSL ensures a high level of local democracy. This is guaranteed by competent and thrifty people, sensitive to the needs and desires of the inhabitants of each of these surroundings, each of these communities and regions. We create efficient and decent government so that, in every place, all around the country prosperity for all is built, so that all Poles have a chance for development and a good life.*
>
> *Protection of life from conception to natural death, marriage as a union between man and woman, the rights of parents to bring up their children, but also material support of families is therefore an important part of our program.*
>
> *We will actively stand up against efforts to legalize euthanasia. We will support the development of hospice care.*
>
> *KDH supports families based on the principles of personal responsibility, responsibility for one's own family, and also the principles of subsidiarity and solidarity between generations. The goal of KDH's family policy is to choose a favorable environment for families with kids, meeting their material and spiritual needs, as well as eliminating discrimination against families with more children. We want to motivate young people to partake in responsible behavior and encourage them to prepare for marriage and parenthood. KDH's family policy has two basic attributes: the protection of families and the support of families. Every healthy society protects the institution of marriage, thus protecting the common good of a man and a woman, as well as their children. This is also why we suggest a constitutional law for the protection of marriage.*

Parties: KDU 2013, PSL 2007, KDH 2006, KDH 2010, KDH 2012, SNS 2012, SNS 2010, Smer 2010, SDKU 2006, SKDU 2010, PiS 2005, OL 2012, ODS 2013

2.8 Support of national culture

The state should play an active role in cultivating, but mainly in producing national culture. In this process, the educational system should be involved in order to educate citizens on the features of national culture. This means, for example, the construction of new monuments, or the support of cultural diplomacy in foreign relations.

Examples

We will promote the long-term restoration of historical heritage so that we can preserve monuments for future generations and improve conditions for tourism. In terms of historical and cultural heritage, we will accentuate the Christian tradition in the legislative and executive form.
Slovakia, founded upon the story of our homeland.

Parties: KDH 2010, KDH 2012, SLD 2005, SLD 2007, PSL 2007, PiS 2005, SNS 2010, Smer 2010

2.9 Support of national identity building

The party demonstrates explicit aims for the development of national culture and perceives this as a necessary part of inculcating belonging. In this case, the state should play an active role in cultivating but mainly in producing national culture. In this process, the educational system should be involved in the promotion of patriotic values in education.

Examples:

Cultural heritage is a spiritual and material treasure which should be cherished, made more accessible to ordinary people and passed on to younger generations. CSSD is aware of the importance of maintaining and constantly cultivating the national language for the development of cultural activities and the creation of cultural heritage. For this reason we will prioritize the development of the mother tongue and the specifics of national culture, the support of new authors and interpreters, as well as the protection of the spheres of informational, educational, and entertainment activities, from anti-spiritual and cheap commercialization.
"The National program of Slovak revival", which is the program of the rigorous defense of national interest in areas of societal life.

Parties: PSL 2007, PiS 2005, SNS 2006, SNS 2012, ČSSD 2006

2.10 Soil as proof of nation

>The party proves the primordial aspect of national identity. This means that it is understood that cultural and contextual (geographical and economic) aspects are given to the particular nation. The nation, according to this understanding, is unique.

Examples:

There is a risk that if further land, forest and water is sold out, we will be one of very few countries in the world that have defined their own territory, while not being the owners of its natural resources and soil.

Parties: SNS 2006

2.11 Christian values

>The party supports the participation of the Church in societal development and desires the state's active support of the Church. In addition to this, the party considers Christian values to have a positive influence of on the cultivation both of society and the nation.

- Support of Church

    To engender wider understanding of Christianity, the party encourages the Church to participate in public life and spread its values

- Church as an integral part of state

    The party understands the Church as deeply rooted in the society. In this context, activities of Church and state should be complementary to each other. Emphasis is given to the promotion and defense of traditional values.

Examples:

National, Christian, and social program for Slovakia

SNS is determined to defend Christian values on the continent through a tough stance against the policy of multiculturalism, Islamization of Europe, and liberal migration policy favoring a disproportionate support of nonconformist ethnic groups.

KDH is a conservative party, which is committed to Slovak national tradition, especially the legacy of Andrej Hlinka during the shaping of Slovakia's fate. The state should have a strong stance in protection of freedom, law and order. However, it cannot abuse its power for unwarranted interference into the natural environment of the individual, family, religion, and society.

Parties: SNS 2006, SNS 2010, SNS 2012, HZDS 2012, KDH 2006, KDH 2010, KDH 2012, KDU 2006, PiS 2005, PSL 2007, PO 2005

2.12 Nation is threatened

> The party openly stresses the rejection of other cultures and influences that it regards as a threat the nation. In addition to this, the party strictly rejects foreign influence. The party uses these emotions to evoke fear that the nation is threatened. In this context, it can be understood as a policy against national minorities, as well as against immigrants. The main argument behind the anti-immigrant position is the danger that immigration poses to the nation.

Examples:

We cannot underestimate the ongoing threats to the sovereignty and integrity of Slovakia from the side of our southern neighbor.

Parties: SNS 2012

III) Minorities

This area covers various topics connected with different kinds of minorities. Although the main focus is given to national minorities, the area covers immigration policy or gender minorities as well. Attention is given to the level of their recognition by the majority society, i.e. political parties; if the party supports the right to self-determination and supports the developing minority's sense of

208 IDENTITY FORMATION

belonging. On the other hand, to what extent the party stresses their integration into majority society/culture.

The list of codes was set as follows:

3.1 Inclusiveness

The party promotes the culture of different minorities and encourages them in the developing of their own identity as well as a sense of belonging. The minorities are perceived as bringing gains to society and enriching the majority culture.

Examples:

Slovakia is a place of understanding and peaceful coexistence between the majority nation and national minorities. Slovakia is a multi-ethnic country and other alternatives to the cooperation in this field do not exist.
Political party MOST-HÍD is a party for the reconciliation between the Hungarians and Slovaks, between the Hungarians themselves, and among other national minorities and ethnic groups.
Same-sex couples are a reality in our society, with such couples in cohabitation in institutionalized life partnership being a realization of the rights of these persons to a full family life and the elements of individual freedom, which we want to promote within the realms of our values.
In addition, apart from this measure, being able to increase the undisputed quality of the daily lives of these couples, simultaneously, it will bring benefits for the entire society, since it will increase the level of its responsibility and social stability.
The long-term cumulated problem of "socially excluded localities" has gotten to the stage, where in some regions it is creating significant social, civic and local tensions. It is therefore necessary to make progress in the practical implementation of integration of people from these localities into society – particularly through pressure for the return of the long-time unemployed and excluded back to the labor market.
Increased attention must be paid to the quality of performance of public administration, protection of the safety of citizens and property, and the reduction of crime and criminality in concentrated areas of the excluded localities. A truly effective solution must be based upon two principles, which also dictate our policy:
1) Respect for the dignity of every person as a unique being
2) It must be more convenient to work or to prepare oneself for employment, than to live solely off of social benefits.

Parties: Most 2010, Most 2012, SaS 2010, SaS 2012, KDU 2010, SLD 2007

3.2 Protection of minorities

Ensuring the protection of specific minority groups (Roma), and strictly against minority demonisation within the public discourse. Focus is given to their cultural and rights.

Examples:

We support the establishment of a mutually tolerant atmosphere between the Roma and the majority of the population, and do not show understanding nor tolerance for violations of the rules of social coexistence nor for crimes.
It will be necessary to closely monitor the use of various kinds of social assistance so as to reach the addressed. We will support the missionary service of the Church to be extended to the Roma population.
In order to increase public safety, we propose the establishment of Roma patrols.
Political party MOST-HÍD supports the key competencies proposed by the Council of Europe:
- *Communication in the mother tongue*
- *Communication in foreign languages*

Parties: Most 2010, Most 2012, SaS 2010, SaS 2012, KDU 2010, Smer 2010, Smer 2012, TOP 09 2010, SDKU 2010, ODS 2010

3.3 Dialogue with minorities

The party's focus on the given situation — whether the minority is part of the state and should not be excluded from political and social life. To develop peaceful relations in this area, dialogue is necessary.

Examples:

In relation to migration and following the negative experiences in some member states, we will require adequate language and cultural integration of migrants.
We will actively work to develop the concept of integration of employed, upstanding, and tax-paying foreigners within Czech territory, including the concept of the impact on the labor market.

Parties: Most 2010, SaS 2012, KDU 2013, KDH 2012

3.4 Limited immigration

The party supports immigration from certain geographical or cultural areas that do not cause serious conflict within society. In addition to this, the party supports immigration of highly qualified people for the benefit of the country. The party perceives immigration from Arab and African countries as a threat to the cultural unity of the state.

Examples:

We will ensure the establishment of clear rules for selective immigration so that only those who really wish to become Czech citizens will be able to settle in the Czech Republic permanently.

We also have to pay more attention to the coexistence of various cultures and philosophies. No one can have another's culture forced upon them and simultaneously, rules that fundamentally change and limit the behavior of people should not be imported anywhere.

We will carry out a single national migration policy in harmony with EU guidelines. We will set up an immigration office in which we will unite hitherto fragmented activities of the Foreign Police and other departments of the Ministry of Interior, the Ministry of Social Affairs, and will add the activities of NGOs to it.

Our country is ready to provide asylum for the persecuted and suffering. A condition for immigration must be the obligation to respect general European moral values and to learn the language of the country. European countries must also commit to taking responsibility for immigrants, to whom they granted entry into the territory of the European Union. With the exception of primarily university-educated experts from around the world, we will prefer immigrants only (mainly) from Slavic countries of South and Southeast Europe.

We support the EU's efforts in creating a common immigration and asylum policy. It will be crucial to ensure legal migration and all the while fight against illegal migration.

Parties: ČSSD 2010, KDU 2013, KDU 2010, ODS 2010, ODS 2013, VV 2010

3.5 Limited rights for minorities

> The party supports the majority nation order within the state. The minority should accept the rules of a majority; this is presented as an issue of political representation. This covers the case of a Roma minority when mixed with Hungarians in Slovakia — Roma should not have the same minority rights. Also, this entails the rejection of the claims of any state/ethnic group against the state, such as Sudeten Germans.

Examples:

> *We reject the targeted assimilation of Slovak citizens and other non-Hungarian nationalities and the Roma ethnic group, as well as the regional policy of the Hungarian Coalition. We also reject the policy of social ignorance championed by the current coalition in the current government, since this policy is dangerous in terms of the future of the country and its citizens.*

Parties: SNS 2006

3.6 Against immigration

> The party rejects integration of incoming immigrants and develops tools to decrease the number of immigrants. This might be added to the rejection of EU immigration policy.

Examples

> *In the area of asylum policy, we will support a strict asylum policy; we will back a high level of protection of the institution of asylum from abuse. We will promote the preservation of sovereignty of member states on EU land during the decision-making process regarding asylum and during checks on external borders of the Union.*

Parties: KDH 2006

3.7 Against minority rights

> The party develops feelings that certain national groups are not welcome in the state and draws a clear line between 'us' and 'them'. In other words, the party rejects their integration; in some cases followed by forced assimilation. This entails provisions to secure ethnic Slovaks instead of all people living in Slovakia.

Examples:

> SNS is committed, without harmful emotions and definitely with the awareness of full responsibility, to face political pressure by chauvinistic and revanchist interpretations of the rights of national minorities. The rejection of any foreign interference of pressure groups, including associations with lingering requirements of displaced Germans into the internal affairs of CZ, as well as the questioning of the Beneš Decrees.

Parties: KSCM 2013, SNS 2006

IV) World

This section focuses on international affairs with the exception of the EU. The focus is given to stressing cooperation with any particular country or geographical area. In addition to this, attention is paid to the role of values in its foreign policy as the party claims; mainly in the case of human rights promotion. The second main area of focus is the relation to globalization and capitalism.

The list of codes was set as follows:

4.1 Support of the EU

The party shows general support of participation of European values without deeper specification and their further accommodation in a national context. The code indicates general support of the country's integration efforts and its anchoring in the so-called European legacy.

Examples:

> CZ is experiencing growth thanks to its membership in the EU.
> Following the accession to the EU, including the eurozone and the Schengen area, today's common challenge is the responsible fulfilment of institutional reform and effective response to global challenges. We want to bring the Slovak stance more actively to the decision-making process of the EU. At the same time we want to cultivate the European consciousness of "we are also the EU" in Slovakia, because the European Union is not a classic external stakeholder.

> *We are strong advocates but also guarantors of the completion of the European integration of Slovakia. We are fully engaged in efforts to adopt the euro on 1.1.2009 – entry into the eurozone will increase the growth of our economy, increase employment, and improve living standards.*

Parties: SDKU 2006, SDKU 2012, ODS 2006, KDH 2010

4.2 Openness towards world

> Globalization is perceived as a positive thing and as a chance for further development. This means openness towards immigrants with emphasis on respect for individuality.

Examples:

> *No matter how carefully we register negative elements, which globalization brings about, the social essence of the process is irreversible. Objective trends cannot completely be resisted, they can be respected and policies can be adapted so that the negative is suppressed, and instead an opportunity could then be used. We believe that the adaptation of our country to globalization offers a huge chance. We do not have the natural resources, but we are a nation of active, hard-working, and qualified people. The application of our work does not have national obstacles. European markets and other territories are opening. Foreign investors, who want to take advantage of our quality work and stable economic environment, are coming.*

Parties: ČSSD 2006

4.2.2 International solidarity

> The party considers its political and social values as transferable to regions/states where it is needed. This is the case of transformation assistance for Balkan countries from the perspective of V4 countries.

Examples:

> *Particular attention will be paid to the South East European region where Slovakia has a specific, favorable position (intensive political dialogue with Croatia and exchange of integration experiences and the reform process with Serbia and Montenegro and with Macedonia).*

Parties: SLD 2007, SKDU 2006

4.2.3 Pushing for human rights in foreign policy

The party defines its foreign policy based on liberal values; more specifically, human rights are an integral part of foreign policy. This is evident in the case of states that are targeted in regards to transformation assistance as priority ones. In the case of V4 countries, this includes Belarus and the Western Balkan.

Examples:

We will promote the spread of democratic principles and the protection of human rights in Eastern European countries (Belarus and Moldova).

Parties: SDKU 2006

4.3 Western orientation

This is understood as a proof of belonging to certain world values' systems and to the commitment of further development. In this regard, the US are perceived as a guarantee of a Western values' system.

Examples:

The meaning of the USA for KDH does not lie only in economic and security cooperation. The USA is a country with which we share many common values. In the complex international security situation, we consider it necessary to take steps toward the removal of alienation between Europe and the United States.
We have to be a trustworthy partner even in the framework of NATO and other international organizations; we will continue our participation in various peacekeeping missions, proportionately and effectively.

Parties: SDKU 2006, KDH 2006, ANO 2013, ODS 2006, KDU 2006, PO 2011, PSL 2011, TOP 09 2013, ODS 2010, ODS 2013, ČSSD 2013, KDH 2012, KDU 2013, Smer 2012, Smer 2010, Smer 2006, Most 2010, KDU 2010, KDU 2006, SLD 2007, PSL 2007, Palikot 2011

4.4 Central European identity

The party shows interest in a specific region or country that should be supported a priori to other countries/regions. In the context of V4 countries, the perception of a shared CEE spirit is significant. In this case, the party stresses shared social development as well as the transformation experience.

Examples:

The Slovak Republic, in accordance with the intention of strategic partnerships promoting and enforcing the national interests of Slovakia, will continue to actively participate within the realms of the V4; the aim of Slovakia will be to strengthen regional cooperation also with the other new EU countries (Romania and Bulgaria) and together will promote common themes and interests within the European Union.
We will support the traditionally good cooperation with the Czech Republic, the development of good neighborly relations with all neighboring states, with the aim to increase the weight of the region on the international stage and with supranational organizations. We will support the development of cross-border cooperation of municipalities and regions in border areas.

Parties: Smer 2012, SDKU 2012, SaS 2012, OL 2012

4.5 Positive perception of Germany

Germany is perceived as an important economic and political partner in the EU. In addition to this, Germany is perceived as a model for particular reforms.

Parties: SLD 2011

4.6 Negative perception of the EU

The connotations of the party's references to the EU appeal to negative emotions like the fear of a threat to national sovereignty, traditional values, national economy etc. The emphasis is given to the EU as such, not specific policy fields.

Examples:

We do not want the transfer of power to Brussels. We will defend sovereignty in the area of tax and budgetary policy.

The developments in Europe in recent years, and particularly the euro crisis, made it clear that our realistic approach toward European integration is correct. We are aware that European integration brings the Czech Republic a number of advantages, but we need to approach it in such a manner that it doesn't proceed at the expense of some of its members. We do not wish to act irresponsibly by leaving the EU, but this isn't to say that we will blindly accept everything that comes from Brussels. We will measure every element of the European integration with Czech eyes and from the angle of Czech national interests. We want the EU as a space for economic freedom and not as a space for European bureaucracy. We want the Czech Republic to act as a proud and confident country in Europe. We will ensure that Czech representatives represent the Czech Republic in Brussels and not Brussels in the Czech Republic.

Parties: Úsvit 2013, SNS 2012, SaS 2012, PiS 2005, ODS 2013

4.7 Positive connotation of RU

Russia described as a strong and important partner in foreign policy; one that has to be respected and with whom relations have to be cultivated. In this case, supporting Russia as a state means representing certain values that should be followed.

Examples:

Reinforcing bilateral cooperation, with other partners in the international community, particularly with the Russian federation.

Parties: SNS 2006, Smer 2010, Smer 2012

4.8 Perceived foreign economic threat

Openness towards the world brings also some negative aspects — threats to the economy, inflows of immigrants, less control over borders. This perception takes in various policy fields such as agriculture, mineral resources, water management etc.

Examples:

Prevent the draining of the brains out of the Czech Republic and build a CZ scientific-technical centre.
Prevent excessive dependence of the Czech economy on foreign capital; broaden trade; promotion of food security and self-sufficiency by the state; restoration of stringent food quality standards.

Parties: ODS 2010, KDU 2010, PSL 2007, PiS 2005, Most 2012, Most 2010, KDH 2010, Smer 2010, Usvit 2013, ODS 2013, KDH 2010, ANO 2013, KSCM 2013, KDU 2010, KSCM 2010, SNS 2006, SNS 2010, SNS 2013

4.9 Stressing sovereignty

The national state and its sovereignty is understood as a value that should be cultivated and preserved against foreign influences as well as against those that do not respect the superiority of state sovereignty.

Examples:

KDU has an interest in preventing historical questions and traumas from burdening the development of Slovak-Hungarian relations. In the spirit of responsibility, KDH will also seek the symbolic reconciliation between Slovakia and Hungary. We will support dialogue at all levels – governmental and non-governmental. We will not accept interference in the sovereignty of the Slovak Republic, such as the creation of new institutional links between the Hungarian state and Slovak citizens of Hungarian nationality, as well as the adoption of extraterritorial legal norms in Hungary. KDH refuses the spread of extremism and revisionism from Hungary to Slovakia. We will support the initiative for parallel texts from common history, which are being prepared by a mixed commission of historians, to become an auxiliary part of the learning process in both countries.

Slovakia will be an integral part of the competition of the international community, with other global security threats, such as the proliferation of weapons of mass destruction, accumulation of conventional weapons or international terrorism. As a primary means of achieving the objective in the area of Common Security and Defense Policy (CSDP) of the EU, the Slovak Republic will look into building on it.

Parties: SNS 2012, Smer 2010, Smer 2006, KDH 2010, KDH 2012, SaS 2012

4.10 Pacifism

> The party rejects the state's membership in NATO and calls for the abolishment of an aggressive foreign policy. In addition, the party rejects military presence in any foreign country.

Examples:

Pause the Czech Republic's membership in the military-security structure of NATO and subsequently withdraw its membership.
Stop the participation of the Czech Republic and its army in foreign military missions carried out by the USA and NATO, which damage world peace, human rights and democracy.

Parties: KSČM 2013, KSČM 2010

4.11 Slavs positive

Slavs and Slavic nations are perceived as special compared to other nations and ethnicities. The party argues that Slavs share the same social features, which should be further cultivated. This means, for instance, developing special bilateral ties and cooperation.

Parties: SNS 2012

4.12 Negative attitudes towards neighbouring country

> The party shows negative attitudes in a specific region or country that should be supported a priori to other countries/regions. This is the case of states that are influenced by the presence of national minorities from neighbouring countries such as Slovakia versus Hungary.

220 IDENTITY FORMATION

Examples:

> *SNS will not be like other parties that conceal threats from expansion of cross-border policies and accept extraterritorial laws. SNS will not allow the taking of a section of the Slovak citizenry by Hungary. We protest against such provocative steps, interfering with the sovereign rights of Slovakia.*

Parties: SNS 2012, OL 2012, SNS 2010, KDH 2012

4.13 Western orientation negative

The party refuses state participation in the cultivation of Western values. The state should focus on national based values and traditions and pay less attention to the environment behind the border. Contradictorily, this position involves developing a more cooperative relationship with Russia.

Examples:

Demand for the abolition of NATO as a long-term goal and as the minimum target performance of CZ from its military structures.
The concept of security in the CZ and Europe, in a pan-European dimension and on the basis of global security.
Revision of the unacceptable practices of NATO from the year 1999, which includes "the right to preemptive strike" and to exert influence far beyond the borders of member countries, even without a mandate according to international law.

Parties KSCM 2013

4.14 Otherness as a threat

The party openly stresses the rejection of other cultures and influences that might be already present in the state. In addition to this, the party strictly rejects foreign influence. In this context, it can be understood as a policy against national minorities, as well as against immigrants.

Examples:

We will not accept the interference with the sovereignty of the Slovak Republic, with adopted extraterritorial norms in Hungary. We refuse the production of non-standard institutional and legal links between the Hungarian state and the Hungarian national citizens in Slovakia, as well as the spread of extremism and revisionism from Hungary onto Slovakia. We want to deal with the conflicting question of citizenship with a specific intergovernmental agreement between the Slovak Republic and Hungary, which would define the conditions for obtaining a dual citizenship.

Parties: KDH 2012, SNS 2012

4.15 Militarization

The national identity (state) should be defended with the use of military. The party strongly supports the development of an ethnically based identity. This identification is based on national values and rejects any external involvement.

Examples:

We cannot underestimate the ongoing threats to sovereignty and integrity of Slovakia from the side of its southern neighbor.

Parties: SNS 2012

13. Appendix C:

Groups of positive and negative categories

The Manifesto Project

Positive categories:	Negative categories:
101: Foreign Special Relationships: Positive	102: Foreign Special Relationships: Negative
107: Internationalism: Positive	109: Internationalism: Negative
108: European Community/Union: Positive	110: European Community/Union: Negative
602: National Way of Life: Negative	601: National Way of Life: Positive

The Grounded Theory

Positive categories:	Negative categories:
1. 1 Support of deeper integration	1. 4 Europe of nations
1. 2 Support of the EU but not deeper integration	1. 5 Against the EU, leaving possible
2. 1 Support of new emancipation movements, open society	2. 7 Support of national culture
2. 1. 1 Nationalism negative	2. 8 support of national identity building
2. 1 Pluralism	2. 9 Soil as proof of nation
2. 2 Individualism and freedom as a values	2. 11 Nation is threatened

2. 3 Human rights as a value

3. 1 Inclusiveness

3. 2 Protection of minorities

3. 3 Dialogue with minority

4. 1 Support of the EU

4. 2 Openness towards world

4. 2. 2 International solidarity

4. 2. 3 Pushing for human rights in foreign policy

4. 3 Western orientation

4. 5 Positive connotation of Germany

3. 4 Limited immigration

3. 5 Limited rights for minorities

3. 6 Against immigration

4. 6 Negative perception of EU

4. 8 Perceived foreign economic threat

4. 9 Stressing sovereignty

4. 11 Slavs positive

4. 12 Negative towards neighboring country

4. 13 West orientation negative

4. 14 Otherness as a threat

4. 15 Militarization

14. List of Tables

Table 1:	Overview of codes	64
Table 2:	Pearson correlation coefficients for the various methods of measuring the party policy positions	78
Table 3:	Pearson correlation coefficients for the political parties' emphasis on transnational cooperation and national identity and weighted number of occupied positions within the EU structures by its nominees	81
Table 4:	Overview of new parties' using national identity in general elections	84
Table 5:	Overview of national identity relevant issues	87
Table 6:	Overview of Czech parties covered and their election gains	90
Table 7:	Overview of parties' positions on selected issues	92
Table 8:	Overview of development of policy of national identity of ČSSD	98
Table 9:	Overview of development of policy of national identity of ODS	101
Table 10:	Overview of development of policy of national identity of KDU-ČSL	104
Table 11:	Overview of development of policy of national identity of KSČM	106
Table 12:	Overview of development of policy of national identity of TOP09	108
Table 13:	Overview of development of policy of national identity of ANO2011	109
Table 14:	Overview of development of policy of national identity of Úsvit	111
Table 15:	Overview of development of policy of national identity of SZ	112
Table 16:	Overview of development of policy of national identity of VV	114
Table 17:	Overview of Czech parties covered and their election gains	116
Table 18:	Overview of issues in the election manifestos	119
Table 19:	Parties' positions on national identity relevant issues (2014)	122
Table 20:	Overview of development of policy of national identity of PO	125
Table 21:	Overview of development of policy of national identity of PiS	127
Table 22:	Overview of development of policy of national identity of SLD	130
Table 23:	Overview of development of policy of national identity of PSL	132
Table 24:	Overview of development of policy of national identity of LPR	134
Table 25:	Overview of development of policy of national identity of SRP	136
Table 26:	Overview of development of policy of national identity of TR	138

Table 27: Overview of political parties and their support 139
Table 28: Overview of parties' positions on selected issues 141
Table 29: Overview of development of policy of national
identity of Směr-SD 146
Table 30: Overview of development of policy of national
identity of KDH 149
Table 31: Overview of development of policy of national
identity SDKÚ-DS 152
Table 32: Overview of development of policy of national
identity of SaS 154
Table 33: Overview of development of policy of national
identity of Most-Híd 156
Table 34: Overview of development of policy of national identity OL 158
Table 35: Overview of development of policy of national identity of SNS .. 160
Table 36: Overview of development of policy of national
identity of HZDS 163
Table 37: Overview of parties covered by research and
number of parties reaching over 3 % public support 166
Table 38: Results of analysis 168
Table 39: Results of analysis 174
Table 40: Results of analysis 180

15. List of Abbreviations

ANO2011	Action of Dissatisfied Citizens 2011 (Akce nespokojených občanů 2011)
AWS	Solidarity Electoral Action
CEE	Central East Europe
ČSSD	Czech Social Democratic Party (Česká strana sociálně demokratická)
DS/DSSS	(Dělnická strana sociální spravedlnosti)
ECB	European Central Bank
ECOSOC	European Economic and Social Committee
EPP	European Peoples's Party
ERG	European Reforminst Group
EU	European Union
KDH	Christian-Democratic Movement (Krestansko-demokraticke hnuti)
KDU-ČSL	Christian and Democratic Union-Czechoslovak People´s Party (Křesťanská a demokratická unie-Československá strana lidová)
KNP	Congress of New Right (Kongres Nowej Prawycy)
KSČM	Communist party of Bohemia and Moravia (Komunistická strana Čech a Moravy)
LPR	The League of Polish Families (Liga Polskich Rodzin)
ĽS-HZDS	(Ľudová strana-Hnutie za demokratické Slovensko)
MP	Member of Parliament
NATO	North Atlantic Treaty Organisation
ODS	Civic Democratic Party (Občanská demokratická strana)
OĽaNO	Ordinary People (Obyčajní ľudia)
PiS	Law and Justice (Prawo i Sprawiedliwość)
PO	Civic Platform (Platforma Obywatelska)
PSL	Polish People's Party (Polske Stronictwo Ludowe)
SaS	Freedom and Solidarity (Sloboda a Solidarita)

SDKÚ-DS	Slovak Democratic and Christian Union-Democratic Party (Slovenská demokratická a kresťanská únia-Demokratická strana)
SdRP	Social Democracy of the Polish Republic (Socjaldemokracja Rzeczypospolitej Polskiej)
SLD	Alliance of the Democratic Left (Sojusz Lewicy Demokratycznej)
Smer-SD	Direction-Social democracy (Smer-Sociálna demokracia)
SMK	Party of Hungarian Coalition (Strana Maďarské Koalice)
SNS	Slovak National Party (Slovenská národná strana)
SRP	Self-defense of Polish Republic (Samoobrona Rzeczpospolitej Polskiej)
SZ	Greens (Strana zelených)
TOP09	Tradition Responsibility Prosperity 09 (Tradice, Odpovědnost, Prosperita 09)
TR	Your Movement (Twoj Ruch)
UP	Labor Union (Unia Pracy)
UW	Freedom Union (Unia Wolnosci)
Úsvit	Tomio Okamura's Dawn of Direct Democracy (Hnutí úsvit přímé demokracie Tomia Okamury)
UK	United Kingdom
VPN	Society against Violence (Verejnosť proti násiliu)
VV	Public Affairs (Věci veřejné)
ZLN	United People's Party (Zjednoczono Stronnictwo Ludowe)

16. References

Ágh, A. 2016. *The Decline of Democracy in East-Central Europe*. Problems of Post-Communism, 7(2), pp. 4–33. doi: 10.1080/10758216.2015.1113383.

Almeida, D. 2012. *The Impact of European Integration on Political Parties: Beyond the Permissive Consensus*. London: Routledge.

Alonso, S., Volkens, A. and Gómez, B. 2012. *Content-analyzing Political texts: A Quantitative Approach*. Madrid: Centro de Investigaciones Sociológicas.

Anderson, B.O.R. 2006. *Imagined Communities: Reflections on the Origin and Spread of Nationalism*. New York: Verso Books.

Antikomplex. 2007. *Zmizelé Sudety*. Praha: Antikomplex

Bakker, R., de Vries, C., Edwards, E., Hooghe, L., Jolly, S., Marks, G., Polk, J., Rovny, J., Steenbergen, M. and Vachudova, M.A. 2012. "Measuring Party Positions in Europe: The Chapel Hill Expert Survey Trend file, 1999-2010." *Party Politics*, 21(1): pp. 1-15. doi: 10.1177/1354068812462931.

Bandelj, N., Finley, K. and Radu, B. (2015) "Democracy in Central and Eastern Europe: Test of Early Impact." *East European Politics*, 31(2): pp. 129–148. doi: 10.1080/21599165.2015.1007959.

Baran, M. 2016. *We Made Him Dangerous*. Available at http://www.cee identity.eu/news/we-made-him, (Accessed: November 16, 2016).

Bartolini, S. 2005. *Restructuring Europe: Centre formation, System Building, and Political Structuring Between the Nation State and the European Union*. Oxford: Oxford University Press.

Beck, U. 2007. *Vynalézání politiky: K teorii reflexivní modernizace*, Praha: Sociologické nakladatelství.

Bélanger, É. and Meguid, B., M. (2008) "Issue Salience, Issue Ownership, and Issue-Based Vote Choice." *Electoral Studies* 27(3): pp. 477–491a doi: 10.1016/j.electstud.2008.01.001.

Bell, D., A. 2003. *The Cult of the Nation in France: Inventing Nationalism, 1680 - 1800*. 2nd edn. Cambridge: Cambridge University Press.

Benoit, K. and Laver, M. (2006) *Party Policy in Modern Democracies*. London: Routledge.

Benoit, K. and Laver, M. 2012. "The Dimensionality of Political Space: Epistemological and Methodological Considerations." *European Union Politics* 13(2): pp. 194–218. doi: 10.1177/1465116511434618.

Benoit, K. and Laver, M. 2007. "Estimating Party Policy Positions: Comparing Expert Surveys and Hand-Coded Content Analysis." *Electoral Studies* 26 (1): pp. 90-107.

Bilčík, V. and Buzalka, J. 2012. *Slovakia In: Life in Post-communist Eastern Europe after EU membership: Happy Ever After?*, edited by Beachain, O., D., Sheridan, V. and Stan, S. London: Routledge, pp. 95-115.

Birch, S. 2007. *Parliamentary Elections and Party Landscape in the Visegrád Group Countries*, edited by Hloušek, V., and Chytilek, R., Brno: Centrum pro stadium demokracie a kultury.

Bochsler, D. 2010. *Territory and Electoral Rules in Post-Communist Democracies*. Hampshire: Palgrave Macmillan.

Bornischier, S. 2009. *Cleavage Politics in Old and New Democracies*, University of Zurich. Avaliable at https://www.ethz.ch/content/dam/ethz/special-interest/gess/cis/cis-dam/CIS_DAM_2015/WorkingPapers/Living_R eviews_Democracy/Bornschier.pdf, (Accessed November 16, 2016).

Börzel, T. and Risse, T. 2003. *Conceptualizing the Domestic Impact of Europe*, in *The Politics of Europeanization*, edited by Featherstone K, and Radaelli C., Oxford: Oxford University Press, pp. 55-78.

Börzel, T. and Risse, T. 2007. *Europeanization: The Domestic Impact of EU Politics*, in *Handbook of European Union Politics*, edited by Joergensen, K., E., Pollack, M. A., and Rosamond, B., London: Sage, pp. 483-504.

Börzel, T., A. 2005. *Mind the Gap: European Integration between Level and Scope*, Journal of European Public Policy, 12(2), pp. 1-20.

Börzel, T., A. 2009. *After Accession: Escaping the Low Capacity Trap*, in *Coping with Accession to the European Union: New modes of environmental governance*, edited by Börzel, T. A. Basingstoke: Palgrave Macmillan, pp. 192-210.

Börzel, T., A. 2010. *The Transformative Power of Europe Reloaded: The Limits of External Europeanization*, No. 11, Kolleg-Forschergruppe (KFG), Freie Universität Berlin.

Börzel, T., A. 2011. *Comparative Regionalism - A New Research Agenda*, No. 15, Kolleg-Forschergruppe (KFG), Freie Universität Berlin.

Braun, M. 2008. *Modernisation Unchallenged: The Czech Discourse on European Unity*. Praha: Institute of International Relations.

Bechhofer, F. and McCrone, D. 2010. *Choosing National Identity*, Sociological Research Online, 15 (3) 3. Available at: http://www.soc resonline.org.uk/15/3/3.html (Accessed: 15 November 2016).

Breuilly, J. 1993. *Nationalism and the State*. 2nd edn. Chicago: University of Chicago Press.

Brubaker, R. 1996. *Nationalism Reframed: Nationhood and the National Question Reframed in the New Europe*. Cambridge: Cambridge University Press.

Budge, I., Klingemann, H.-D., Volkens, A., Bara, J. and Tanenbaum, E. (2001) *Mapping Policy Preferences: Estimates for Parties, Electors, and Governments, 1945-1998*. Oxford: Oxford University Press.

Canovan, M. 1999. "Trust the People! Populism and the Two Faces of Democracy." *Political Studies* 47(1): pp. 2–16. doi: 10.1111/1467-9248.00184.

Canovan, M. 2002. "The People, the Masses, and the Mobilization of Power: The Paradox of Hannah Arendt's "Populism"." *Social Research* 69(2): pp. 403–422. doi: 10.2307/40971555.

Carter, E. and Poguntke, T. 2010. "How European Integration Changes National Parties: Evidence from a 15-Country Study." *West European Politics* 33(2): pp. 297–324. doi: 10.1080/01402380903538930.

Castells, M. 2010. *The Rise of the Network Society: With a New Preface*. London: Wiley-Blackwell.

ceeidentity.eu. 2014. *The Czech Republic*, EUROPEUM. Available at: http://www.ceeidentity.eu/sites/default/files/downloads/cs_-_cs.pdf (Accessed: 15 November 2016).

ceeidentity.eu. 2016a. *Czech Social Democratic Party*, EUROPEUM. Available at: http://ceeidentity.eu/database/manifestoescoun/czech-social (Accessed: 15 November 2016).

ceeidentity.eu. 2016b. *Civic Democratic Party*, EUROPEUM. Available at: http://ceeidentity.eu/database/manifestoescoun/civic (Accessed: 15 November 2016).

ceeidentity.eu. 2016c. *Communist Party of Bohemia and Moravia*, EUROPEUM. Available at: http://www.ceeidentity.eu/database/manifestoescoun/communist-party (Accessed: 15 November 2016).

ceeidentity.eu. 2016d. *Tradition Responsibility Prosperity 09*, EUROPEUM. Available at: http://ceeidentity.eu/database/manifestoescoun/tradition (Accessed: 15 November 2016).

ceeidentity.eu. 2016e. *Action of Dissatisfied Citizens 2011*, EUROPEUM. Available at: http://ceeidentity.eu/database/manifestoescoun/action (Accessed: 15 November 2016).

ceeidentity.eu. 2016f. *Public Affairs*, EUROPEUM. Available at: http://ceeidentity.eu/database/manifestoescoun/public-affairs (Accessed: 15 November 2016).

ceeidentity.eu. 2016h. *Interview with Prof. Jan Rydel about role of state in history education, politicizing of national mythology, and forecast for Polish general election*, EUROPEUM. Available at: http://www.ceeiden tity.eu/news/interview-prof (Accessed: 15 November 2016).

ceeidentity.eu. 2016k. *Fico and the Question of Slovak National Identity*, EUROPEUM. Available at: http://www.ceeidentity.eu/news/ficoand, (Accessed: 15 November 2016).

ceeidentity.eu. 2016l. *Christian-Democratic Movement*, EUROPEUM. Available at: http://ceeidentity.eu/database/manifestoescoun/christian-0 (Accessed: 15 November 2016).

ceeidentity.eu. 2016o. *Freedom and Solidarity*, EUROPEUM. Available at: http://ceeidentity.eu/database/manifestoescoun/freedom-and (Accessed: 15 November 2016).

ceeidentity.eu. 2016p. *Most – Híd*, EUROPEUM. Available at: http://cee identity.eu/database/manifestoescoun/most-h-d-bridge (Accessed: 15 November 2016).

ceeidentity.eu. 2016q. *Ordinary People*, EUROPEUM. Available at: http://ceeidentity.eu/database/manifestoescoun/ordinary-people (Accessed: 15 November 2016).

ceskatelevize.cz. 2011. *Slovensko dotáhlo euroval k vítěznému konci*, Česká Televize.Available at: http://www.ceskatelevize.cz/ct24/ekonomi ka/1238240-slovensko-dotahlo-euroval-k-viteznemu-konci, (Accessed: 15 November 2016).

Cibulka, F. 2012. '"The Czech Republic." In *Life in Post-CommunistEastern Europe after EU membership: Happy Ever After?* Beachain, O., D., Sheridan, V. and Stan, S., London: Routledge, pp. 31-54.

Cianciara, A. 2015. *European pPlicy of Law and Justice Government: Change or Continuity?*, CEU Budapest. Avaliable at https://cens.ceu.edu/artic le/2016-01-07/effects-elections-cee-countries-eu-governance-papersconference (Accessed: 15 November 2016).

Connor, W. 1978. *A Nation is a Nation, is a State, is an Ethnic Group is a …*, Ethnic and Racial Studies, 1(4), pp. 377–400. doi: 10.1080/01419870.1978.9993240.

Černoch, F., Husák, J., Schütz, O. and Vít, M. (2011) *Political Parties and Nationalism in Visegrad Countries*. Brno: Masarykova univerzita, Mezinárodní politologický ústav.

Dančák, B. 2002. "Republika Polsko." In *Politické strany ve střední a východní Evropě: Ideově-politický profil, pozice a role politických stran v postkomunistických zemích*, edited by Fiala, P., Holzer, J., Strmiska, M. Brno: Masarykova univerzita.

Decker, F. 2007. *Populismus: Gefahr für die Demokratie oder nützliches Korrektiv?*, Bonn: Bundeszetrale für Politische Bildung.

REFERENCES 233

de Vries, C., E. 2007. *Sleeping giant: Fact or Fairytale? How European Integration Affects National Elections*, European Union Politics, 8(3), pp. 363-385. doi: 10.1177/1465116507079546.

Deegan-Krause, K. 2010. *2010 Slovak Parliamentary Elections: Post-Election Report*, The Monkey Cage. Available at: http://themonkeycage.org/2010/07/2010_slovak_parliamentary_elec/(Accessed: 15 November 2016).

Deegan-Krause, K. and Haughton, T. 2014. *Hurricane Season: Systems of instability in Central and East European Party Politics*, APSA, Annual Meeting Paper.Available at: https://ssrn.com/abstract=2452275 (Accessed: 15 November 2016).

Deutsch, K. W. 1966. *The Nerves of Government: Models of Political Communication and Control*. New York: The Free Press.

Deutsch, K. W. 1954. *Political Community at theInternationalLevel: Problems of Definition and Measurement*. New York: Doubleday.

Diez, T. 2004 .*Europe's Others and the Return of Geopolitics*, Cambridge Review of International Affairs, 17(2), pp. 319-335. doi: 10.1080/0955757042000245924.

Eibl, O. 2010. *Issues in Czech politics*. Available at: http://is.muni.cz/th/65581/fss_d/ (Accessed: 15 November 2016).

Eibl, O. 2013. *České prezidentské volby v roce 2013*, in Šedo, J., Brno (ed.): Centrum pro studium demokracie a kultury.

Eriksen, T. H. 2010. *Ethnicity and Nationalism: Anthropological Perspectives*. 3rd edn. New York: Pluto press.

EUROPEUM Institute for European Policy. 2014. *Czech and Polish Political Parties and National Identity*. Praha.

Evans, G. and Whitefield, S. 1993. "Identifying the Bases of Party Competition in Eastern Europe." *British Journal of Political Science* 23(4): pp. 521-548. doi: 10.2307/194215.

Flora, P., ed. 1999. *State Formation, Nation-Building, and Mass Politics in Europe: The Theory of Stein Rokkan: Based on His Collected Works*, Oxford: Oxford University Press.

Freyburg, T. and Richter, S. 2010. "National Identity Matters: The Limited Impact of EU Political Conditionality in the Western Balkan.", *Journal of European Public Policy* 17(2): pp. 263-281. doi: 10.1080/13501760903561450.

Fuchs, D 1999. *Die demokratische Gemeinschaft in den USA und in Deutschland*. Berlin: SSG Sozialwissenschaften. Available at: http://www.ssoar.info/ssoar/handle/document/12523 (Accessed: 15 November 2016).

Fuchs, D. and Klingemann, H.-D., ed. 2011. *Cultural Diversity, European Identity and the Legitimacy of the EU*. Cheltenham: Edward Elgar Publishing.

Galaxie, D. and Hubé, N. 2013. "On National and Ideological Background of Elites' Attitudes toward European Institutions." In *A Political Sociology of Transnational Europe*, edited by Kauppi, N. Colchester: Columbia University Press, pp. 165-191.

Gellner, E. 2009. *Nations and Nationalism*. United States: Cornell University Press.

Gjuričová, A., Kopeček, M., Roubal, P., Suk, J., Zahradníček, T. 2011. *Rozděleni minulostí. Vytváření politických identit v České republice po roce 1989*. Praha: Ústav pro soudobé dějiny AV ČR, v. v. i.

Glaser, B., G. 2002. *Constructivist Grounded Theory*, Forum Qualitative Sozialforschung / Forum: Qualitative Social Research, 3(3), avaliable at http://www.qualitative-research.net/index.php/fqs/article/view/825/1792 (Accesed November 15 2016).

Glaser, B., G. 2002. "Conceptualization: On Theory and Theorizing Using Grounded Theory." *International Journal of Qualitative Methods* 1(2). Avaliable at https://sites.ualberta.ca/~iiqm/backissues/1_2Final/pdf/glaser.pdf (Accessed November 15 2016).

Glaser, B., G. and Strauss, A., L. 1967. *The Discovery of Grounded Theory: Strategies for Qualitative Research*. New York: Chicago, Aldine Pub. Co.

Gressel, G. 2015. *Understanding Eastern European Attitudes on Refugees*, European Council on Foreign Relations. Available at http://www.ecfr.eu/article/commentary_understanding_eastern_european_attitudes_on_refugees4019 (Accessed 15 November, 2016).

Grew, R. 2003. *Konstrukce národní identity*, In *Pohledy na národ a nacionalismus*, edited by Hroch, M., Praha: Sociologické nakladatelství, pp. 203-216.

Guibernau, M. 2000. "Nationalism and Intellectuals in Nations without States: The Catalan Case." *Political Studies* 48(5): pp. 989-1005. doi: 10.1111/1467-9248.00291.

Guzzini, S. 2000. "A Reconstruction of Constructivism in International Relations." *European Journal of International Relations* 6(2): pp. 147-182. doi: 10.1177/1354066100006002001.

Gyarfášová, O. 2011. "Slovenské parlamentné voľby 2010: nacionálna agenda na ústupe?" *Středoevropské politické studie*, 13(1), pp. 65-84.

Gynnild, A. and Martin, V., B. , eds., 2011. *Grounded Theory: The Philosophy, Method, and Work of Barney Glaser*. Boca Raton: Universal Publishers.

References

Hanley, D. 2007. *Beyond the Nation State: Parties in the Era of European Integration*. Basingstoke: Palgrave Macmillan.

Hanley, S. N. 2015. Review Article: 'We All Fall Down: The Prospects for Established Parties in Europe and Beyond.' *Government and Opposition*, 50(2): pp. 300-323.

Hanley, S., Szczerbiak, A., Haughton, T., and Fowler, B. 2008. "Sticking together: explaining comparative centre-right party success in post-communist Central and Eastern Europe" *Party Politics*, 14 (4): pp. 407-434.

Hanley, S. N. 2011. *The New Right In The New Europe: Czech Transformation and Right-Wing Politics, 1989-2006*. London: Taylor & Francis.

Hanley, S. N. and Sikk, A. 2013. "Economy, Corruption or Promiscuous Voters? Explaining the Success of Anti-Establishment Reform Parties in Eastern Europe." COMPASSS WP Series 2013-75. Available at: http://www.compasss.org/wpseries/HanleySikk2013.pdf (Accessed: 15 November 2016).

Haughton, T. 2004. "Explaining the Limited Success of the Communist-Successor Left in Slovakia: The Case of the Party of the Democratic Left (SDL)." *Party Politics* 10(2): pp. 177-191. doi: 10.1177/1354068804040499.

Haughton, T. 2009. "For Business, for Pleasure or for Necessity: The Czech Republic's Choices for Europe." *Europe-Asia Studies* 61: pp. 1371-1392.

Haughton, T. 2010. "Zranitelnost, povstupní kocovina a role předsednictví: formování národních preferencí nových členských států EU." *Mezinárodní vztahy* 45(4): pp. 11-28.

Haughton, T. 2013. "Battlefields, Ammunition and Uniforms: the {ast and Politics in Post-Communist Central and Eastern Europe." *Comparative European Politics* 11 (2): pp. 249-260.

Haughton, T., ed., 2011. *Party Politics in Central and Eastern Europe: Does EU Membership Matter?* London: Routledge.

Haughton, T. and Rybář, M. 2008. "A Change of Direction: the 2006 Parliamentary Elections and the Dynamics of Party Politics in Slovakia." *Journal of Communist Studies and Transition Politics* 24 (2): pp. 232-255.

Haughton, T. and Rybář, M. 2009. "A Tool in the Toolbox: Assessing the Impact of EU Membership on Party Politics in Slovakia", *Journal of Communist Studies and Transition Politics* 25(4): pp. 540-563. doi: 10.1080/13523270903310928.

Havlík, V. 2008. „Jak je měřit? Přístupy a metody analýzy postojů politických stran k evropské integraci." *Středoevropské politické studie* 10 (4): pp. 365-387.

Havlík, V. 2014. "The 2013 Parliamentary Election in the Czech Republic." *European Electoral Studies*. Avaliable at: http://www.volebnistudia.cz/wp-content/uploads/EVS_2014_1-3.pdf (Accessed: 15 November 2016).

Havlík, V. et. al. 2014. *Volby do Poslanecké sněmovny 2013*, Brno: Munipress.

Havlík, V. and Voda, P. 2014. *Lost stability? Re-Alignment of party politics and the rise of new political parties in the Czech Republic*. In APSA Annual Meeting.

Hearl, D., ed., 1987. *Ideology, strategy and party change: A spatial analysis of post-war electoral programmes in nineteen democracies*, Cambridge: Cambridge University Press.

Hearn, J., S. 2006. *Rethinking Nationalism: A Criticallintroduction*. Basingstoke: Palgrave Macmillan.

Henderson, K. 2004. "EU Accession and the New Slovak Consensus." *West European Politics* 27 (4): pp. 652-670.

Hloušek, V. 2005. "Česko." In *Politické strany moderní Evropy. Analýza stranicko-politických system*. Strmiska, M.; Hloušek, V., Kopeček, L., Chytilek, R. Praha: Portál, pp. 438 – 452.

Hloušek, V. and Chytilek, R. 2007. *Parliamentary Elections and Party Landscape in the Visegrád group countries*. Brno: Centrum pro studium demokracie a kultury.

Hloušek, V. and Kopeček, L. 2008. "Cleavages in Contemporary Czech and Slovak Politics: Between Persistence and Change."*East European Politics and Societies* 22(3): pp. 518-552.

Hloušek, V., Kopeček, L. 2010. *Politické strany. Původ, ideologie a transformace politic-kých stran v západní a střední Evropě*. Praha: Grada Publishing.

Hloušek, V. and Procházková, I. 2013. "Významnost tématu evropské integrace: obsahová analýza programů českých stran pro parlamentní volby 2006 a 2010." *European Electoral Studies* 8(2): pp. 113–132.

Hloušek, V. and Pšeja, P. 2009. "Europeanization of Political Parties and the Party System in the Czech Republic." In *Party Politics in Central and Eastern Europe. Does EU membership Matter?*, edited by Haughton, T. London: Routledge, pp. 101-128.

Hloušek, V. and Šipulová, K. 2012. *Rozdielne cesty tranzitívnej spravodlivosti – prípady Českej republiky*, Středoevropské politické studie, 14(1), pp. 55-89.

Hobsbawn, E. 1996. "Identity Politics and the Left." New Left Review, pp. 38-47.

Hooghe, L., Marks, G. and Wilson, C. J. 2002. "Does Left/Right Structure Party Positions on European integration?" *Comparative Political Studies* 35(8): pp. 965–989. doi: 10.1177/001041402236310.

Hroch, M., ed., 2003. *Pohledy na národ a nacionalismus: Čítanka textů*. Praha: Sociologické nakladatelství (SLON).

Hroch, M. 2009. *Národy nejsou dílem náhody: Příčiny a předpoklady utváření moderních evropských národů*. Praha: Sociologické nakladatelství (SLON).

Checkel, J. T. 2007. "Constructivism and EU Politics." In *The Sage Handbook of European Union Politics*, edited by Jorgensen, K. E., Pollack, M., and Rosamond, B. J. London: Sage Publications Ltd, pp. 57–76.

Checkel, J. T., ed., 2007. *International Institutions and Socialization in Europe: An International Organization Reader*. Cambridge: Cambridge University Press.

Chudžíková, A. 2014. *Case Study Slovakia*, National Identity in CEE Countries. Available at: http://www.ceeidentity.eu/sites/default/files/downloads/cs_-_sk.pdf (Accessed: 15 November 2016).

Idnes.cz. 2010. *Fico odhalil v Komárně sousoší věrozvěstů. Fuj! Křičeli na něj místní*. Available at: http://zpravy.idnes.cz/fico-odhalil-v-komarne-sousosi-verozvestu-fuj-kriceli-na-nej-mistni-115-/zahranicni.aspx?c=A100704_200046_zahranicni_btw (Accessed: 16 November 2016).

Idnes.cz. 2013. *Pusťte nás na ně, skandoval v Budějovicích dav. Marně*. Available at: http://zpravy.idnes.cz/druha-demonstrace-proti-romum-v-ceskych-budejovicich-pd2-/domaci.aspx?c=A130706_102941_budejovice-zpravy_kol (Accessed: 16 November 2016).

Ihned.cz. 2014. *Neúspěšný politik Paroubek. Sponzoři ale LEV 21 milují, poslali 43 milionů*. Available at: http://archiv.ihned.cz/c1-63243590-neuspesny-politik-paroubek-sponzori-ale-lev-21-miluji-poslali-43-milionu (Accessed: 16 November 2016).

Ihned.cz. 2014. *Tápající ODS rozhoduje o budoucnosti. Krize strany vyjádřená v 5 grafech*. Available at: http://domaci.ihned.cz/c1-61574770-krize-ods-v-peti-grafech (Accessed: 16 November 2016).

Inglehart, R., F. 1989. *Culture Shift in Advanced Industrial Society*. San Francisco: Princeton University Press.

Inglehart, R., F. 2007. "Mapping Global Values". In *Measuring and Mapping Cultures: 25 years of Comparative Value Surveys*, edited by Yilmaz, E., Pettersson, T. Leiden: Brill Academic Publishers, pp. 11-32.

Interview with Boguslav Sonik, September 2014.

Interview with Ivan Gabal, September 2015.

Jarausch K., H. and Lindenberger T., eds., 2007. *Conflicted Memories. Europeanizing Contemporary Histories*. Berghahn Books.

jeseniky.ceeidenetity.eu 2016. *Politics of Exclusion in the Czech Regional Politics*. Available at http://jeseniky.ceeidentity.eu/project-overview (Accessed: 16 November 2016).

Jörissen, B. and Zirfas, J. , ed.s, 2010, *Schlüsselwerke der Identitätsforschung*. Wiesbaden: VS Verlag für Sozialwissenschaften/GWV Fachverlage GmbH, Wiesbaden.

Kasprowicz, D. 2014. *Filling in the Niche: The Populist Radical Right and the Concept of Solidarity*. Available at: http://www.eurozine.com/articles/2014-02-14-kasprowicz-en.html (Accessed: 16 November 2016).

Kasprowicz, D. 2016. *Introduction into Polish Politics*. Pedagogical University Krakow (*manuscript*).

Katzenstein, P. 1996. "Introduction: Alternative Perspectives on National Security." In *The Culture of National Security*. edited by Katzenstein, P. New York. Columbia University Press, pp. 1-32.

Kauppi, N. 2013. *A Political Sociology of Transnational Europe*. Colchester, United Kingdom: Columbia University Press.

Kelle, U. 2005. "Emergence vs. Forcing of Empirical Data? A Crucial Problem of "Grounded Theory" Reconsidered." *Forum Qualitative Social Research* 6(2).

Kitschelt, H. 1992. "The Formation of Party Systems in East Central Europe." *Politics Society* 20(1): pp. 7–50. doi: 10.1177/0032329292020001003.

Klíma, M. 2015. *Od totality k defektní demokracii: Privatizace a kolonizace politických stran netransparentním byznysem*, Praha: Sociologické nakladatelství (SLON).

Klingemann, H. D., Volkens, A., Bara, J., Budge, I. And Macdonald, M., eds., 2006. *Mapping Policy Preferences II: Estimates for Parties, Electors and Governments in Central and Eastern Europe, European Union and OECD 1990-2003*. Oxford: Oxford University Press.

Klingemann, H. D., Hofferbert, R. I. and Budge, I. 1994. *Parties, Policies, and Democracy*. Boulder, CO: Westview Press.

Klingemann, H. D., Fuchs, D. and Zielonka, J., eds., 2006. *Democracy and Political Culture in Eastern Europe*. London: Routledge.

Klingemann, H. D., 2014. "Dissatisfied Democrats: Democratic Maturation in Old and New Democracies." In *The Civic Culture Transformed: From Allegiant to Assertive Citizens*, edited by Russell J. D., Welzel, C. Cambridge: Cambridge University Press.

Kluknavská, A., and Zagibová, L. 2013. "Neprispôsobiví Rómovia a slušná väčšina? Spravodajský diskurz po násilných udalostiach na severe Českej republiky 2011." *Středoevropské politické studie* 15(4): 300–323.

Knill, Ch. 2001. *The Europeanisation of National Administrations: Patterns of Institutional Change and Persistence*. Cambridge: Cambridge University Press.

Kocúr, M. and Mesežnikov, G. 2015. *Extremism vs. Democracy in Central Europe*. Bratislava: Inštitut pre verejné otázky.

König, T., Marbach, M. and Osnabrugge, M. 2013. "Estimating Party Positions across Countries and Time-A Dynamic Latent Variable Model for Manifesto Data". Political Analysis, 21(4): pp. 1–24. doi: 10.1093/pan/mpt003.

Kopecký, J. 2014. *Odkaz na reformní komunismus v nové zahraniční politice dráždí ODS*. Available at: https://zpravy.idnes.cz/ods-vadi-odkaz-na-reformni-komunismus-v-nove-zahranicni-politice-ph7-/domaci.a spx?c=A141209_134702_domaci_kop (Accessed: 15 November 2016).

Kopecký, P. 2006. "The Rise of the Power Monopoly: Political Parties in the Czech Republic." In *Post-Communist EU Member States. Parties and Party Systems*, edited by Jungerstam-Mulders, S. Aldershot: Ashgate.

Kopeček, L. 2005. "Slovensko." In *Politické strany moderní Evropy. Analýza stranicko-politických systémů*, Strmiska, M.; Hloušek, V.; Kopeček, L.; Chytilek, R., Praha: Portál, pp. 438 – 479.

Kopeček, L. 2012. *Fenomén Václav Klaus. Politická biografie*. Brno: Barrister & Principal.

Koremenos, B., Lipson, C. and Snidal, D. 2001."The Rational Design of International Institutions." *International Organization* 55(4): pp. 761–799. doi: 10.1162/002081801317193592.

Kriesi, H. 2006. *Globalization and the transformation of the national political space: six European countries compared*, European Journal of Political Research 45, pp. 921-957

Kriesi, H. 2006. *West European Politics in the Age of Globalization*, Cambridge University Press.

Krastev, I., Leonard, M. 2015. :The New European Disorder." *European Council on Foreign Relations*. Avaliable at http://www.ecfr.eu/publications/summary/the_new_european_disorder322 (Accesed: November 15 2016).

Krastev, I. 2016. "What's Wrong with East-Central Europe? Liberalism's Failure to Deliver." *Journal of Democracy* 27(01): pp. 35–39.

Krouwel, A. P. M. 2004. *Partisan States. Legal Regulation of Political Parties in France, Germany, The Netherlands and the United Kingdom.* Nijmegen: Ars Aequi Libri/Wolf Legal Publishers.

Kubicek, P. J. 2003. *The European Union & Democratization: Reluctant states.* London: Routledge.

Kupka, P., Laryš, M. and Smolík, J. 2009. *Krajní pravice ve vybraných zemích střední a východní Evropy: Slovensko, Polsko, Ukrajina, Bělorusko, Rusko.* Brno: Masarykova univerzita.

Ladrech, R. 2012. "Understanding Causality and Change in Party Politics." In *Research Design in European Studies*, edited by Exadyctilos, T. and Radaelli, C. London: Palgrave MacMillan, pp. 178–194.

Lasheras, F. .2016. *Return to Instability: How Migration And Great Power Politics Threaten the Western Balkans*, European Council on Foreign Relations. Available at http://www.ecfr.eu/page/-/ECFR_163_RETURN_TO_INSTABILITY.pdf (Accessed: 15 November 2016).

Laver, M. and Garry, J. 2000. "Estimating Policy Positions from Political Texts."*American Journal of Political Science* 44(3): pp. 619–634. doi: 10.2307/2669268.

Laver, M., Benoit, K. and Garry, J. 2003. "Extracting Policy Positions from Political Texts Using Words as Data." *American Political Science Review* 97(02), pp. 311–331. doi: 10.1017/s0003055403000698.

Lewis, P. 2000. *Political Parties in Post-Communist Eastern Europe.* London: Routledge.

Lochocki, T. 2012. „Immigrationsfragen: Sprungbrett rechtspopulistischer Parteien." *Aus Politik und Zeitgeschichte*, 5-6. Available at: http://www.bpb.de/apuz/75858/immigrationsfragen-sprungbrett-rechtspopulistischer-parteien?p=all (Accessed: 15 November 2016).

Mair, P. 2000. "The Limited Impact of Europe on National Party Systems." *West European Politics* 23(4): 27-51. DOI: 10.1080/01402380008425399

Mansfeldová, Z., ed., 2006. *Participace a zájmové organizace v České republice*, Praha: Sociologické nakladatelství (SLON).

Mareš, M. 2000. *Problematika menšin jako profilové téma pravicového extremismu v České republice*, Středoevropské politické studie, 2(3). Availabl at: https://journals.muni.cz/cepsr/article/view/3826 (Accessed: 15 November 2016).

March, J., G. and Olsen, J., P. 1998. "The Institutional Dynamics of International Political Orders." *International Organization* 52(4): pp. 943–969. doi: 10.1162/002081898550699.

Mau, S. and Mewes, J. 2012. "Horizontal Europeanisation in Contextual Perspective." *European Societies* 14(1): pp. 7-34. doi: 10.1080/14616696.2011.638083.

Maull, H., W. 1990. "Germany and Japan: The New Civilian Powers". *Foreign Affairs* 69(5): pp. 91-106. doi: 10.2307/20044603.

McCrone, D. and Bechhofer, F., ed., 2009. *National Identity, Nationalism and Constitutional Change*. London: Palgrave Macmillan.

McDonald, M., and Mendés, S. 2001. "The Policy Space of Party Manifestos." In *Estimating the Policy Position of Political Actors*, edited by Michael Laver. London: Routledge, pp. 90-114.

McDonald, M. D. and Budge, I. 2005. *Elections, Parties, Democracy: Conferring the Median Mandate*. Oxford: Oxford University Press.

McLaren, L. 2005. *Explaining Mass-Level Euroskepticism: Identity, Interests, and Institutional Distrust*, Amsterdam.

McLaren, L., M. 2005. *Identity,Interests, and Attitudes to European Integration*. Basingstoke, Hampshire: Palgrave Macmillan.

Mikhaylov, S., Laver, M. and Benoit, K., R. 2012. "Coder Reliability and Misclassification in the Human Coding of Party Manifestos." *Political Analysis* 20(1): pp. 78-91. doi: 10.1093/pan/mpr047.

Millard, F. 2008. "Poland: Parties without a Party system." *Politics & Policy* 37 (4): pp. 781-798.

Moravcsik, A. and Vachudova, M., A. 2003. "National interests, state power, and EU enlargement." *East European Politics and Societies* 17(1): pp. 42-57. doi: 10.1177/0888325402239682.

Morley, D. 2001. "Belongings: Place, Space and Identity in a Mediated World." *European Journal of Cultural Studies* 4(4): pp. 425-448. doi: 10.1177/136754940100400404.

Müller, H. 2004. "Arguing, bargaining and all that: Communicative action, rationalist theory and the logic of appropriateness in international relations." *European Journal of International Relations* 10(3): pp. 395-435. doi: 10.1177/1354066104045542.

Müller-Werner, J. 2016. *Was ist Populismus?*, Bonn: Bundeszentrale für Politische Bildung.

Navrátilová, A. 1986. *Etnické procesy v nově osídlených oblastech na Moravě: na příkladu vybraných obcí v Jihomoravském a Severomoravském kraji*, Strážnice: Ústav lidového umění.

Neumann, S. and Pujkalo, A. 2011. *Sprache und Identität. Herausforderungen in der deutsch-polnischen Erinnerungsdebatte. Plädoyer für ein Wörterbuch der deutsch-polnischen Missverständnisse* In *Erinnerungskultur des 20. Jahrhunderts*, Warsaw: Museum des Warschauer Aufstands.

Oakeshott, M. J. 1975. *On Human Conduct.* Oxford: Oxford University Press.

Olson, D. M., Crowther, W. E. and Box-Steffensmeier, J. M., ed., 2002. *Committees in Post-Communist Democratic Parliaments: Comparative institutionalization.* Columbus, OH: Ohio State University Press.

Nemčok, M., Vít, M. 2016. *Attitudes towards Nationalism and European Integration: Are Political Parties Behaving consistently in the European Arena and within the Nation State?.* manuscript.

Norris, P. 2005. "Political Parties and Democracy in Theoretical and Practical Perspectives" *The National Democratic Institute for International Affairs.* https://www.hks.harvard.edu/fs/pnorris/Acrobat/NDI%20Final%20booklet%20-%20Communications.pdf (Accessed: 15 November 2016).

Paasi, A. 2001. "Europe as a Social Process and Discourse: Considerations of Place, Boundaries and Identity." *European Urban and Regional Studies* 8(1): pp. 7–28. doi: 10.1177/096977640100800102.

Paasi, A. 2009. "Bounded spaces in a 'borderless world'? Border studies, power, and the anatomy of the territory." *Journal of Power* 2(2): pp. 213-234.

Paciorek-Herrmann, D. 2012. *Doing Socialization after Accession, L'Europe en Formation* (2): pp. 343 - 364. doi: 10.3917/eufor.364.0343.

Ther, P. 2015. *Nový pořádek na stareém kontinente: Příbeh neoliberální Evropy,* Praha: Libri.

Pierson, P. 2000. "Increasing returns, path dependence, and the study of politics." *The American Political Science Review* 94(2): pp. 251. doi: 10.2307/2586011.

Pierson, P. 2004. *Politics in Time: History, Institutions, and Social Analysis.* New York, United States: Princeton University Press.

Pink, M. and Valterová, A. 2010. "Volby do Poslanecké sněmovny České republiky 2010 a jejich „alternativní" výstupy." *Středoevropské politické studie* 12(2).

Pridham, G. and Lewis, P. G., ed., 1996. *Stabilising Fragile Democracies: Comparing New Party Systems in Southern and Eastern Europe.* London: Taylor & Francis.

Pridham, G. 2002. "EU Enlargement and Consolidating Democracy in Post–Communist States - Formality and Reality." *Journal of Common Market Studies.* Blackwell Publishers, pp. 953-973.

Pridham, G. 2005. *Designing Democracy. EU Enlargement and Regime Change in Post-Communist Europe.* London: Palgrave Macmillan.

Radaelli, C. 2003. *The Politics of Europeanization.* Oxford: Oxford University Press.

Radaelli, C., Exadaktlyos T., eds., 2012. *Research Design in European Studies Establishing Causality in Europeanization.* London: Palgrave MacMillan.

Risse, T. 2002. "Constructivism and International Institutions. toward Conversations accross Paradigms." In *Political Science as Discipline: Reconsidering Power, Choice, and the State at the Century's End,* edited by Katznelson, I, Milner, H. New York: W. W. Norton, pp. 597-623.

Risse, T. 2010. *A Community of Europeans? Transnational Identities and Public Spheres.* Ithaca NY: Cornell University Press.

Rohrschneider, R. and Whitefield, S. 2006. "Political Parties, Public Opinion and European Integration in Post-Communist Countries: The State of the Art." *European Union Politics* 7(1): pp. 141 – 160.

Rohrschneider, R. and Whitefield, S. 2007. "Representation in new democracies: Party stances on European integration in post-communist eastern Europe." *The Journal of Politics,* 69(4), pp. 1133–1146. doi: 10.1111/j.1468-2508.2007.00613.x.

Rohrschneider, S. and Whitefield, R. 2011. *The Europeanization of Political Parties in Central and Eastern Europe? The Impact of EU Entry on Issue Stances, Salience and Programmatic coherence,* In *Party Politics in Central and Eastern Europe. Does EU membership Matter?,* edited by Haughton, .T, London: Routledge, pp. 152-172.

Rohrschneider, R. and Whitefield, S. 2012. *The Strain of Representation: How Parties Represent Diverse Voters in Western and Eastern Europe.* Oxford: Oxford University Press.

Rovný, J. 2012. "Who Emphasizes and Who Blurs? Party Strategies in Multidimensional Competition." *European Union Politics* 13(2): pp. 1–24. doi: 10.1177/1465116511435822.

Rovný, J. 2015a. "Party Competition Structure in Eastern Europe: Aggregate Uniformity Versus Idiosyncratic Diversity?." *East European Politics & Societies* 29(1), pp. 1–24. doi: 10.1177/0888325414567535.

Rovný, J. 2015b. "Riker and Rokkan: Remarks on the strategy and structure of party competition." *Party Politics* 21(6): pp. 912–918. doi: 10.1177/1354068815602588.

Rovný, J. and Edwards, E. E. 2012. "Struggle over Dimensionality: Party Competition in Western and Eastern Europe." *East European Politics & Societies* 26(1): pp. 56–74. doi: 10.1177/0888325410387635.

Rozner, A., Vit, M. 2014. *Zagrożone mniejszości – rozmowa z prof. Janem Hartmanem,* Liberté. Available at http://liberte.pl/tozsamosc-narodowa-6/, (Accessed November 16, 2016).

Ruedin, D. 2013. *Why Aren't They There? The Political Representation of Women, Ethnic Groups and Issue Positions in Legislatures*. Colchester: ECPR Press.

Rumelili, B. 2004. "Constructing Identity and Relating to Difference: Understanding the EU's Mode of Differentiation." *Review of International Studies* 30(1): pp. 27–47. doi: 10.2307/20097897.

Rupnik, J. and Zielonka, J. 2012. "Democracy in Central and Eastern Europe: The State of the Art." *East European Politics & Societies* 27(1), pp. 3–25. doi: 10.1177/0888325412465110.

Scully, R. 2005. *Becoming Europeans? Attitudes, behaviour, and socialization in the European parliament*. Oxford: Oxford University Press.

Sarcinelli, U. 2009. *Politische Kommunikation in Deutschland. Zur Politikvermittlung im demokratischen System*. Wiesbaden: VS Verlag für Sozialwissenschaften.

Sean, H. 2015. "All Fall Down? The Prospects for Established Parties in Europe and Beyond." *Government and Opposition*. Avaliable at https://www.cambridge.org/core/journals/government-and-opposition/article/all-fall-down-the-prospects-for-established-parties-in-europe-and-beyond/91971CCCBEC47A38133E7E1553703BD4 (Accessed: November 15 2016).

Sedelmeier, U. 2009. "Post-Accession Compliance with EU Gender Equality Legislation in Post-Communist New Member States." In *Post-Accession Compliance in the EU's New Member States, European Integration Online Papers*, edited by Schimmelfennig, F., Trauner, F. Special Issue 2, Vol. 13.

Schimmelfennig, F., Engert, S., Knobel, H. and Egan, M. 2006. "International Socialization in Europe: European Organizations,Ppolitical Conditionality and Democratic Change." In *Palgrave Studies in European Union Politics series*, edited by Paterson, W., E. New York: Palgrave Macmillan.

Schöpflin, G. 1999. *Nations, Identity, Power*. New York: New York University Press.

Simmons, O. E. 2010. "Is that Real Theory or Did You Just Make it Up?" *The Grounded Theory Review* 9(2): pp. 15–39.

Sitter, N. 2003. "Euro-scepticism as party strategy: Persistence and change in party-based opposition to European integration." *EUSA 8th International Biennial Conference*. Avaliable at http://aei.pitt.edu/2952/ (Accessed: November 15 2016)

Spirova, M. 2007. *Political Parties in Post-Communist Systems: Formation, Persistence, and Change*. New York: Palgrave Macmillan.

Spirova M. 2012. European Integration and Minority Politics: Ethnic Parties at the EP Elections. *East European Politics* 28(1): 76-93.

Strážay, T. 2015. "Ten Years of Membership in the European Union" Slovakia. In *European Integration of the Western Balkans - Can the Visegrad Group Countries Serve as Role models? European Movement in Serbia*, pp. 33 – 45.

Szcerbiak, A. 2011. "When in Doubt, (Re-)turn to Domestic Politics? The (Non-) Impact of the EU on Party Politics in Poland." In *Party Politics in Central and Eastern Europe. Does EU membership Matter?*, ed. by Haughton, T. London: Routledge.

Szczerbiak, A. 2012. *Poland within the European Union: New Awkward Partner or New Heart of Europe?*, London: Routledge.

Szczepanik, M. 2011. "Between a Romantic "Mission in the East" and Minimalism: Polish Policy Towards the Eastern Neighbourhood." *Perspectives Review of International Affairs* 19(2), pp. 45–67.

Szpala, M. 2015. *Ten years of Membership in the European Union – Poland.* in European integration of the Western Balkans - Can the Visegrad Group countries serve as role models? European Movement in Serbia, pp. 64 – 78.

Taggart, P. A. and Szczerbiak, A. 2013. "Coming in from the Cold? Euroscepticism and Government Participation and Party Positions on Europe." *Journal of Common Market Studies* 51 (1): pp. 17-37.

Taggart, P. A. 1996. *The New Populism and the New Politics: New Protest Parties in Sweden in a Comparative Perspective*. New York: Palgrave.

Taggart, P. A. 2002. *Populism and the Pathology of Representative Politics.*, In *Democracies and the Populist Challenge*, edited by Meny Yves and Surel Yves. Basingstoke: Palgrave Macmillan, pp. 62-80.

Topaloff, L. K. 2012. *Political parties and Euroscepticism*. New York: Palgrave Macmillan.

Tóth, C. 2014. "Full text of Viktor Orbán's speech at Băile Tușnad (Tusnádfürdő) of 26 July 2014". *Budapest Beacon*. Available at http://budapest beacon.com/public-policy/full-text-of-viktor-orbans-speech-at-baile -tusnad-tusnadfurdo-of-26-july-2014/10592 (Accessed: 15 November 2016).

Triandafyllidou, A. 1998. "National identity and the "Other"." *Ethnic and Racial Studies* 21(4): pp. 593–612. doi: 10.1080/014198798329784.

Troebst, S. 2013. *Erinnerungskultur, Kulturgeschichte, Geschichtsregion: Ostmitteleuropa in Europa*. Stuttgart: Franz Steiner Verlag Wiesbaden GmbH.

Tulmets, E. 2012. "Introduction: Identity and Solidarity in the Foreign Policy of EU Members: Renewing the Research Agenda." *Perspectives Review of International Affairs* 19(2): pp. 5–27.

Učeň, P. 2011. "Competitive Lines in the Slovak Parliamentary Elections 2010." In *Visegrad Elections 2010. Domestic Impact and European Consequences*, edited by Gyárfášová, O., Mesežnikov, G. Bratislava: Inštitut pre verejné otázky, pp. 79-98.

Vachudova, M. 2005. *Europe Undivided: Democracy, Leverage and Integration after Communism.* Oxford: Oxford University Press.

Van der Brug, W. 2004 "Issue Ownership and Party Choice." *Electoral Studies* 23(2): pp. 209–233. doi: 10.1016/S0261-3794(02)00061-6.

van Kessel, S. 2015. *Populist Parties in Europe: Agents of Discontent?* New York: Palgrave Macmillan.

Vít, M. 2014a. "Ludowe mity – rozmowa z Jerzym Stefaniukiem." Liberté. Available at http://lberte.pl/tozsamosc-narodowa-2/, (Accessed: 16 November, 2016).

Vít, M. 2014b. "Brytyjska BNP to prymitywny nacjonalizm – rozmowa z Krzysztofem Bosakiem." *Liberté.* Available at http://liberte.pl/tozsam osc-narodowa-1/, (Accessed: 16 November, 2016).

Vít, M. 2014c. "Historyczna narracja SLD – rozmowa z prof. Andrzejem Jaeschke." *Liberté.* Available at http://liberte.pl/tozsamosc-narodowa-7/, (Accessed: 16 November, 2016).

Vít, M. 2014d. "New Political Movements in the Czech Politics: Reshaping Political Space?" *Warsaw: SPACE, Elipsa*, pp. 112 – 124.

Vít, M. 2016. *Metanaratives of Russian Propaganda in Czech Online Media*, in *Fog or Falsehood?*, edited by Pynnöniemi, K., Rácz, A. Finish Institute of International Affairs, pp. 25 – 289.

Voda, P. 2015. *Jaká je role postkomunismu? Volební geografie České a Rakouské republiky v letech 1990-2013.* Brno: Centrum pro studium demokracie.

Vodička, K. 2010. *Das politische System Tschechiens*, in *Die politischen Systeme Osteuropas*, edited by Ismayr, W., Wiesbaden: Verlag Für Sozialwissenschaften.

Volkens, A., Bara, J. and Budge, I. 2009. *Data Quality in Content Analysis. The Case of the Comparative Manifestos Project*, Historical Social Research / Historische Sozialforschung, 34(1), pp. 234–251.

Volkens, A. 2015a. *The Manifesto Data Collection,* Manifesto Project (MRG/CMP/MARPOR). Version 2015a.

Volkens, A. 2015b. *The Manifesto Project Dataset – Codebook,* Manifesto Project (MRG/ CMP / MARPOR). Version 2015a.

Von dem Berge, B., Poguntke, T. 2013. "The Influence of Europarties on Central and Eastern European Partner Parties: A Theoretical and Analytical Model." *European Political Science Review* 5(2), 311-334. doi: 10.1017/S1755773912000264

Walsch, Ch. 2015. *Aufbruch nach Europa*. Herne: Gabriele Schäfer Verlag.

Webb, P. and White, S. 2007. *Party Politics in New Democracies*. Oxford: Oxford University Press.

Wegs, R. J. and Ladrech, R. 2002. *Evropa po roce 1945*. Praha: Vyšehrad.

Wendt, A. 1999. *Social Theory of International Politics*. Cambridge University Press.

Whitehead, L. 2002. *Democratization: Theory and Experience*. Oxford: Oxford University Press.

Wojtas, K. 2012. "Polsko." In *Populist Political Parties in East-Central Europe*, edited by Havlík, V., Pinková, A., Balcere, I., Cholova, B., Havlík, V., Smrčková, M., Spáč, P., Wojtas, K., and Krašovec, A. Brno: Masaryk University, International Institute of Political Science.

Zalan, E. 2016. "Can Europe Stand-up to Its Own Strongmen?" *Foreign Policy*. Avaliable at https://foreignpolicy.com/2016/03/10/can-europe-stand-up-to-its-own-strongmen/ (Accessed: November 15, 2016).

Zürn, M. 1998. *Regieren jenseits des Nationalstaates: Globalisierung und Denationalisierung als chance*. Frankfurt a. M.: Suhrkamp.

Election manifestos

Action of Dissatisfied Citizens (2013): Volebný program.

Alliance of the Democratic Left (2005): Sprawiedliwość Społeczna i Praca Programowa.

Alliance of the Democratic Left (2007): Polska Demokratyczna i Socjalna. Konstytucja Programowa Sojuszu Lewicy Demokratycznej.

Alliance of the Democratic Left (2011): Polska Demokratyczna i Socjalna. Konstytucja Programowa Sojuszu Lewicy Demokratycznej.

Bridge (2010): Volebný program.

Brigde (2012): Volebný program.

Civic Democratic Party (2013): Volební program pro parlamentní volby 2013.

Civic Democratic Party (2010): Řešení, která pomáhají, program pro volby 2006.

Civic Democratic Party (2006): Společně pro lepší život 2010.

Christian-Democratic Movement (2006): Volebný program.

Christian-Democratic Movement (2010): Volebný program.

Christian-Democratic Movement (2012): Volebný program.

Christian and Democratic Union – Czechoslovak People's Party (2006): Volební program KDU-ČSL 2006.

Christian and Democratic Union – Czechoslovak People's Party (2010): Volební program 2010 – 2014.

Christian and Democratic Union – Czechoslovak People's Party (2013): Volební program KDU-ČSL 2013

Communist Party off Bohemia and Moravia (2006): Program KSČM pro volby do Poslanecké sněmovny 2006.

Communist Party off Bohemia and Moravia (2010): Otevřený volební program KSČM pro volby do PS PČR 2010.

Communist Party off Bohemia and Moravia (2013): Program KSČM pro volby do Poslanecké sněmovny 2013.

Czech Social Democratic Party (2006): Program změny a naděje 2006.

Czech Social Democratic Party (2010): Jistoty pro lidi, naděje pro zemi 2010.

Czech Social Democratic Party (2010): Jistoty pro lidi, naděje pro zemi 2013.

Direction - Social Democracy (2006): Volebný program.

Direction - Social Democracy (2010): Volebný program.

Direction - Social Democracy (2012): Volebný program.

Green Party (2006): Volební program Strany zelených volby do Poslanecké sněmovny 2006

Green Party (2010): Volební program Strany zelenýchvolby do Poslanecké sněmovny 2010

Green Party (2013): Volební program Strany zelenýchvolby do Poslanecké sněmovny 2013

Law and Justice (2005): IV RZECZPOSPOLITA Sprawiedliwość dla Wszystkich

Law and Justice (2007): PROGRAM PRAWA I SPRAWIEDLIWOŚCI

Law and Justice (2011): PROGRAM PRAWA I SPRAWIEDLIWOŚCI

League of Polish Families (2005): Program wyborczy.

League of polish Families (2007): Program wyborczy.

Ordinary People (2010): Volebný program.

Ordinary People (2012): Volebný program.

People's Party – Movement for a Democratic Slovakia (2006): Volebný program.

People's Party – Movement for a Democratic Slovakia (2010): Volebný program.

People's Party - Movement for a Democratic Slovakia (2012): Volebný program.
Polish People's Party (2005): Program wyborczy.
Polish People's Party (2007): Program wyborczy.
Polish People's Party (2011): Program wyborczy.
Public Affairs (2010): Politický program 2010.
Freedom and Solidarity (2010): Volebný program.
Freedom and Solidarity (2012): Volebný program.
Self-defence (2005): Program wyborczy.
Self-defence (2007): Program wyborczy.
Slovak Democratic and Christian Union - Democratic Party (2006): Volebný program.
Slovak Democratic and Christian Union - Democratic Party (2010): Volebný program.
Slovak Democratic and Christian Union - Democratic Party (2013): Volebný program.
Slovak National Party (2006): Volebný program.
Slovak National Party (2010): Volebný program.
Slovak National Party (2012): Volebný program.
Tomio Okamura's Dawn of Direct Democracy (Hnutí úsvit přímé demokracie Tomia Okamury): Volební program 2013.
Tradition, Responsibility, Prosperity (2010): Volební program 2010.
Tradition, Responsibility, Prosperity (2013): Volební program 2013.
The Civic Platform (2005): PAŃSTWO DLA OBYWATELI PLAN RZĄDZENIA 2005 - 2009.
The Civic Platform (2007): Program PO Polska zasługuje na cud gospodarczy.
The Civic Platform (2011): Program PO Polska zasługuje na cud gospodarczy.
Your Movement (2011): Program wyborczy.

SOVIET AND POST-SOVIET POLITICS AND SOCIETY
Edited by Dr. Andreas Umland | ISSN 1614-3515

1   Андреас Умланд (ред.) | Воплощение Европейской конвенции по правам человека в России. Философские, юридические и эмпирические исследования | ISBN 3-89821-387-0

2   Christian Wipperfürth | Russland – ein vertrauenswürdiger Partner? Grundlagen, Hintergründe und Praxis gegenwärtiger russischer Außenpolitik | Mit einem Vorwort von Heinz Timmermann | ISBN 3-89821-401-X

3   Manja Hussner | Die Übernahme internationalen Rechts in die russische und deutsche Rechtsordnung. Eine vergleichende Analyse zur Völkerrechtsfreundlichkeit der Verfassungen der Russländischen Föderation und der Bundesrepublik Deutschland | Mit einem Vorwort von Rainer Arnold | ISBN 3-89821-438-9

4   Matthew Tejada | Bulgaria's Democratic Consolidation and the Kozloduy Nuclear Power Plant (KNPP). The Unattainability of Closure | With a foreword by Richard J. Crampton | ISBN 3-89821-439-7

5   Марк Григорьевич Меерович | Квадратные метры, определяющие сознание. Государственная жилищная политика в СССР. 1921 – 1941 гг | ISBN 3-89821-474-5

6   Andrei P. Tsygankov, Pavel A. Tsygankov (Eds.) | New Directions in Russian International Studies | ISBN 3-89821-422-2

7   Марк Григорьевич Меерович | Как власть народ к труду приучала. Жилище в СССР – средство управления людьми. 1917 – 1941 гг. | С предисловием Елены Осокиной | ISBN 3-89821-495-8

8   David J. Galbreath | Nation-Building and Minority Politics in Post-Socialist States. Interests, Influence and Identities in Estonia and Latvia | With a foreword by David J. Smith | ISBN 3-89821-467-2

9   Алексей Юрьевич Безугольный | Народы Кавказа в Вооруженных силах СССР в годы Великой Отечественной войны 1941-1945 гг. | С предисловием Николая Бугая | ISBN 3-89821-475-3

10 Вячеслав Лихачев и Владимир Прибыловский (ред.) | Русское Национальное Единство, 1990-2000. В 2-х томах | ISBN 3-89821-523-7

11 Николай Бугай (ред.) | Народы стран Балтии в условиях сталинизма (1940-е – 1950-е годы). Документированная история | ISBN 3-89821-525-3

12 Ingmar Bredies (Hrsg.) | Zur Anatomie der Orange Revolution in der Ukraine. Wechsel des Elitenregimes oder Triumph des Parlamentarismus?| ISBN 3-89821-524-5

13 Anastasia V. Mitrofanova | The Politicization of Russian Orthodoxy. Actors and Ideas | With a foreword by William C. Gay | ISBN 3-89821-481-8

14 Nathan D. Larson | Alexander Solzhenitsyn and the Russo-Jewish Question | ISBN 3-89821-483-4

15 Guido Houben | Kulturpolitik und Ethnizität. Staatliche Kunstförderung im Russland der neunziger Jahre | Mit einem Vorwort von Gert Weisskirchen | ISBN 3-89821-542-3

16 Leonid Luks | Der russische „Sonderweg"? Aufsätze zur neuesten Geschichte Russlands im europäischen Kontext | ISBN 3-89821-496-6

17 Евгений Мороз | История «Мёртвой воды» – от страшной сказки к большой политике. Политическое неоязычество в постсоветской России | ISBN 3-89821-551-2

18 Александр Верховский и Галина Кожевникова (ред.) | Этническая и религиозная интолерантность в российских СМИ. Результаты мониторинга 2001-2004 гг. | ISBN 3-89821-569-5

19 Christian Ganzer | Sowjetisches Erbe und ukrainische Nation. Das Museum der Geschichte des Zaporoger Kosakentums auf der Insel Chortycja | Mit einem Vorwort von Frank Golczewski | ISBN 3-89821-504-0

20 Эльза-Баир Гучинова | Помнить нельзя забыть. Антропология депортационной травмы калмыков | С предисловием Кэролайн Хамфри | ISBN 3-89821-506-1

21 Юлия Лидерман | Мотивы «проверки» и «испытания» в постсоветской культуре. Советское прошлое в российском кинематографе 1990-х годов | С предисловием Евгения Марголита | ISBN 3-89821-511-3

22 Tanya Lokshina, Ray Thomas, Mary Mayer (Eds.) | The Imposition of a Fake Political Settlement in the Northern Caucasus. The 2003 Chechen Presidential Election | ISBN 3-89821-436-2

23 Timothy McCajor Hall, Rosie Read (Eds.) | Changes in the Heart of Europe. Recent Ethnographies of Czechs, Slovaks, Roma, and Sorbs | With an afterword by Zdeněk Salzmann | ISBN 3-89821-606-5

24 *Christian Autengruber* | Die politischen Parteien in Bulgarien und Rumänien. Eine vergleichende Analyse seit Beginn der 90er Jahre | Mit einem Vorwort von Dorothée de Nève | ISBN 3-89821-476-1

25 *Annette Freyberg-Inan with Radu Cristescu* | The Ghosts in Our Classrooms, or: John Dewey Meets Ceauşescu. The Promise and the Failures of Civic Education in Romania | ISBN 3-89821-416-8

26 *John B. Dunlop* | The 2002 Dubrovka and 2004 Beslan Hostage Crises. A Critique of Russian Counter-Terrorism | With a foreword by Donald N. Jensen | ISBN 3-89821-608-X

27 *Peter Koller* | Das touristische Potenzial von Kam''janec'–Podil's'kyj. Eine fremdenverkehrsgeographische Untersuchung der Zukunftsperspektiven und Maßnahmenplanung zur Destinationsentwicklung des „ukrainischen Rothenburg" | Mit einem Vorwort von Kristiane Klemm | ISBN 3-89821-640-3

28 *Françoise Daucé, Elisabeth Sieca-Kozlowski (Eds.)* | Dedovshchina in the Post-Soviet Military. Hazing of Russian Army Conscripts in a Comparative Perspective | With a foreword by Dale Herspring | ISBN 3-89821-616-0

29 *Florian Strasser* | Zivilgesellschaftliche Einflüsse auf die Orange Revolution. Die gewaltlose Massenbewegung und die ukrainische Wahlkrise 2004 | Mit einem Vorwort von Egbert Jahn | ISBN 3-89821-648-9

30 *Rebecca S. Katz* | The Georgian Regime Crisis of 2003-2004. A Case Study in Post-Soviet Media Representation of Politics, Crime and Corruption | ISBN 3-89821-413-3

31 *Vladimir Kantor* | Willkür oder Freiheit. Beiträge zur russischen Geschichtsphilosophie | Ediert von Dagmar Herrmann sowie mit einem Vorwort versehen von Leonid Luks | ISBN 3-89821-589-X

32 *Laura A. Victoir* | The Russian Land Estate Today. A Case Study of Cultural Politics in Post-Soviet Russia | With a foreword by Priscilla Roosevelt | ISBN 3-89821-426-5

33 *Ivan Katchanovski* | Cleft Countries. Regional Political Divisions and Cultures in Post-Soviet Ukraine and Moldova | With a foreword by Francis Fukuyama | ISBN 3-89821-558-X

34 *Florian Mühlfried* | Postsowjetische Feiern. Das Georgische Bankett im Wandel | Mit einem Vorwort von Kevin Tuite | ISBN 3-89821-601-2

35 *Roger Griffin, Werner Loh, Andreas Umland (Eds.)* | Fascism Past and Present, West and East. An International Debate on Concepts and Cases in the Comparative Study of the Extreme Right | With an afterword by Walter Laqueur | ISBN 3-89821-674-8

36 *Sebastian Schlegel* | Der „Weiße Archipel". Sowjetische Atomstädte 1945-1991 | Mit einem Geleitwort von Thomas Bohn | ISBN 3-89821-679-9

37 *Vyacheslav Likhachev* | Political Anti-Semitism in Post-Soviet Russia. Actors and Ideas in 1991-2003 | Edited and translated from Russian by Eugene Veklerov | ISBN 3-89821-529-6

38 *Josette Baer (Ed.)* | Preparing Liberty in Central Europe. Political Texts from the Spring of Nations 1848 to the Spring of Prague 1968 | With a foreword by Zdeněk V. David | ISBN 3-89821-546-6

39 *Михаил Лукьянов* | Российский консерватизм и реформа, 1907-1914 | С предисловием Марка Д. Стейнберга | ISBN 3-89821-503-2

40 *Nicola Melloni* | Market Without Economy. The 1998 Russian Financial Crisis | With a foreword by Eiji Furukawa | ISBN 3-89821-407-9

41 *Dmitrij Chmelnizki* | Die Architektur Stalins | Bd. 1: Studien zu Ideologie und Stil | Bd. 2: Bilddokumentation | Mit einem Vorwort von Bruno Flierl | ISBN 3-89821-515-6

42 *Katja Yafimava* | Post-Soviet Russian-Belarussian Relationships. The Role of Gas Transit Pipelines | With a foreword by Jonathan P. Stern | ISBN 3-89821-655-1

43 *Boris Chavkin* | Verflechtungen der deutschen und russischen Zeitgeschichte. Aufsätze und Archivfunde zu den Beziehungen Deutschlands und der Sowjetunion von 1917 bis 1991 | Ediert von Markus Edlinger sowie mit einem Vorwort versehen von Leonid Luks | ISBN 3-89821-756-6

44 *Anastasija Grynenko in Zusammenarbeit mit Claudia Dathe* | Die Terminologie des Gerichtswesens der Ukraine und Deutschlands im Vergleich. Eine übersetzungswissenschaftliche Analyse juristischer Fachbegriffe im Deutschen, Ukrainischen und Russischen | Mit einem Vorwort von Ulrich Hartmann | ISBN 3-89821-691-8

45 *Anton Burkov* | The Impact of the European Convention on Human Rights on Russian Law. Legislation and Application in 1996-2006 | With a foreword by Françoise Hampson | ISBN 978-3-89821-639-5

46 *Stina Torjesen, Indra Overland (Eds.)* | International Election Observers in Post-Soviet Azerbaijan. Geopolitical Pawns or Agents of Change? | ISBN 978-3-89821-743-9

47 *Taras Kuzio* | Ukraine – Crimea – Russia. Triangle of Conflict | ISBN 978-3-89821-761-3

48 *Claudia Šabić* | "Ich erinnere mich nicht, aber L'viv!" Zur Funktion kultureller Faktoren für die Institutionalisierung und Entwicklung einer ukrainischen Region | Mit einem Vorwort von Melanie Tatur | ISBN 978-3-89821-752-1

49 *Marlies Bilz* | Tatarstan in der Transformation. Nationaler Diskurs und Politische Praxis 1988-1994 | Mit einem Vorwort von Frank Golczewski | ISBN 978-3-89821-722-4

50 *Марлен Ларюэль (ред.)* | Современные интерпретации русского национализма | ISBN 978-3-89821-795-8

51 *Sonja Schüler* | Die ethnische Dimension der Armut. Roma im postsozialistischen Rumänien | Mit einem Vorwort von Anton Sterbling | ISBN 978-3-89821-776-7

52 *Галина Кожевникова* | Радикальный национализм в России и противодействие ему. Сборник докладов Центра «Сова» за 2004-2007 гг. | С предисловием Александра Верховского | ISBN 978-3-89821-721-7

53 *Галина Кожевникова и Владимир Прибыловский* | Российская власть в биографиях I. Высшие должностные лица РФ в 2004 г. | ISBN 978-3-89821-796-5

54 *Галина Кожевникова и Владимир Прибыловский* | Российская власть в биографиях II. Члены Правительства РФ в 2004 г. | ISBN 978-3-89821-797-2

55 *Галина Кожевникова и Владимир Прибыловский* | Российская власть в биографиях III. Руководители федеральных служб и агентств РФ в 2004 г.| ISBN 978-3-89821-798-9

56 *Ileana Petroniu* | Privatisierung in Transformationsökonomien. Determinanten der Restrukturierungs-Bereitschaft am Beispiel Polens, Rumäniens und der Ukraine | Mit einem Vorwort von Rainer W. Schäfer | ISBN 978-3-89821-790-3

57 *Christian Wipperfürth* | Russland und seine GUS-Nachbarn. Hintergründe, aktuelle Entwicklungen und Konflikte in einer ressourcenreichen Region| ISBN 978-3-89821-801-6

58 *Togzhan Kassenova* | From Antagonism to Partnership. The Uneasy Path of the U.S.-Russian Cooperative Threat Reduction | With a foreword by Christoph Bluth | ISBN 978-3-89821-707-1

59 *Alexander Höllwerth* | Das sakrale eurasische Imperium des Aleksandr Dugin. Eine Diskursanalyse zum postsowjetischen russischen Rechtsextremismus | Mit einem Vorwort von Dirk Uffelmann | ISBN 978-3-89821-813-9

60 *Олег Рябов* | «Россия-Матушка». Национализм, гендер и война в России XX века | С предисловием Елены Гощило | ISBN 978-3-89821-487-2

61 *Ivan Maistrenko* | Borot'bism. A Chapter in the History of the Ukrainian Revolution | With a new Introduction by Chris Ford | Translated by George S. N. Luckyj with the assistance of Ivan L. Rudnytsky | Second, Revised and Expanded Edition ISBN 978-3-8382-1107-7

62 *Maryna Romanets* | Anamorphosic Texts and Reconfigured Visions. Improvised Traditions in Contemporary Ukrainian and Irish Literature | ISBN 978-3-89821-576-3

63 *Paul D'Anieri and Taras Kuzio (Eds.)* | Aspects of the Orange Revolution I. Democratization and Elections in Post-Communist Ukraine | ISBN 978-3-89821-698-2

64 *Bohdan Harasymiw in collaboration with Oleh S. Ilnytzkyj (Eds.)* | Aspects of the Orange Revolution II. Information and Manipulation Strategies in the 2004 Ukrainian Presidential Elections | ISBN 978-3-89821-699-9

65 *Ingmar Bredies, Andreas Umland and Valentin Yakushik (Eds.)* | Aspects of the Orange Revolution III. The Context and Dynamics of the 2004 Ukrainian Presidential Elections | ISBN 978-3-89821-803-0

66 *Ingmar Bredies, Andreas Umland and Valentin Yakushik (Eds.)* | Aspects of the Orange Revolution IV. Foreign Assistance and Civic Action in the 2004 Ukrainian Presidential Elections | ISBN 978-3-89821-808-5

67 *Ingmar Bredies, Andreas Umland and Valentin Yakushik (Eds.)* | Aspects of the Orange Revolution V. Institutional Observation Reports on the 2004 Ukrainian Presidential Elections | ISBN 978-3-89821-809-2

68 *Taras Kuzio (Ed.)* | Aspects of the Orange Revolution VI. Post-Communist Democratic Revolutions in Comparative Perspective | ISBN 978-3-89821-820-7

69 *Tim Bohse* | Autoritarismus statt Selbstverwaltung. Die Transformation der kommunalen Politik in der Stadt Kaliningrad 1990-2005 | Mit einem Geleitwort von Stefan Troebst | ISBN 978-3-89821-782-8

70 *David Rupp* | Die Rußländische Föderation und die russischsprachige Minderheit in Lettland. Eine Fallstudie zur Anwaltspolitik Moskaus gegenüber den russophonen Minderheiten im „Nahen Ausland" von 1991 bis 2002 | Mit einem Vorwort von Helmut Wagner | ISBN 978-3-89821-778-1

71 *Taras Kuzio* | Theoretical and Comparative Perspectives on Nationalism. New Directions in Cross-Cultural and Post-Communist Studies | With a foreword by Paul Robert Magocsi | ISBN 978-3-89821-815-7

72 *Christine Teichmann* | Die Hochschultransformation im heutigen Osteuropa. Kontinuität und Wandel bei der Entwicklung des postkommunistischen Universitätswesens | Mit einem Vorwort von Oskar Anweiler | ISBN 978-3-89821-842-9

73 *Julia Kusznir* | Der politische Einfluss von Wirtschaftseliten in russischen Regionen. Eine Analyse am Beispiel der Erdöl- und Erdgasindustrie, 1992-2005 | Mit einem Vorwort von Wolfgang Eichwede | ISBN 978-3-89821-821-4

74 *Alena Vysotskaya* | Russland, Belarus und die EU-Osterweiterung. Zur Minderheitenfrage und zum Problem der Freizügigkeit des Personenverkehrs | Mit einem Vorwort von Katlijn Malfliet | ISBN 978-3-89821-822-1

75 *Heiko Pleines (Hrsg.)* | Corporate Governance in post-sozialistischen Volkswirtschaften | ISBN 978-3-89821-766-8

76 *Stefan Ihrig* | Wer sind die Moldawier? Rumänismus versus Moldowanismus in Historiographie und Schulbüchern der Republik Moldova, 1991-2006 | Mit einem Vorwort von Holm Sundhaussen | ISBN 978-3-89821-466-7

77 *Galina Kozhevnikova in collaboration with Alexander Verkhovsky and Eugene Veklerov* | Ultra-Nationalism and Hate Crimes in Contemporary Russia. The 2004-2006 Annual Reports of Moscow's SOVA Center | With a foreword by Stephen D. Shenfield | ISBN 978-3-89821-868-9

78 *Florian Küchler* | The Role of the European Union in Moldova's Transnistria Conflict | With a foreword by Christopher Hill | ISBN 978-3-89821-850-4

79 *Bernd Rechel* | The Long Way Back to Europe. Minority Protection in Bulgaria | With a foreword by Richard Crampton | ISBN 978-3-89821-863-4

80 *Peter W. Rodgers* | Nation, Region and History in Post-Communist Transitions. Identity Politics in Ukraine, 1991-2006 | With a foreword by Vera Tolz | ISBN 978-3-89821-903-7

81 *Stephanie Solywoda* | The Life and Work of Semen L. Frank. A Study of Russian Religious Philosophy | With a foreword by Philip Walters | ISBN 978-3-89821-457-5

82 *Vera Sokolova* | Cultural Politics of Ethnicity. Discourses on Roma in Communist Czechoslovakia | ISBN 978-3-89821-864-1

83 *Natalya Shevchik Ketenci* | Kazakhstani Enterprises in Transition. The Role of Historical Regional Development in Kazakhstan's Post-Soviet Economic Transformation | ISBN 978-3-89821-831-3

84 *Martin Malek, Anna Schor-Tschudnowskaja (Hgg.)* | Europa im Tschetschenienkrieg. Zwischen politischer Ohnmacht und Gleichgültigkeit | Mit einem Vorwort von Lipchan Basajewa | ISBN 978-3-89821-676-0

85 *Stefan Meister* | Das postsowjetische Universitätswesen zwischen nationalem und internationalem Wandel. Die Entwicklung der regionalen Hochschule in Russland als Gradmesser der Systemtransformation | Mit einem Vorwort von Joan DeBardeleben | ISBN 978-3-89821-891-7

86 *Konstantin Sheiko in collaboration with Stephen Brown* | Nationalist Imaginings of the Russian Past. Anatolii Fomenko and the Rise of Alternative History in Post-Communist Russia | With a foreword by Donald Ostrowski | ISBN 978-3-89821-915-0

87 *Sabine Jenni* | Wie stark ist das „Einige Russland"? Zur Parteibindung der Eliten und zum Wahlerfolg der Machtpartei im Dezember 2007 | Mit einem Vorwort von Klaus Armingeon | ISBN 978-3-89821-961-7

88 *Thomas Borén* | Meeting-Places of Transformation. Urban Identity, Spatial Representations and Local Politics in Post-Soviet St Petersburg | ISBN 978-3-89821-739-2

89 *Aygul Ashirova* | Stalinismus und Stalin-Kult in Zentralasien. Turkmenistan 1924-1953 | Mit einem Vorwort von Leonid Luks | ISBN 978-3-89821-987-7

90 *Leonid Luks* | Freiheit oder imperiale Größe? Essays zu einem russischen Dilemma | ISBN 978-3-8382-0011-8

91 *Christopher Gilley* | The 'Change of Signposts' in the Ukrainian Emigration. A Contribution to the History of Sovietophilism in the 1920s | With a foreword by Frank Golczewski | ISBN 978-3-89821-965-5

92 *Philipp Casula, Jeronim Perovic (Eds.)* | Identities and Politics During the Putin Presidency. The Discursive Foundations of Russia's Stability | With a foreword by Heiko Haumann | ISBN 978-3-8382-0015-6

93 *Marcel Viëtor* | Europa und die Frage nach seinen Grenzen im Osten. Zur Konstruktion ‚europäischer Identität' in Geschichte und Gegenwart | Mit einem Vorwort von Albrecht Lehmann | ISBN 978-3-8382-0045-3

94 *Ben Hellman, Andrei Rogachevskii* | Filming the Unfilmable. Casper Wrede's 'One Day in the Life of Ivan Denisovich' | Second, Revised and Expanded Edition | ISBN 978-3-8382-0044-6

95 *Eva Fuchslocher* | Vaterland, Sprache, Glaube. Orthodoxie und Nationenbildung am Beispiel Georgiens | Mit einem Vorwort von Christina von Braun | ISBN 978-3-89821-884-9

96 *Vladimir Kantor* | Das Westlertum und der Weg Russlands. Zur Entwicklung der russischen Literatur und Philosophie | Ediert von Dagmar Herrmann | Mit einem Beitrag von Nikolaus Lobkowicz | ISBN 978-3-8382-0102-3

97 *Kamran Musayev* | Die postsowjetische Transformation im Baltikum und Südkaukasus. Eine vergleichende Untersuchung der politischen Entwicklung Lettlands und Aserbaidschans 1985-2009 | Mit einem Vorwort von Leonid Luks | Ediert von Sandro Henschel | ISBN 978-3-8382-0103-0

98 *Tatiana Zhurzhenko* | Borderlands into Bordered Lands. Geopolitics of Identity in Post-Soviet Ukraine | With a foreword by Dieter Segert | ISBN 978-3-8382-0042-2

99 *Кирилл Галушко, Лидия Смола (ред.)* | Пределы падения – варианты украинского будущего. Аналитико-прогностические исследования | ISBN 978-3-8382-0148-1

100 *Michael Minkenberg (Ed.)* | Historical Legacies and the Radical Right in Post-Cold War Central and Eastern Europe | With an afterword by Sabrina P. Ramet | ISBN 978-3-8382-0124-5

101 *David-Emil Wickström* | Rocking St. Petersburg. Transcultural Flows and Identity Politics in the St. Petersburg Popular Music Scene | With a foreword by Yngvar B. Steinholt | Second, Revised and Expanded Edition | ISBN 978-3-8382-0100-9

102 *Eva Zabka* | Eine neue „Zeit der Wirren"? Der spät- und postsowjetische Systemwandel 1985-2000 im Spiegel russischer gesellschaftspolitischer Diskurse | Mit einem Vorwort von Margareta Mommsen | ISBN 978-3-8382-0161-0

103 *Ulrike Ziemer* | Ethnic Belonging, Gender and Cultural Practices. Youth Identitites in Contemporary Russia | With a foreword by Anoop Nayak | ISBN 978-3-8382-0152-8

104 *Ksenia Chepikova* | ‚Einiges Russland' - eine zweite KPdSU? Aspekte der Identitätskonstruktion einer postsowjetischen „Partei der Macht" | Mit einem Vorwort von Torsten Oppelland | ISBN 978-3-8382-0311-9

105 *Леонид Люкс* | Западничество или евразийство? Демократия или идеократия? Сборник статей об исторических дилеммах России | С предисловием Владимира Кантора | ISBN 978-3-8382-0211-2

106 *Anna Dost* | Das russische Verfassungsrecht auf dem Weg zum Föderalismus und zurück. Zum Konflikt von Rechtsnormen und -wirklichkeit in der Russländischen Föderation von 1991 bis 2009 | Mit einem Vorwort von Alexander Blankenagel | ISBN 978-3-8382-0292-1

107 *Philipp Herzog* | Sozialistische Völkerfreundschaft, nationaler Widerstand oder harmloser Zeitvertreib? Zur politischen Funktion der Volkskunst im sowjetischen Estland | Mit einem Vorwort von Andreas Kappeler | ISBN 978-3-8382-0216-7

108 *Marlène Laruelle (Ed.)* | Russian Nationalism, Foreign Policy, and Identity Debates in Putin's Russia. New Ideological Patterns after the Orange Revolution | ISBN 978-3-8382-0325-6

109 *Michail Logvinov* | Russlands Kampf gegen den internationalen Terrorismus. Eine kritische Bestandsaufnahme des Bekämpfungsansatzes | Mit einem Geleitwort von Hans-Henning Schröder und einem Vorwort von Eckhard Jesse | ISBN 978-3-8382-0329-4

110 *John B. Dunlop* | The Moscow Bombings of September 1999. Examinations of Russian Terrorist Attacks at the Onset of Vladimir Putin's Rule | Second, Revised and Expanded Edition | ISBN 978-3-8382-0388-1

111 *Андрей А. Ковалёв* | Свидетельство из-за кулис российской политики I. Можно ли делать добро из зла? (Воспоминания и размышления о последних советских и первых послесоветских годах) | With a foreword by Peter Reddaway | ISBN 978-3-8382-0302-7

112 *Андрей А. Ковалёв* | Свидетельство из-за кулис российской политики II. Угроза для себя и окружающих (Наблюдения и предостережения относительно происходящего после 2000 г.) | ISBN 978-3-8382-0303-4

113 *Bernd Kappenberg* | Zeichen setzen für Europa. Der Gebrauch europäischer lateinischer Sonderzeichen in der deutschen Öffentlichkeit | Mit einem Vorwort von Peter Schlobinski | ISBN 978-3-89821-749-1

114 *Ivo Mijnssen* | The Quest for an Ideal Youth in Putin's Russia I. Back to Our Future! History, Modernity, and Patriotism according to Nashi, 2005-2013 | With a foreword by Jeronim Perović | Second, Revised and Expanded Edition | ISBN 978-3-8382-0368-3

115 *Jussi Lassila* | The Quest for an Ideal Youth in Putin's Russia II. The Search for Distinctive Conformism in the Political Communication of Nashi, 2005-2009 | With a foreword by Kirill Postoutenko | Second, Revised and Expanded Edition | ISBN 978-3-8382-0415-4

116 *Valerio Trabandt* | Neue Nachbarn, gute Nachbarschaft? Die EU als internationaler Akteur am Beispiel ihrer Demokratieförderung in Belarus und der Ukraine 2004-2009 | Mit einem Vorwort von Jutta Joachim | ISBN 978-3-8382-0437-6

117 *Fabian Pfeiffer* | Estlands Außen- und Sicherheitspolitik I. Der estnische Atlantizismus nach der wiedererlangten Unabhängigkeit 1991-2004 | Mit einem Vorwort von Helmut Hubel | ISBN 978-3-8382-0127-6

118 *Jana Podßuweit* | Estlands Außen- und Sicherheitspolitik II. Handlungsoptionen eines Kleinstaates im Rahmen seiner EU-Mitgliedschaft (2004-2008) | Mit einem Vorwort von Helmut Hubel | ISBN 978-3-8382-0440-6

119 *Karin Pointner* | Estlands Außen- und Sicherheitspolitik III. Eine gedächtnispolitische Analyse estnischer Entwicklungskooperation 2006-2010 | Mit einem Vorwort von Karin Liebhart | ISBN 978-3-8382-0435-2

120 *Ruslana Vovk* | Die Offenheit der ukrainischen Verfassung für das Völkerrecht und die europäische Integration | Mit einem Vorwort von Alexander Blankenagel | ISBN 978-3-8382-0481-9

121 *Mykhaylo Banakh* | Die Relevanz der Zivilgesellschaft bei den postkommunistischen Transformationsprozessen in mittel- und osteuropäischen Ländern. Das Beispiel der spät- und postsowjetischen Ukraine 1986-2009 | Mit einem Vorwort von Gerhard Simon | ISBN 978-3-8382-0499-4

122 *Michael Moser* | Language Policy and the Discourse on Languages in Ukraine under President Viktor Yanukovych (25 February 2010–28 October 2012) | ISBN 978-3-8382-0497-0 (Paperback edition) | ISBN 978-3-8382-0507-6 (Hardcover edition)

123 *Nicole Krome* | Russischer Netzwerkkapitalismus Restrukturierungsprozesse in der Russischen Föderation am Beispiel des Luftfahrtunternehmens "Aviastar" | Mit einem Vorwort von Petra Stykow | ISBN 978-3-8382-0534-2

124 *David R. Marples* | 'Our Glorious Past'. Lukashenka's Belarus and the Great Patriotic War | ISBN 978-3-8382-0574-8 (Paperback edition) | ISBN 978-3-8382-0675-2 (Hardcover edition)

125 *Ulf Walther* | Russlands "neuer Adel". Die Macht des Geheimdienstes von Gorbatschow bis Putin | Mit einem Vorwort von Hans-Georg Wieck | ISBN 978-3-8382-0584-7

126 *Simon Geissbühler (Hrsg.)* | Kiew – Revolution 3.0. Der Euromaidan 2013/14 und die Zukunftsperspektiven der Ukraine | ISBN 978-3-8382-0581-6 (Paperback edition) | ISBN 978-3-8382-0681-3 (Hardcover edition)

127 *Andrey Makarychev* | Russia and the EU in a Multipolar World. Discourses, Identities, Norms | With a foreword by Klaus Segbers | ISBN 978-3-8382-0629-5

128 *Roland Scharff* | Kasachstan als postsowjetischer Wohlfahrtsstaat. Die Transformation des sozialen Schutzsystems | Mit einem Vorwort von Joachim Ahrens | ISBN 978-3-8382-0622-6

129 *Katja Grupp* | Bild Lücke Deutschland. Kaliningrader Studierende sprechen über Deutschland | Mit einem Vorwort von Martin Schulz | ISBN 978-3-8382-0552-6

130 *Konstantin Sheiko, Stephen Brown* | History as Therapy. Alternative History and Nationalist Imaginings in Russia, 1991-2014 | ISBN 978-3-8382-0665-3

131 *Elisa Kriza* | Alexander Solzhenitsyn: Cold War Icon, Gulag Author, Russian Nationalist? A Study of the Western Reception of his Literary Writings, Historical Interpretations, and Political Ideas | With a foreword by Andrei Rogatchevski | ISBN 978-3-8382-0589-2 (Paperback edition) | ISBN 978-3-8382-0690-5 (Hardcover edition)

132 *Serghei Golunov* | The Elephant in the Room. Corruption and Cheating in Russian Universities | ISBN 978-3-8382-0570-0

133 *Manja Hussner, Rainer Arnold (Hgg.)* | Verfassungsgerichtsbarkeit in Zentralasien I. Sammlung von Verfassungstexten | ISBN 978-3-8382-0595-3

134 *Nikolay Mitrokhin* | Die "Russische Partei". Die Bewegung der russischen Nationalisten in der UdSSR 1953-1985 | Aus dem Russischen übertragen von einem Übersetzerteam unter der Leitung von Larisa Schippel | ISBN 978-3-8382-0024-8

135 *Manja Hussner, Rainer Arnold (Hgg.)* | Verfassungsgerichtsbarkeit in Zentralasien II. Sammlung von Verfassungstexten | ISBN 978-3-8382-0597-7

136 *Manfred Zeller* | Das sowjetische Fieber. Fußballfans im poststalinistischen Vielvölkerreich | Mit einem Vorwort von Nikolaus Katzer | ISBN 978-3-8382-0757-5

137 *Kristin Schreiter* | Stellung und Entwicklungspotential zivilgesellschaftlicher Gruppen in Russland. Menschenrechtsorganisationen im Vergleich | ISBN 978-3-8382-0673-8

138 *David R. Marples, Frederick V. Mills (Eds.)* | Ukraine's Euromaidan. Analyses of a Civil Revolution | ISBN 978-3-8382-0660-8

139 *Bernd Kappenberg* | Setting Signs for Europe. Why Diacritics Matter for European Integration | With a foreword by Peter Schlobinski | ISBN 978-3-8382-0663-9

140 *René Lenz* | Internationalisierung, Kooperation und Transfer. Externe bildungspolitische Akteure in der Russischen Föderation | Mit einem Vorwort von Frank Ettrich | ISBN 978-3-8382-0751-3

141 *Juri Plusnin, Yana Zausaeva, Natalia Zhidkevich, Artemy Pozanenko* | Wandering Workers. Mores, Behavior, Way of Life, and Political Status of Domestic Russian Labor Migrants | Translated by Julia Kazantseva | ISBN 978-3-8382-0653-0

142 *David J. Smith (Eds.)* | Latvia – A Work in Progress? 100 Years of State- and Nation-Building | ISBN 978-3-8382-0648-6

143 *Инна Чувычкина (ред.)* | Экспортные нефте- и газопроводы на постсоветском пространстве. Анализ трубопроводной политики в свете теории международных отношений | ISBN 978-3-8382-0822-0

144 Johann Zajaczkowski | Russland – eine pragmatische Großmacht? Eine rollentheoretische Untersuchung russischer Außenpolitik am Beispiel der Zusammenarbeit mit den USA nach 9/11 und des Georgienkrieges von 2008 | Mit einem Vorwort von Siegfried Schieder | ISBN 978-3-8382-0837-4

145 Boris Popivanov | Changing Images of the Left in Bulgaria. The Challenge of Post-Communism in the Early 21st Century | ISBN 978-3-8382-0667-7

146 Lenka Krátká | A History of the Czechoslovak Ocean Shipping Company 1948-1989. How a Small, Landlocked Country Ran Maritime Business During the Cold War | ISBN 978-3-8382-0666-0

147 Alexander Sergunin | Explaining Russian Foreign Policy Behavior. Theory and Practice | ISBN 978-3-8382-0752-0

148 Darya Malyutina | Migrant Friendships in a Super-Diverse City. Russian-Speakers and their Social Relationships in London in the 21st Century | With a foreword by Claire Dwyer | ISBN 978-3-8382-0652-3

149 Alexander Sergunin, Valery Konyshev | Russia in the Arctic. Hard or Soft Power? | ISBN 978-3-8382-0753-7

150 John J. Maresca | Helsinki Revisited. A Key U.S. Negotiator's Memoirs on the Development of the CSCE into the OSCE | With a foreword by Hafiz Pashayev | ISBN 978-3-8382-0852-7

151 Jardar Østbø | The New Third Rome. Readings of a Russian Nationalist Myth | With a foreword by Pål Kolstø | ISBN 978-3-8382-0870-1

152 Simon Kordonsky | Socio-Economic Foundations of the Russian Post-Soviet Regime. The Resource-Based Economy and Estate-Based Social Structure of Contemporary Russia | With a foreword by Svetlana Barsukova | ISBN 978-3-8382-0775-9

153 Duncan Leitch | Assisting Reform in Post-Communist Ukraine 2000–2012. The Illusions of Donors and the Disillusion of Beneficiaries | With a foreword by Kataryna Wolczuk | ISBN 978-3-8382-0844-2

154 Abel Polese | Limits of a Post-Soviet State. How Informality Replaces, Renegotiates, and Reshapes Governance in Contemporary Ukraine | With a foreword by Colin Williams | ISBN 978-3-8382-0845-9

155 Mikhail Suslov (Ed.) | Digital Orthodoxy in the Post-Soviet World. The Russian Orthodox Church and Web 2.0 | With a foreword by Father Cyril Hovorun | ISBN 978-3-8382-0871-8

156 Leonid Luks | Zwei „Sonderwege"? Russisch-deutsche Parallelen und Kontraste (1917-2014). Vergleichende Essays | ISBN 978-3-8382-0823-7

157 Vladimir V. Karacharovskiy, Ovsey I. Shkaratan, Gordey A. Yastrebov | Towards a New Russian Work Culture. Can Western Companies and Expatriates Change Russian Society? | With a foreword by Elena N. Danilova | Translated by Julia Kazantseva | ISBN 978-3-8382-0902-9

158 Edmund Griffiths | Aleksandr Prokhanov and Post-Soviet Esotericism | ISBN 978-3-8382-0903-6

159 Timm Beichelt, Susann Worschech (Eds.) | Transnational Ukraine? Networks and Ties that Influence(d) Contemporary Ukraine | ISBN 978-3-8382-0944-9

160 Mieste Hotopp-Riecke | Die Tataren der Krim zwischen Assimilation und Selbstbehauptung. Der Aufbau des krimtatarischen Bildungswesens nach Deportation und Heimkehr (1990-2005) | Mit einem Vorwort von Swetlana Czerwonnaja | ISBN 978-3-89821-940-2

161 Olga Bertelsen (Ed.) | Revolution and War in Contemporary Ukraine. The Challenge of Change | ISBN 978-3-8382-1016-2

162 Natalya Ryabinska | Ukraine's Post-Communist Mass Media. Between Capture and Commercialization | With a foreword by Marta Dyczok | ISBN 978-3-8382-1011-7

163 Alexandra Cotofana, James M. Nyce (Eds.) | Religion and Magic in Socialist and Post-Socialist Contexts. Historic and Ethnographic Case Studies of Orthodoxy, Heterodoxy, and Alternative Spirituality | With a foreword by Patrick L. Michelson | ISBN 978-3-8382-0989-0

164 Nozima Akhrarkhodjaeva | The Instrumentalisation of Mass Media in Electoral Authoritarian Regimes. Evidence from Russia's Presidential Election Campaigns of 2000 and 2008 | ISBN 978-3-8382-1013-1

165 Yulia Krasheninnikova | Informal Healthcare in Contemporary Russia. Sociographic Essays on the Post-Soviet Infrastructure for Alternative Healing Practices | ISBN 978-3-8382-0970-8

166 Peter Kaiser | Das Schachbrett der Macht. Die Handlungsspielräume eines sowjetischen Funktionärs unter Stalin am Beispiel des Generalsekretärs des Komsomol Aleksandr Kosarev (1929-1938) | Mit einem Vorwort von Dietmar Neutatz | ISBN 978-3-8382-1052-0

167 Oksana Kim | The Effects and Implications of Kazakhstan's Adoption of International Financial Reporting Standards. A Resource Dependence Perspective | With a foreword by Svetlana Vlady | ISBN 978-3-8382-0987-6

168 *Anna Sanina* | Patriotic Education in Contemporary Russia. Sociological Studies in the Making of the Post-Soviet Citizen | With a foreword by Anna Oldfield | ISBN 978-3-8382-0993-7

169 *Rudolf Wolters* | Spezialist in Sibirien Faksimile der 1933 erschienenen ersten Ausgabe | Mit einem Vorwort von Dmitrij Chmelnizki | ISBN 978-3-8382-0515-1

170 *Michal Vít, Magdalena M. Baran (Eds.)* | Transregional versus National Perspectives on Contemporary Central European History. Studies on the Building of Nation-States and Their Cooperation in the 20th and 21st Century | With a foreword by Petr Vágner | ISBN 978-3-8382-1015-5

171 *Philip Gamaghelyan* | Conflict Resolution Beyond the International Relations Paradigm. Evolving Designs as a Transformative Practice in Nagorno-Karabakh and Syria | With a foreword by Susan Allen | ISBN 978-3-8382-1057-5

172 *Maria Shagina* | Joining a Prestigious Club. Cooperation with Europarties and Its Impact on Party Development in Georgia, Moldova, and Ukraine 2004–2015 | With a foreword by Kataryna Wolczuk | ISBN 978-3-8382-1084-1

173 *Alexandra Cotofana, James M. Nyce (Eds.)* | Religion and Magic in Socialist and Post-Socialist Contexts II. Baltic, Eastern European, and Post-USSR Case Studies | With a foreword by Anita Stasulane | ISBN 978-3-8382-0990-6

174 *Barbara Kunz* | Kind Words, Cruise Missiles, and Everything in Between. The Use of Power Resources in U.S. Policies towards Poland, Ukraine, and Belarus 1989–2008 | With a foreword by William Hill | ISBN 978-3-8382-1065-0

175 *Eduard Klein* | Bildungskorruption in Russland und der Ukraine. Eine komparative Analyse der Performanz staatlicher Antikorruptionsmaßnahmen im Hochschulsektor am Beispiel universitärer Aufnahmeprüfungen | Mit einem Vorwort von Heiko Pleines | ISBN 978-3-8382-0995-1

176 *Markus Soldner* | Politischer Kapitalismus im postsowjetischen Russland. Die politische, wirtschaftliche und mediale Transformation in den 1990er Jahren | Mit einem Vorwort von Wolfgang Ismayr | ISBN 978-3-8382-1222-7

177 *Anton Oleinik* | Building Ukraine from Within. A Sociological, Institutional, and Economic Analysis of a Nation-State in the Making | ISBN 978-3-8382-1150-3

178 *Peter Rollberg, Marlene Laruelle (Eds.)* | Mass Media in the Post-Soviet World. Market Forces, State Actors, and Political Manipulation in the Informational Environment after Communism | ISBN 978-3-8382-1116-9

179 *Mikhail Minakov* | Development and Dystopia Studies in Post-Soviet Ukraine and Eastern Europe | With a foreword by Alexander Etkind | ISBN 978-3-8382-1112-1

180 *Aijan Sharshenova* | The European Union's Democracy Promotion in Central Asia A Study of Political Interests, Influence, and Development in Kazakhstan and Kyrgyzstan in 2007–2013 | With a foreword by Gordon Crawford | ISBN 978-3-8382-1151-0

181 *Andrey Makarychev, Alexandra Yatsyk (Eds.)* | Boris Nemtsov and Russian Politics. Power and Resistance | With a foreword by Zhanna Nemtsova | ISBN 978-3-8382-1122-0

182 *Sophie Falsini* | The Euromaidan's Effect on Civil Society. Why and How Ukrainian Social Capital Increased after the Revolution of Dignity | With a foreword by Susann Worschech | ISBN 978-3-8382-1131-2

183 *Andreas Umland (Ed.)* | Ukraine's Decentralization. Challenges and Implications of the Local Governance Reform after the Euromaidan Revolution | ISBN 978-3-8382-1162-6

184 *Leonid Luks* | A Fateful Triangle. Essays on Contemporary Russian, German and Polish History | ISBN 978-3-8382-1143-5

185 *John B. Dunlop* | The February 2015 Assassination of Boris Nemtsov and the Flawed Trial of his Alleged Killers. An Exploration of Russia's "Crime of the 21st Century" | ISBN 978-3-8382-1188-6

186 *Vasile Rotaru* | Russia, the EU, and the Eastern Partnership. Building Bridges or Digging Trenches? | ISBN 978-3-8382-1134-3

187 *Marina Lebedeva* | Russian Studies of International Relations. From the Soviet Past to the Post-Cold-War Present | With a foreword by Andrei P. Tsygankov | ISBN 978-3-8382-0851-0

188 *Tomasz Stępniewski, George Soroka (Eds.)* | Ukraine after Maidan. Revisiting Domestic and Regional Security | ISBN 978-3-8382-1075-9

189 *Petar Cholakov* | Ethnic Entrepreneurs Unmasked. Political Institutions and Ethnic Conflicts in Contemporary Bulgaria | ISBN 978-3-8382-1189-3

190 *A. Salem, G. Hazeldine, D. Morgan (Eds.)* | Higher Education in Post-Communist States. Comparative and Sociological Perspectives | ISBN 978-3-8382-1183-1

191 *Igor Torbakov* | After Empire. Nationalist Imagination and Symbolic Politics in Russia and Eurasia in the Twentieth and Twenty-First Century | With a foreword by Serhii Plokhy | ISBN 978-3-8382-1217-3

192 *Aleksandr Burakovskiy* | Jewish-Ukrainian Relations in Late and Post-Soviet Ukraine. Articles, Lectures and Essays from 1986 to 2016 | ISBN 978-3-8382-1210-4

193 *Natalia Shapovalova, Olga Burlyuk (Eds.)* | Civil Society in Post-Euromaidan Ukraine. From Revolution to Consolidation | With a foreword by Richard Youngs | ISBN 978-3-8382-1216-6

194 *Franz Preissler* | Positionsverteidigung, Imperialismus oder Irredentismus? Russland und die „Russischsprachigen", 1991–2015 | ISBN 978-3-8382-1262-3

195 *Marian Madeła* | Der Reformprozess in der Ukraine 2014-2017. Eine Fallstudie zur Reform der öffentlichen Verwaltung | Mit einem Vorwort von Martin Malek | ISBN 978-3-8382-1266-1

196 *Anke Giesen* | „Wie kann denn der Sieger ein Verbrecher sein?" Eine diskursanalytische Untersuchung der russlandweiten Debatte über Konzept und Verstaatlichungsprozess der Lagergedenkstätte „Perm'-36" im Ural | ISBN 978-3-8382-1284-5

197 *Alla Leukavets* | The Integration Policies of Belarus and Ukraine vis-à-vis the EU and Russia. A Comparative Case Study Through the Prism of a Two-Level Game Approach | ISBN 978-3-8382-1247-0

198 *Oksana Kim* | The Development and Challenges of Russian Corporate Governance I. The Roles and Functions of Boards of Directors | With a foreword by Sheila M. Puffer | ISBN 978-3-8382-1287-6

199 *Thomas D. Grant* | International Law and the Post-Soviet Space I. Essays on Chechnya and the Baltic States | With a foreword by Stephen M. Schwebel | ISBN 978-3-8382-1279-1

200 *Thomas D. Grant* | International Law and the Post-Soviet Space II. Essays on Ukraine, Intervention, and Non-Proliferation | ISBN 978-3-8382-1280-7

201 *Slavomír Michálek, Michal Štefansky* | The Age of Fear. The Cold War and Its Influence on Czechoslovakia 1945–1968 | ISBN 978-3-8382-1285-2

202 *Iulia-Sabina Joja* | Romania's Strategic Culture 1990–2014. Continuity and Change in a Post-Communist Country's Evolution of National Interests and Security Policies | With a foreword by Heiko Biehl | ISBN 978-3-8382-1286-9

203 *Andrei Rogatchevski, Yngvar B. Steinholt, Arve Hansen, David-Emil Wickström* | War of Songs. Popular Music and Recent Russia-Ukraine Relations | With a foreword by Artemy Troitsky | ISBN 978-3-8382-1173-2

204 *Maria Lipman (ed.)* | Russian Voices on Post-Crimea Russia. An Almanac of Counterpoint Essays from 2015–2018 | ISBN 978-3-8382-1251-7

205 *Ksenia Maksimovtsova* | Language Conflicts in Contemporary Estonia, Latvia, and Ukraine. A Comparative Exploration of Discourses in Post-Soviet Russian-Language Digital Media | With a foreword by Ammon Cheskin | ISBN 978-3-8382-1282-1

206 *Michal Vít* | The EU's Impact on Identity Formation in East-Central Europe between 2004 and 2013. Perceptions of the Nation and Europe in Political Parties of the Czech Republic, Poland, and Slovakia | With a foreword by Andrea Pető | ISBN 978-3-8382-1275-3

ibidem.eu